Finding Home

Finding Home

How Americans Prevail

SALLY OOMS

Home Free Publishing

SAN FRANCISCO

Home Free Publishing

Home Free Publishing LLC
P.O. Box 225053
San Francisco, CA 94122

www.findinghomestories.com
www.homefreepublishing.com

Printed in the United States of America

ISBN: 978-0-9883479-0-8

First Edition
18 17 16 15 14 13   10 9 8 7 6 5 4 3 2 1

Project management, design, and composition by Steven Hiatt / Hiatt & Dragon, San Francisco   Copyediting: Steven Hiatt   Proofreading: Tom Hassett
Cover Design: Stewart Cauley Design

For all the people on these pages
who generously shared their stories.

For all those who are still on
the quest to find home.

For all those who are helping
them on their journey.

There's more than one way home,
Ain't no right way, ain't no wrong.
Whatever road you might be on
Find your own way
'Cuz there's more than one way home.

Keb' Mo'

Contents

Preface

Displacement as Mirror

The evening of May 20, 1957, when I was ten and still in pigtails, I ate a chicken pot pie upstairs in my parents' bedroom. My parents were entertaining friends from out of town in the dining room. I tried to watch the TV Western my father and I had an affinity for, but the local station kept interrupting the program to air the weatherman's report on tornado sightings in the Kansas City vicinity.

We lived in the center of the city in a house that my great uncle had built, a two-story with a basement and an attic. Forty-foot elms lined the streets. I wasn't allowed to watch much television, but I had seen *The Wizard of Oz* at least five times.

The weatherman's predictions became increasingly dire: a monster tornado was headed for the city. I ran downstairs to tell everyone that the television said we should all go to the basement. Since my parents were inured to tornado warnings and knew that predicting where a tornado was going to hit was an inaccurate science at best, they told me not to worry about it. There had been plenty of false alarms that season.

I went back upstairs and listened to the weatherman some more. He wasn't fooling around. I hung my head out a window. Everything was calm. Too calm. That is one of the signs of an approaching tornado. I was convinced we should go to the basement.

Back in the dining room, my parents and their guests were laughing and filled with bravado. Everything was going to be all right, they said. My father had a theory that tornados never went through the center of cities, a belief that was dashed the next year when one swept through downtown

Topeka. The couple visiting from New York State smiled at me and were as cavalier as their hosts.

Upstairs again I listened to the reports and I thought, "What do people from New York know about tornados?" The weatherman was passing on information from eyewitnesses who had called him and given him an idea of where the tornado was on the ground. The wind started to kick up outside our house and after about twenty minutes the elm trees began to bow.

I pleaded with my parents this time. "Come look at the trees," I said, jabbing my fingers against the dining room bay window. The lights went out at that point, leaving the party in candlelight. The flames wavered a few seconds from the breath of an unseen source. It alarmed me, but it just seemed to excite the grown-ups.

I felt my way to my room and snatched up my dachshund, a flashlight and the transistor radio I had received for Christmas. I thought I knew where in the laundry room I was supposed to be when the tornado struck: next to the wall on the northeast side.

It smelled like mothballed blankets and dank wall plaster. I sat on a chair I dragged from another basement room, one that people used when they talked on the phone down there. I had lifted the receiver of the phone briefly and heard no dial tone. That increased my terror. My dog, Madel, stayed close, her hair brushing my legs. I could still hear the wind. Now there was the splat of furious rain and hail as it landed in the window wells. Mostly I heard my own rapid heartbeat in my head.

No one came to join me, and the tornado did not hit us. I went back upstairs about half an hour later when the weather calmed down, the lights flashed back on, and my mother called for me to come get some dessert.

But in those thirty minutes alone in the basement, I had time to imagine my family and their friends being ripped away from our house. Our house itself gone. My home. Everything I loved was up there. The people I loved were not protecting themselves. I was powerless. The tornado had all the power, and it would decide whether it would take my parents and my house away or not.

It decided to go to the Kansas City suburb of Ruskin Heights instead, where it killed forty-six people. No doubt some of them were other people's parents. I read the papers and looked at the photos of the high school and junior high in complete wreckage. One gym wall still stood. From the letters that once spelled "RUSKIN," the tornado had left the letters spelling "RUIN."

There were so many stories about the capriciousness of tornados. One house in a block would be left intact while all the others were completely demolished. One woman claimed a tornado whistled in and tore away most of the clothing in her closet, but left several dresses. Some of the stories stretched one's credulity. But one thing was for certain: tornados had the upper hand. There was no way to defy them or prevent them. You just had to cower in your basement, and hope and pray.

I sometimes wonder: Did that one incident develop in me a hypersensitivity to people who find themselves without a home?

As a teen I did what was referred to as "charity work" and went weekly to the cerebral palsy center in midtown Kansas City to push afflicted kids around a few blocks in their wheelchairs. I was horrified to discover that these teens did not live at home with their parents. They lived there at the center, a commercial building makeover permeated with the odor of urine-soaked mattresses. Their caretakers seemed nice, but …

In my journalism career, I have had the most passion for stories involving people who couldn't defend themselves. I see now that the concept of home was the basis for more than a few of those feature articles. I investigated boarding homes in a state mental hospital town whose owners were ripping off and mistreating the patients who had left the institution.

I reported on a college high-rise dorm that students said was a firetrap and where emergency doors were bolted shut at night.

As a freelancer, I went to Oklahoma to interview Wilma Mankiller, then chief of the Cherokee Nation. I read about the Cherokee Trail of Tears when most of the tribe was driven from its homeland in the South to Oklahoma and thousands died along the way.

The topic of displacement repeatedly caught my attention.

When New Orleans was flooded after Hurricane Katrina, I watched television along with millions of Americans who saw masses of people, predominantly black, being neglected. It brought up issues of race and poverty, but it also highlighted gaps in human interaction that troubled me. When the government that is supposed to represent us doesn't adequately assist people in dire straits, what then is my role as a citizen and human?

To supplement my writing income, I had bought a 1991 Cadillac stretch limousine and was running my own one-car business. My first impulse in reaction to the New Orleans disaster was to drive my car to the Crescent

City, pick up some people and drive them away. I pondered how I would get into the city. Who would I pick up? People who ran toward me needing a ride? Where would I take them? The more I considered it, wanting to do something productive with what I had at hand, the more unrealistic it sounded to me. The result was that I did nothing.

When it became apparent that New Orleaneans wanted to rebuild, there was a hue and cry. Were people really meant to live in areas that depended on levees to keep them from floating away? But New Orleans has deep and multifaceted traditions rooted in music, religious customs, food and attitude. The large Catholic families in the Lower Ninth Ward, for example, were at home there, and most of them wanted to come back home. All over the city, New Orleaneans began efforts to re-establish their way of life.

Two years after Katrina, an EF5 tornado, the largest of its kind in history, wiped out all but a couple of blocks of Greensburg, Kansas, a town of 1,400 people. I was acquainted with a few people in Greensburg, having stopped and stayed at their motel and shared meals at a café on the way from my childhood home in Kansas City to my adult home in New Mexico. Only eleven people died in Greensburg because there were better storm alarms and alerts than in my youth and because people heeded them. But the town itself was no more.

Again, there was negativity about the townspeople's abilities to rebuild their hometown. What surfaced in Greensburg was a determination not only to rebuild but an imperative to construct a town that incorporated green building. I went to cover a story about University of Kansas architecture students who were erecting a prototype LEED Platinum building in the heart of town. A LEED (Leadership in Energy and Environment Design) Platinum rating is the top standard of the internationally recognized U.S. Green Building Council.

The townspeople took up the torch and re-invented Greensburg. In the process, they have attracted young people eager to be part of their avant-guard undertaking and now host thousands of visitors annually who are interested in green building.

My mother always made the distinction between the words "house" and "home." She was incensed when realtors advertised homes. "It's not a home until the people move in and make it one. Until then, it's just a house," she said.

So what is a home? It is not just a structure, a physical dwelling. In my explorations for this book, I've discovered a wealth of definitions. Included are life partners, family, friends and community. For some home means being part of a heritage, religion or culture. For others it signifies a spiritual space. Sometimes it is a place found only in the mind. Sometimes it is a place solely in the heart. For a few, home simply involves feeling right within one's own skin.

No matter how home is defined, I have come to realize that the concept is hooked into a person's identity—into self—and into feelings of worth. And that the need for a home is ubiquitous.

When I first hatched the idea of talking to people who were or had been displaced—or who felt alienated and isolated from society—I carried with me a list of the categories of people I thought I might interview. I listed the groupings that wound up in the book, but there were originally so many more. Included were prisoners, handicapped people, monks, victims of eminent domain, someone in the witness protection program (good luck on that) and refugees. Whenever I showed friends and associates the list, they would invariably snatch it from me and say, "You've got to have this person" or "Here is a group you haven't thought of." The list grew to thirty, then forty, then fifty categories. The last person to scribble an idea on the sheet wrote down "Evangelical Christians." She could tell you about the alienation, she said. She was one herself.

Whoa, I thought. There are more people than I imagined who feel they are not a part of the mainstream, who feel neglected or misunderstood or put into a category where they are easily dismissed.

I started to pare down the categories and do interviews. The groups, over three or four years, have metamorphosed into the ten parts you find in this book, each with interviewees addressing similar struggles.

I found people through referrals from organizations assisting the displaced. I mined the Internet—from Wikipedia to blogs—for contacts. I heard about potential interviewees from friends, friends of friends and people whom friends had met. An old school buddy told me about a woman in Ocean Beach, California, who ran a bed and breakfast and was "doing something with kids that might fit into your book."

That lead turned out to be the avenue to speaking with former foster kids who are overcoming their disadvantaged childhoods and getting college educations through a special scholarship program.

I met a man in a Minneola, Kansas, motel breakfast room who was traveling by motorcycle. After I ran my book idea by him, he told me briefly about Navajos he had defended against unfair labor practices and handed me a card that said, "We sue railroads."

"Give me a call if you want to talk about it," he said. That prompted me to research the Navajo and Hopi Nation peoples' fight to retain their homelands and survive on their land.

Increasingly, the book became about people who were searching for, or trying to retain, a home. Sometimes a new one. Or one to replace the old one. Sometimes battling to keep the old one. Sometimes re-examining the old one and on a quest for the new one. All variations on that theme. It has become a book about people who have come off their center and about how they have righted themselves. I also welcomed the stories of individuals who are helping others "find home." So often they have undergone the same trials and understand how to give a hand up. They also serve to offer ideas on how we might involve ourselves.

I really didn't write this book. The interviewees did. Most of them chose to use their own names—either first name only, or first and last name. A few elected to use an assumed name—a first name or first and surname.

There really is no sensational aspect to this book. The media often present individuals' hardships and ordeals one day, then drop them and their "issues" the next.

I didn't want to publish a gloom-and-doom book: "Woe is me. I lost my home." We hear plenty of depressing stories in America. I wanted to showcase people who are pretty much everyday Americans dealing with the problems our society is handing us on a daily basis. They are doing more than just coping. They are innovators in their own lives. They are unstoppable. They are prevailing.

Author Gretchen Rubin, who has done extensive research on the nature of happiness, says that she has read studies, theories, and great books, tapping into great minds dealing with her topic. But she found greater value in what people have told her about what "worked for them, than in any other kind of argument—and that's true even when we seem to have nothing in common."

I find that to be spot on. A person on the subway, or in the bank line or grocery store, can slip me an experience from his or her life that resonates with me more than any generic study or great philosopher can implant. If I had just superficially judged that person before any exchange, I would not have dreamed there would be any merit to a conversation.

So you might meet any one of the people I have interviewed on the street any day and not recognize how much you have in common with them. I find their stories uplifting. I recognize some of their struggles as my own. I respect the others who have undergone things I can barely imagine. Whatever feelings their stories elicit, I feel privileged to have made their acquaintance. I hope you do too.

The ache for home lives in all of us, the safe place where we can go as we are and not be questioned.

Maya Angelou

1 Rough Start

Alecia

Alecia has just finished speaking to a crowd of fellow former foster kids at a Fostering Opportunities Dollars for Scholars luncheon. She is twenty-three, one of the scholarship organization's recipients, and graduating from college. She spoke about the importance of education in reversing the ill effect the foster care system has on so many young people. Now she elaborates on that theme and talks about her life.

I was number four out of five children. I am the only one to get a degree. I spent nine years in foster care where we were always told we were not going to make it. We were going to get pregnant. We would never succeed.

I am first-generation American. My parents moved from Iraq. My father had a high school diploma. My mother went through second grade. My father came to the United States and got a green card. He married my mother in an arranged marriage. Married life was the only life she knew. She had no friends. She worked once in the schools, sewing costumes. That was freedom, an escape.

I'm one of five girls; I have a twin sister. We were born in Michigan and moved to East County *(San Diego County)* when I was two years old. I don't remember anything about Michigan. I didn't know anything other than there was warm sunshine here.

My father was incarcerated for domestic violence. My parents were Catholic. Chaldean. My father was asked to leave Michigan, where he was jailed eighteen times. Every time it was for domestic violence.

I was nine years old when I was put in foster care. My father murdered my mother. He was thirteen years older. She was thirty-nine when she

1

passed. He was given twenty-six years to life, but he has spent fifteen years in prison and is up for parole in two years for good behavior. It's scary. All of us sisters are going to testify against him.

My mother never went against my father. She could have gotten a divorce but it is against Chaldean culture. So many in my family say, "Leave it up to God. It is His will," but I'm blessed to be away from that. I am living, breathing, healthy, getting an education. I have a job.

Immediately after the murder, we went to the police station. I remember looking down at the floor and seeing a puddle of water from my tears. Then we went to stay with a family friend who had two girls of his own. Then there was a Hispanic man, a defense attorney with six kids of his own, who took us in. That didn't work out. We were there a year. There was a ton of favoritism toward their own kids. We were immediately ostracized at school. Or there was pity. I didn't like that. Everyone knew what had happened to my mother.

My mother's brother from Jordan had a visa. He learned to speak English and took twelve months of foster parent training. He became certified and became a citizen. He got a job working graveyard shifts replacing windshields and took us all in, including my eighteen-year-old sister because she was certified to be a foster parent.

It was the first time since my mother died that we had been with our own family, our own blood. We had never known what my mother's parents' children looked like, what her childhood had been like, and he was able to tell us. He was fun-loving and it was good until I was eleven years old. He married a Chaldean woman who was really into the culture.

"No shorts. You can't go out in this." (*She points to her short-sleeved, V-neck blouse.*) I couldn't show cleavage. I was supposed to cook and clean. Education was not a priority. She made me wear baggy clothes around men.

She told me nothing about menstrual cycles. She asked one time why I hugged a guy after class. She demanded fingerprints of every member of a house where I was to go to spend the night. It was a long time before I could be open and get to know people after that. I had four sisters. They were my friends.

I couldn't go to a dance. I talked back. The social worker took me and my older sister away to another foster home when we were rebellious. This was another Hispanic family where the parents were seventy-two and seventy-five. They were the greatest people. We still keep in touch.

My aunt had made me mop the floor because I had bad grades. These people said: "Go to the library." They valued education. The mother was a teacher at my school. He was a fisherman. She used to sit on his lap and kiss him before dinner. She actually peeled him grapes. It is the first time I saw love. They held hands at the mall. He opened her door. I saw that love could last for years.

They had one son and, other than that, always fostered kids. They fostered sixteen kids in twenty-five years. I went to a gathering with the people who had been their foster youth.

There was never any physical violence. We had already seen the highest level of physical violence. There was no verbal abuse. It was huge for us. We always tried hard to communicate. Number one in any family or living situation is communication.

People have no idea what a group home is like. Fifty-five percent become homeless after they age out. Eighty percent of the people who go through the foster care system have been jailed.

The older you get when you are fostered in a private home, the more your foster parents are funded. When you are aging out, you are worth $1,200 a month. It sucks to think that way. The parents can be picky with who they take in. Then they can go buy brand-new cars. Foster homes kick you out on your eighteenth birthday or make you start paying rent.

As a foster kid, you can complain. But so many social workers are nine-to-fivers. They don't care. The county ones came and went. There were so many. I remember one had a red car. One month and she was gone. One had a phone in her car. One had a dog she walked. The social workers are always just moving on.

In some families there is a countdown to your eighteenth birthday. But they don't have to wait to get rid of us. The family can call anytime they don't want a kid any more. We're an item.

It's different with Fostering Opportunities, our scholarship mentors. Some of them will stay up and work with you until two in the morning. They have an abundance of love. They could be out with their grandkids. They choose us.

My older sister and I tried to make it on our own. I worked for Rave Girl, a clothing company. We ate Top Ramen for dinner. I had several credit cards and was in debt. The younger kids stayed with my aunt and uncle. My twin was so absorbed and brainwashed. When I would call to ask her to go to the movies, she would have to be back at 10:30.

I learned how to save money for rent and not fritter it away. How to buy groceries. I had no idea how to shop. I bought a watermelon on sale but didn't know what to do with it. I threw it away a week later. I learned that just because you have a coupon for something you don't necessarily need it. And I learned that you don't need lots of clothes in your closet. A black pencil skirt will always last. A white shirt will always last.

I have rules. I clean my home. No happy hour for me until I am done with the laundry. I was on my own for three years trying to make it. I went to Grossmont Community College. But I was in debt. I was working in a bank. We're talking 401(k)s and eating $9 cheeseburgers. Out for a drink after work.

I opened up to financial aid. People said, "Hey, there's lots available for former foster kids. Housing. Medical insurance." I applied and ever since doors have been opening. I connected with all the scholarships out there. Now I'm all about resources. When I saw I was accepted for the first scholarship, I melted on the floor of the bank where I worked.

When I turned eighteen I didn't want anyone to help me. I didn't know how to shop, how to get a Social Security number. I didn't want anybody to know I had been a foster kid. They throw these statistics at you about how many have failed. You want to show you can do it on your own. I didn't know the appropriate way to ask for help.

I had a surge of happiness when I opened up. At eighteen, I was scared every day. Now I can't wait for today.

I have had a huge amount of support. I had six scholarships coming in at one time. I was able to quit my job and just work on my schooling. That's something normal students often can't even do.

I got a job at a group home with fifty foster youth between the ages of six and twelve. They have behavioral issues. They threw oranges at me, ripped my earrings, but once I showed that I was not scared, that I wanted to be there, it changed.

A girl tried to cut herself. Some don't want to live past eighteen. They don't care. But even when I was leaving crying in the car, I was so looking forward to tomorrow. I need to work with foster youth. One person can make the difference in a kid's life. In the group home I saw mothers come in to visit with bruises and cuts. Marks all over them from shooting meth. The children are so bright. The mothers would just criticize them: "What you're wearing looks so ugly on you."

I talked with the older girls who are aging out. I was able to tell them my story. They said it was good that they could open up and tell theirs.

I have given seven or eight talks to companies and agencies about what it is like to be a foster kid. I am spreading awareness. I know it sounds cheesy, but I say education, education, education. But it's true: it's a way out and up.

I'm not sure what I am going to do next. I have a year to figure it out but I would like to get my master's. In social work probably. It's not much money. My twin sister got her AA. My older sister got her AA. I will be the first to get a bachelor's in my family, my BA from San Diego State.

Today is my younger sister's second wedding anniversary. They are a cute couple. Who knows if the Chaldean way is right or wrong? It's just not for me. But my mom moved here for a reason. That's what I think about when I've had a hard day studying and eat Tater Tots for dinner. I have a spur: the memory of my mom. The things she gave me. She gave me morals and values.

But I can't live by the book. Chaldeans teach that you cannot do anything outside of marriage. For them, it is marry, then fall in love. I want to fall in love, marry, and then fall deeper in love.

Katie Elsbree

Katie Elsbree sits in the sunny breakfast room of her Ocean Beach, California, bed-and-breakfast. The converted Victorian is painted teal and turquoise. Katie sports a lilac top, iris apron and violet earrings.

She puts out tea and homemade muffins before she starts to explain why one of sixteen Dollars for Scholars organizations she has helped start in San Diego County is particularly near and dear to her heart.

I'm always concerned about what happens when foster kids "age out"—when they turn eighteen, that is. They have no place to go. My colleagues and I had seen these young people thrust out of various situations—from county-run homes to family foster homes. It's a challenge for them just trying to keep in the good graces with the foster home they are assigned to. Unless they are very close to graduation, they are put out on the street at eighteen years old.

We said, "We have to do something."

We founded Fostering Opportunities Dollars for Scholars. We trained volunteer mentors. All the mentors have full-time jobs, but they are so dedicated that it is nothing for them to be up until one in the morning helping kids. Our mentors are there for any type of support. One of our first former foster kids was a girl who did not know how to cook. She has two little boys to feed, so we helped her learn. We have helped her for a number of years.

We don't raise enough money to completely sponsor our scholars' education, but we encourage them to find other scholarships and assist with the process. Even so, some of them are working two to three jobs.

Lots of scholarships are awarded to students only for their college freshman year. One big advantage of Fostering Opportunities is that awards are renewable and can extend as long they want to pursue higher education. They can also apply in the middle of their school career. Each year they get renewable scholarships, and we try to make them bigger every time.

We have given scholarships to people who chose two-year vocational training as well as those who are working toward university degrees. One young man in our program wanted to be an auto mechanic. This year we are sponsoring for the first time a young man who wants to be a carpenter.

We had one kid who had been in thirteen schools. First of all we had to find all his credits. In spite of his unstable lifestyle, he had passed the courses he took. He had been in thirteen foster homes since he was two weeks old. He was taken away from his home, along with his brother, who was two years old. They had an unfit mother. The court took the kids away. A foster home adopted him, but the mother died when he was eight. He didn't know any other mother.

He told me, "I was angry because I had another mother abandon me.

I acted out something terrible. I would get sent to a place and say, 'I'll bet I won't last here two weeks.'"

At about age fifteen, a guy from a Boys and Girls Club became his mentor. That turned him around.

He was very handsome. Kind of a playboy. Really good looking. He got himself in college. Around the end of his second year he said, "I'm just gonna drop out of school." I talked to him every week and told him how it was OK if he was just taking a break, but not OK to give up on his schooling. The next semester he applied to California State University at San Marcos. He is now a graduate. He spoke at a graduation party and told people, "She just wouldn't let it go."

I am constantly telling them, "Get this application in now. Your paperwork for this is due now. Apply for this now."

One of our first kids graduated from Mills College, a private liberal arts college in Oakland. We helped her get her master's degree. She had a bachelor's from a state university and wanted to be a journalist. She went to Mills and they said, "You can't go here." She had the academics, yes, but the finances, no.

That young woman didn't give up. She said, "There must be some way—with grants, loans." She sat for a week in their administration office. They finally decided she had been persistent enough and said, "I guess you can go here." They looked at her records and admitted her with student aid.

She and her sister were left homeless at ages twelve and ten. Their mother was involved in drugs, and was in a drug deal that went bad. She was shot. The girls lived with a woman in a wheelchair. They took care of her. The woman moved with them to Arizona. A year later, she accidentally overdosed. Arizona shipped the girls back to a homeless shelter where their dad was.

Drop-dead gorgeous girls, thirteen and eleven. Fortunately, a lawyer from the DA's office was walking through the shelter and saw them and said, "What are they doing here? You can't keep them here. It's inappropriate." He called Child Welfare.

Another woman took them into her home and fostered them through high school. The older girl was so successful at Mills College that she was asked to give the graduation speech. My sister and I attended. She said she had realized that her bachelor's in English had not been enough to pursue her career. That she knew she didn't really fit in at

Mills but she had made it through. She talked about the importance of community.

There was not a dry eye in the house. We were like proud mamas.

There was a girl who got into college and a dorm with a full scholarship but had no home to go to during breaks. She was in with girls whose parents bought them sheets, pillowcases and matching rugs for college. She had saved $500 and bought a car. She just wanted one she could drive around the block. When all the kids went home for Thanksgiving and Christmas breaks, she packed up and pretended she was going home also, but just came back and lived in the dorm. Before the midterm break, an announcement went around that dorms would be closed to redo the floors. She packed up and for six weeks she just drove around in her car.

We were heartbroken when we heard about her. The wheels turned quickly. She is now in housing that never closes, so she can stay.

One hundred and one people sent us donations for Fostering Opportunities Dollars for Scholars this year. People are generous, but we still need more money. The easiest way to raise money is through publicity. We are schoolteachers, social workers, nurses, mostly professional people who have been involved in the social work field. It is difficult for us. We don't have the skills for fundraising.

My sister Mary Jo and I were part of eleven kids. We grew up in Illinois. It used to be that people generally took kids in and took care of them if they saw they were in need. You have a responsibility to the community at large—that was the legacy from my mother.

Our family never went hungry, but we didn't have much variety in our diet. Our mother bought the twenty-four-can cases of beans and gunnysacks of potatoes. We called the dishes she made "some-mora," as in "May I have some-mora beans?" No matter what she had made for us, she made a whole casserole and twenty minutes before we were to eat, one of us got in the car with her and the casserole. She would pull in front of the house of somebody who needed food. Whoever she took with her would ring the doorbell and say, "My mother made this for you for dinner tonight."

My mother was proud and she wanted others to be as well. It was always anonymous. She would get wind of who needed help. She worked in a hospital and would see poor families in the emergency room. "We need to get something over there," she would say. She had their address—there was no HIPPA privacy act at that time—so she knew where to take the meal. Our mother taught us that we were lucky. It was time for us to give back. She wanted to teach us how to pay it forward.

I believe in helping others. Don't just tell me about a problem. Do something about it. Everyone can do something. Walk across the street and help a neighbor. Feed the homeless. You need to be proactive. You need to reach out and help.

I am proud of all the young people I see go through Fostering Opportunities. I feel like a mother. These kids touch your life.

Clifton and Shane

Clifton Hidds and Shane Hidds-Thomas have different fathers but they call one another brother unequivocally. They grew up with their mother until she died. They were thirteen and fifteen, respectively.

Clifton: I have a twin sister, and we have an older sister. We were all sent to Polinsky's Children's Center. It's for kids who have nowhere else to go.

Shane: It was an uncomfortable experience. Awkward.

Clifton: It was not home.

Shane: It was supposed to be a temporary place until they worked out permanent foster care for all four of us. There were about 120 kids at Polinsky's. Different ages in different houses. We got a home-school kind of learning. Instructors came in to teach.

Clifton: We went to a temporary foster home for three months, then we were placed in an academy, a boarding school, where you go to school and live with other foster youth.

Shane: It was better because it was like living in a house. House parents were in the living situations with us. The same staff every day. Familiar faces. There was therapy and social workers. We made friends.

Clifton: We all four wanted to be together. They tried to separate us and put us in different foster homes. You can refuse, and we did.

Shane: They tried to put our sisters in another home, and we found out and said no. So we all stayed together through it all.

Shane: A career advisor at the boarding school told us about scholarships for college and helped us apply. I'm now twenty-one. I'm about to graduate from San Francisco State University in business. I'd like to move around a while before I start my career. Travel.

Clifton: I'm nineteen. I go to San Diego Mesa College. I'm getting a degree in kinesthesiology and athletic training. I plan to be a workout trainer. I'd like to play a part in lowering the obesity level of Americans. And keep myself in shape as well.

Shane: Our sister goes to San Francisco Community College.

Clifton: My twin is studying at California Polytechnic Institute.

Shane: We all attend different colleges, but we get together often. All the time we four siblings get together. We go to someone's house, a common place, for a week or two to hang out.

Clifton: We have our own houses now. I like having my own place. You don't have to worry about the other person's stuff. It's just you.

For our mother's birthday and the day she passed, we go to the same pier where we scattered her ashes. I go more often. I'm closer. On Mother's Day and other occasions.

Dawson

Dawson Marino walks the grounds of Hilton Head Court, the apartment complex where he lives, then settles at a table near the deserted swimming pool. The seventeen-year-old lives with his sister and a friend in the El Cajon, California, complex. His father lives in an adjoining apartment.

I'll turn eighteen in three months, in November. I'm trying to get into the Job Corps to get my high school diploma and join the military, the Army probably.

I was in foster care from eight until I was eleven. When I was six years old, Dad broke up with my mother and remarried. My brother and two sisters and I were living with my mother. Mom's boyfriend came first before us. We were put into foster care. It was in Arkansas. Right before I was twelve, I moved with my brother and two sisters to California. We moved in with my grandma.

My grandma started legal guardianship. She was pretty much milking the system by getting paid for us to be in the house. She was getting food stamps.

Every day for five years, I had to sit in my room. Punishment. I had two friends maybe I hung out with twice. I had no life outside school.

Me and my siblings, my sisters that is—my brother was always on the run—lived together. We had been hit by my grandmother. There was violence. We complained to the social workers and the cops and they ignored the situation. They eventually put her in Mesa Vista, the psychiatric hospital.

They said she was a borderline split personality. She blames everybody but herself.

At one point back in December I had had enough. I left the house on my bike. I went to the beach, the park, the mall. I knew nothing about living on the streets. There were kids sleeping in the elevators at the mall. They took me in. I was homeless about six months. I learned survival skills, how you do what you have to do to survive.

Food? Theft from Walmart or Target. I ate at a friend's house or out of the trashcan in back of Walmart. Out of the churches' trashcans certain days.

Downtown, the drunks coming out of bars—you ask for money and they give it to you. At Ocean Beach I lived with hippies. All the bums called us "The Kids." Eventually one day I got tired of it. One night I was sleeping in a tent in the woods and I said, "I'm tired of this, my own freedom. I want back into the social lifestyle." I called Dad and he picked me up. I've been living near my blood father since then. My father and his girlfriend live in the same complex.

My good friends are on the streets. I still hang out with them all the time. Some are moving around the state, up to San Francisco. I can relate to a lot of the stuff they've been through. One friend's mother has used domestic violence against him. I made sure he was safe on the streets.

The two women I live with, the blonde one is my sister. The one with black hair is her roommate. She's staying with my sister this summer before they return to Northern Arizona University.

My half-brother was taken away by his father. My brother has always been put in juvie and psycho hospitals. At nineteen he got locked up for two years. We were never really close. He is not a part of my life.

Probably the strongest is my older sister. Even when we were little, when Mom was not home, she fed us. She pretty much became mom when I was eight.

There was molestation of one of my siblings. My sisters made it through bad times. Both my sisters were honor roll all the way.

I plan to go to college after serving in the military. I'm going to try to get a master's degree in literature. I always liked writing and reading. In fifth grade through seventh grade I had troubles. I always had a hard time. Me and my brother were not the best with school. One class I would always get an A or B in was English.

I've been trying to find a job since I was fifteen and a half. I worked for the *Union Tribune* selling subscriptions. I'm not the best salesman. I had a job with Dad in his auto detailing business. He had to sell the business. There were not enough customers.

I hope the Job Corps will help. When I was on the run, I lost half a year. If I go back to school, it will probably be back to my sophomore year, so the Job Corps I see as a last resort. I went to an open house for the Job Corps. I need to get all my records back from my grandmother. The Job Corps would help me get a California State ID and fill out a resume. They would help me get my high school diploma. I would live on a campus where everything would be free. It should come through.

As soon as I am done with the military, I will go to college. I'd like to write books. I've always written tons. I go halfway through, and then I don't finish them. I'd like to write something kids my age like to read.

There are those people who say their parents have ruined them and sit around and do nothing while the disadvantaged are taking action to improve themselves. But it's hard to find a job. I pounded the pavement locally, but most people tell you to go home and apply online.

I don't understand why people don't want to meet prospective employees face-to-face. No, you come home and fill out the online application and give them all your information, or print it out yourself and drop it off. You get an online rejection and there you've wasted at least two hours per application. Looking for a job is stressful. And now I am waiting for the Job Corps call. I would start the program in a week. I'm tense waiting for the call. Waiting for one call that can mean so much to change your life.

Denise

Denise is on her lunch hour at Mama's Bakery, a Lebanese restaurant in San Diego. She is twenty-six and a former foster child who recently received a scholarship from Fostering Opportunities Dollars for Scholars.

My mom was a single mom of five. She was an alcoholic and was not able to care for us. We all went into the foster care system. My two brothers were kept together and went to the babysitter we had at the time. My middle sister went to another person who we also knew. That ended up being an abusive situation. That sister is having a hard time in life now. Most of her placements have not been good. The youngest, who was just starting kindergarten, and I went to a friend of the family. This person never had kids and never wanted kids.

It was a month before high school for me. I was fourteen. I wanted to do my own teenage thing, listen to my own music. I acted up, and I got kicked out. My little sister stayed with that same person. The woman adopted her. That woman now has adopted four kids. Looking back, I think I would have had a pretty good time if I had stayed.

I was sent to the Polinsky Children's Center—it's a temporary emergency shelter—and then to foster parents in Santee in east San Diego County. They had biological kids as well. It didn't work out, and I went back to Polinsky.

I didn't want to be in Santee. The community was very different from what I was used to. There was a lot of racism. It was predominantly white. It was abusive as well. Back at Polinsky, I was a sophomore. The school was horrible. They have to do a one-size-fits-all program. The kids have so many different skill levels that they reduce everything down. It's a place where you are sent when you have nowhere else to go. You are fed, there are beds and a school. That's it.

I was in a group home for a week. I went into another foster home where I stayed until I graduated from high school. It was a relative of my brothers' foster parent, our old babysitter. My sister who was by herself ended up coming to live with me. That was nice—I felt like a little small piece of my family was back with me.

When I was eighteen, I packed myself up and went to live with my biological mom. Two months into it, staying in the living room— there was no bed or room for me—I left and went to the shelter at the YWCA. That program you could stay a month. That gave me time to be accepted into a transitional housing program.

My first apartment was in North Park. I had funding resources. There is no way I could have done it otherwise, even with working. I was a shoe salesperson at a shoe store. People used to steal shoes from me all the time. It looked bad and like I allowed people to steal from the store.

While at the shelter I was attending a community college. I had another job working for a woman who was updating law books. I would start at six in the morning and get off about two or three. Then I would take the bus all the way to East County to Grossmont Community College night classes. Since I was exhausted by that time I would just fall asleep on the grass, oftentimes missing my class session. I had the ambition to do school, but not enough motivation.

When the program for my transitional housing ended I was accepted for a different transitional housing program, and I found a place in the same complex as my biological mom. I had not seen her often as a teen. I was expecting my firstborn. I had moved closer to her so she could help. It turned out to be vice versa. I lived with my firstborn in the same apartment complex until I was just about to give birth to my second son. That's when I decided to move in with my mom again.

With my mom it was me and two infants in one bedroom. Then my middle sister moved in. Mom got care of her. My sister is bipolar and depressed. There was an incident where things got so loud that we were kicked out. My sister went into a group home and my mom and I needed to separate, so she went to live with her boyfriend and my children and I went to live with my younger brother and his foster dad, our old babysitter.

I lived there, with my boys, for about a month more. At this time I had two jobs, one of them being a newspaper girl. Crazy hours. Up at

1:30 in the morning and work till 4:30, sometimes 6. Then I went to my day job from 9 to 3. I was doing career advising. I was always tired. I had no thought of school—there was no time.

My mom and I found another two-bedroom apartment and moved in with each other. While we were at this apartment my mom's application for Section 8 housing was granted. Since her name came up for her own apartment I stayed in the apartment with two bedrooms and she moved to another one-bedroom. I was in a lower unit for three years, and I was able to get into the Section 8 housing program. Every year it rained into the bedroom. We moved upstairs in the same complex for one year until there was an issue of domestic violence toward me from the father of my children. Not feeling safe and not being able to stand the confines of that apartment, I decided to move into a three-bedroom, two-bath apartment with washer and dryer and I've been there since January. I'm staying—I am tired of moving all of the time. I want a place to call home, for a while at least. I'd like for my children to have the consistency that I did not have.

In 2007, I got the best job I have ever had as a youth engagement specialist, where I coordinate a Youth Advisory Board. A friend pointed me to the Dollars for Scholars program. They had a walking event and I was able to bring my boys. At this event I met sponsors Mary Jo and Katie. They were friendly, nice ladies with hearts of gold.

At this point in my life I was finally settled, at least settled enough to be able to manage my college education. I decided to start by gradually increasing the number of units I took each semester, so I started with only one class at Cuyamaca Community College. Currently I am taking some classes at Grossmont College. But I don't take a class unless it meshes with my work schedule—it's the only way, but sometimes it means that I don't get to take a class that I would really like to take. I want a degree in sociology. I want to do research. I know I can do it. It is a broad major, so soon I will need to conduct some research on various careers in the sociology field to decide where I would like to focus my attention.

Eventually I would like to manage a youth program, be a resource to different schools, youth programs. Maybe a consultant. I want to be more productive where agencies that work with youth could use me for real tough youth issues. I'd like to do program designing and see more involvement of people at a younger age. I'd like to hear youth voices from the different funding agencies and let young people know about the services available to them and how to overcome barriers.

We kind of have our own lives now—me with work and my kids and school. My baby sister watches the kids sometimes—they're now ages six and four. She is a teenager and an artist. She found an old photo of me with our brothers when we were young, under five, and she glued it to a canvas and is working with my boys to do a painting around the photo. It is very special to me.

My younger sister is feeling some of the same things I was—wanting family together. I knew this when she came to me and asked, "Can we gather everybody together?" Her idea was to have a family reunion at the beach, so she used her artistic skills to create an invitation. I hope everybody's work schedule will allow them to come. We are working on the project together. We could bring a camera to the event, take family photos, and put something artistic together. I want to support her in her art.

I have heard people give speeches about foster care experiences. Sometimes they were much worse than mine, some not as bad. The first time I was a public speaker, I didn't know how to speak about my story strategically. A member of the audience asked what I had wanted most growing up. I said it was to be with my mom. I felt pressured by all of the audience's questions and so I broke down and cried during the speech. My mouth quivered—all I wanted was my mom and my family back. Without them I feel empty and alone, like something from my life is always missing.

Most of my siblings live in East County. I have another brother in Del Mar. My bipolar sister is in treatment in a facility in Alpine. We all have the desire to be connected. There is some emptiness around the fact that we weren't able to grow up and be with one another, even just fight with one another. When we do get together, it is very loving and we laugh. We are living with a sense that everybody is there for one another. It's like we are trying to catch up for the time that we did not have together.

Veronica

Veronica lives in a modest house in San Diego County. She leads the way through the living room where she and the teenage sister she is fostering sleep. An open door on the way to the kitchen shows the one bedroom's occupant, Veronica's ninety-eight-year-old grandfather. On hospice and expected to die in a few days, he is lying in bed.

My mother had been doing drugs. I had been unaware of how bad it was for a long time, but it came to the point when I was thirteen or fourteen that the situation was more out there.

I had a brother who was eight, a one-year-old sister and a two-year-old brother. One day I went to a religious meeting. I came back and I realized my mother had been leaving my siblings alone. Everything at home was in a mess and disarray. I called the police. My mother told the police she had been gone only a few minutes, but they didn't believe her. They found out when they went into our home how bad it was.

The first couple of months after we were taken away from my mother, my younger siblings went to an uncle's house. I lived with a parent-friend. My uncle decided he didn't want to take care of them long term. He didn't want to mess with my biological mother, so we went to a foster home for eight months. I went with them.

She had quite a few men in her life. She left my father when I was three. My younger brother has a different father. The other two have the same father. Biological parents get a second chance, so we went back with her for three weeks. She had moved to a bigger place. She dropped meth one day and fell asleep in front of my school.

My mother still wasn't able to raise us, so my brothers and sister were sent to the same foster home as before but I was left out. They left me with my mother. I don't know why that happened. I was sixteen. I thought I could take care of myself.

After three or four months there, I was trying to find a place away from my mother. My grandparents were in a senior citizens home, so that obviously was not good. I found other parent-friends, now in their fifties. We had a spiritual connection. I am a Jehovah's Witness. I was with them for a good year, then went with my siblings again. I aged out from that foster home. Aging out is when you turn eighteen and the next day you are out on your own.

Through a program, I was offered a place but you had to have a roommate and you had to be home at a certain time. I didn't think I wanted a roommate or a curfew. I mean, if I was out, I wasn't out being wild. I did find an apartment that was for foster youth. I attended Southwestern College in Chula Vista and I was a student worker. Friends gave me a used Chrysler Le Baron so I could drive back and forth to school. At first I wanted to be in computer networking. But I did not apply myself in school. My grandma was not doing well and I used that as an excuse. I fell into a depression. I didn't tell anyone.

I had wanted to be married. I got married. I got married three months before I turned nineteen. It was not a good marriage. I relied on him to supply support. He was seven years older than me, but he was not ready for that. I was independent but I let go and wanted him to catch me. He was also suffering from depression and didn't have good self-esteem.

From November of 2003 to June of 2004 we lived in Eugene, Oregon. He wanted to be somewhere where we did not have family problems around. It was strange. He couldn't find a job. I worked at Walmart at the cash register. He was depressed because he thought he should be paying the bills. I was always a workaholic.

We came back three times to San Diego to visit for a week or two. The last time, we went back to Oregon and right after we vacationed we returned because my grandmother passed away. February of 2004. We moved back four months later and stayed in his grandparents' home for three months, then we found a little studio.

I went to school off and on while we were married. I tried to get back to school in 2005, but my little brother was having problems so I started trying to figure out stuff for him. In 2005 my sister came to live with us. She was eight years old. Two weeks later my husband's brother lost his kids. We took them. A one-month-old, a one-year-old and a four-year-old. I stopped school again. For six months that was our situation. My husband couldn't handle babies. He went to work and slept. But it was so close to home for me. I couldn't allow them to be somewhere else, without family.

Her sister comes in and hangs around the table. There is the tinkling of carnival music. The Good Humor man is coming down the street and she is looking out for him because she wants an ice cream. Veronica watches her as she runs out to meet the truck.

The cockroaches where we were living in Chula Vista were taking over. We moved to a condo in Benita. All we had was his car to carry the kids around, and it wouldn't take all of us. We had to collaborate. Sometimes somebody had to be left behind. We got a van so we could transport everyone.

All the younger children left to live with their mom in 2006. My sister was still with us. We moved to a townhouse in a nicer area. Just the three of us. I was kind of riding it, but our relationship got bad again.

In 2007 I went back to school. My husband and I went through that "I'm leaving, you're leaving" thing. He didn't particularly like that I went back to school. He didn't want me to make more money than he did. He was an insecure and selfish person, but I was in love when I got married. That same year we separated. He was excited about finding his own place. He said he would help me, but he had his own bills.

I had a friend whose parents were moving out of state and suggested we find a house and move in together. We did that in February of 2008. A five-bedroom house for me and my sister, a husband and wife, and their two kids. But my ex-husband stopped paying my car payment after two months and it was a real struggle.

I was working part-time for Casey Family Programs as a youth advocate, teaching classes in independent living skills, but then the grant for the program where I was working went to Access Inc. You have to be a certain age to do that counseling anyway. I was too old to be a youth advocate. It's better if the kids you are counseling are closer in age. I could relate to them, but I was already twenty-four.

April 2008 to July 2008, I had another part-time job in PET—that's Pre-employment Training. I was earning some money. I became a little shopaholic. I was stressed and trying to spend it off. There was still the roller-coaster of the relationship. In October something happened— and kind of didn't—but anyway my husband and I broke apart.

I rented a room for my sister and me, a two-car converted garage. We had things stacked on top of one another, five thirty-two-gallon plastic storage bins and the mattresses on top. We got pretty creative with the space. It was still a roller-coaster. But I got rid of my credit card debt during that period. I was never one to have credit cards. After six months, I financially achieved that.

My husband and I went to couples therapy twice. I was kind of fed up. I was always the one giving, and I became more and more outspoken in therapy. I hurt his feelings. He is a man of unsureness. In his own way he loved me. It just was not what I needed.

I filed for a separation but he turned it back into a divorce. It was going there. No more: yes, maybe, yes, maybe. In June of 2008 it was finalized. I got $175 in alimony. It was more about the principle of it all. Even though I messed up a little. Still, my revenge was that he had to pay me for two years.

In six years we had hurt one another a lot. I don't want to have that experience any more. I learned a lot about myself. I have had no relationships since my ex. Now I want to get my life together and focus on school. I have a lot of friends, friends I have known since I was fifteen. Family that are not blood. I still care about the kids we fostered for a while. I still see them. But my ex has said to me that he wants to be friends. I told him, "Define friends." I've known him since I was fifteen, too. He comes over. He came today. But do I want to choose to stay in communication? I don't know. Now I am all about consistent relationships.

"My house is your house" has always been my way. My ex-husband's way was, "Call me before you come over."

In August of 2009 my sister and I moved to this house. I finally got my own place again. It has been stressful, though, because I have been unemployed and the relationship with my little sister is strained. We have lived on unemployment and I get money as a foster parent. But it came at a good time. It is giving me time to get myself together physically and emotionally. And I know now to be a little more choosey about what I apply for. I'm subbing for a paper route while I apply for city and county business licenses. I want my own business, but it's scary not knowing where the money is coming from. I want to set up a nonprofit that covers a little of everything, to benefit foster and at-risk youth. I'd like to have a group home. I want to have my own foster kids. I tell friends I want twenty kids.

I want to be a financial planner and tax advisor. I'm doing a pilot project with my ex-brother-in-law. I am running their budget. He gives me his paycheck and I am helping to move them out of debt. I love doing people's taxes. I want to get my business administration degree and CPA certification. I would love to get my master's, too, if I can get enough grants and scholarships to support my family. Just to be able to fully study would be great, a luxury.

My sister is thirteen now. Our relationship needs to be better. She needs more of my time and attention.

Her sister and a young female cousin who has come to help with their grandfather for the day come into the kitchen. Veronica hands them a baby food jar of prunes and tells them to feed it to him.
    Cousin: He doesn't want it.
    Veronica: He needs to eat the prunes.
    The girls go back into the bedroom with a spoon.

My grandfather used to live on his own. My mother was his caregiver, but she was not in a good place to take care of him. Three or four months ago she called from jail. The next day he went down onto the floor of his room. An ambulance came and Adult Protective Services was involved. My mom's brother said, "You take care of it, Veronica." My grandfather was in the hospital two weeks and then six weeks in a nursing facility. We wanted to get him into a skilled nursing facility, but it would have required all the family to pay out of pocket.

So he took my sister's room and she and I now use the pullout couches in the living room. He had a stroke a few days ago and he is receiving hospice.

He is a grumpy, funny old man. Now I have to be home. He grounded me a little bit. Sundays and Tuesdays I have religious meetings. My fifteen-year-old cousin comes to help. My sister helps. I change him. He's barely eating. The nurse thinks he will die within days. I'm trying to blend baby food myself but not having much luck.

The girls come back in. Her cousin tells her in Spanish that her grandfather doesn't want to eat the prunes.
    Sister: You should see the face he made when we tried to feed them to him.

Veronica (handing them another jar of baby food, this time chicken):
He'll eat that.

It's a good excuse to be at home. There are lots of nurses in and out.
The house is disarrayed. I've been trying to get a washing machine in
here so I don't have to beg friends to let me wash at their houses or go
to a laundry.

Just last week my grandfather was alert and sitting in this kitchen
talking to me. He was joking about his life. He said, "Boracho, jugador
y faldillero." Drunk, playing cards at the casino—his favorite thing—
and chasing skirts.

I've enjoyed the time he's been here. He is ninety-eight—born on
11/11/1911.

I'm supposed to start school in ten days. This time I'm going to start
with a couple of classes for eight weeks.

*Veronica's grandfather calls out to her and she excuses herself. She talks with
the old man in Spanish in the bedroom, then returns to the kitchen.*

I have to make sure that I appreciate every moment, even though I am
living in a little room. Maybe we'll get a bigger place. I want a bigger
place, but being happy in every moment you are alive is most important. We are not in need of anything, thankfully. We're eating, we have
a car, can put gas in the car.

To find a home, you have to be OK thinking, "It's just me." Instead of
wishing for parents, become one in the future. I'll be there for whoever
needs me. But I have had enough of overextending myself. It's not good
for me.

I have been trying to find or make a home lots of times, but I've
found it has to happen inside me. The only thing I can do is control me.
I'm a spiritual person. I rely on a higher power. But I find that home is
within myself.

2 After Battle

"The greatest casualty is being forgotten."
Wounded Warrior Project slogan

Joe

Joe Barrera retired in 2010 from teaching Ethnic Studies and American South-west literature at the University of Colorado at Colorado Springs. He holds a PhD in English literature from the University of Texas in Austin. He sits in the back corner of a Colorado Springs bookstore and coffee shop, looking the image of a professor in his cap and tweed jacket with elbow patches.

When I was seven, my family moved with my career army dad from Texas, where I was born, to Germany. My father was sent to Germany several times. My family also lived in Hawaii. We were comfortable, as far as you can be moving every two to three years. You had to make new friends. It was tough on my mother. The mother has to create the home.

I kind of liked Army posts. The military is just a huge socialistic life-style. You're given housing, schools, recreation, all one big community. In the fifties and sixties, when I was young, the military communities were more tightly bound. There was more of a culture and a lifestyle. Today the legacy of Vietnam and the ongoing eternal wars act to pull the whole thing apart.

I joined the Army in 1967 after two years of college at the University of Texas–Pan American in Edinburgh, Texas. Dad had been sent back to Germany for the third time. I told him I wasn't going to go. I was going to stay there. But I was not very happy. I was bored. I didn't have a lot of money. I signed up and got sent to Vietnam as an infantryman. It's what I had wanted to do all along.

In the culture of South Texas at that time it was normal to go into the military. Expected. More readiness to do so. The same was true for poor whites in Appalachia and poor blacks in the city. It was a way to get away from the isolation or poverty. A lot of middle class white folks have a problem with that, but that's the way it was.

It's even more true now. The majority of the military is made up of the working class struggling to survive.

I knew a lot about the Army before I joined, but afterward I was seeing it from a different perspective. Before, when I was a military dependent, I had been one of the privileged just watching the soldiers go through training. I could tell it wasn't fun, but as a kid I wanted to do it.

I went to Fort Polk, Louisiana, two months for basic training, then Fort Gordon in Georgia another two months for Advanced Individual Training. After that I was considered trained. I had infantry training and went into the 11 Bravo MOS as a light weapons infantryman or rifleman. I was part of the Fourth Infantry Division in the Central Highlands, flown out of Pleiku Air Force Base in South Vietnam. I ended up in a line company, literally on the line. That became my home. They issued you a rucksack to carry, a poncho, a poncho liner and an air mattress. It was the best that they had. Besides that you had a rifle, ammunition, a helmet, trenching tools—big shovels and little—and grenades.

You walked for months across rivers, swamps, jungles. Every night you would dig a foxhole, or trenches sometimes, and get into your hooch and snap your poncho together with a buddy. It was much like sleeping under a tarp. You couldn't be enclosed because you had to know if there were signs of the enemy. We cut trees down with machetes to build landing zones for the helicopters. There were lots of mosquitoes and other bugs. There was malaria, dengue fever, hepatitis and jungle rot on your skin. I still have some. It was hot, but cool at night on the mountaintops. In December and January they actually had winter. You were only issued a jungle sweater, a wool and nylon lightweight sweater.

Sometimes we went weeks without bathing or changing our clothes. Uniforms were stained with the red mud of the area. They were torn. You could see brine from sweat that made white spots on the uniforms. (*He rubs his chest.*) Everyone lost weight. We ate C rations. Those cans are heavy. Every once in a while we would get Long-Range Recon Patrol rations that the Special Operations forces used—freeze-dried food—on long patrols deep into enemy territory. The others were too heavy for extended missions on foot, when we were going out looking for the enemy.

Part of the job was to wreck the North Vietnamese base camps. I saw a lot of combat against the North Vietnamese, not the Viet Cong. Of course, the natives understood the jungle and knew the terrain much better than the American forces. They were a lot better at erecting bunkers than us. They were built at a perfect ninety-degree angle. No loose dirt. They made huts out of bamboo and thatch. Elaborate bunker complexes. Wonderful bunkers with tables, chairs and beds. Ingenious stoves of mud where they would dig a trench up the hill for a chimney. It was built in a way that the smoke from the fires was dispersed so that it couldn't be detected.

We were messy. We ruined the countryside with our bombing. Americans are very sloppy, dirty people—especially soldiers. We would bulldoze. Cut down trees needlessly. We did a lot of environmental damage. And there was Agent Orange, of course, which destroyed and poisoned huge tracts of pristine forest. B-52 bombers dropped bombs from 30,000 feet causing huge, indiscriminate damage. It was like trying to kill ants with sledgehammers.

The area where we patrolled was not like a Tarzan jungle, but full of enormous hardwood trees that occasionally blocked all the light. There was no underbrush. It was beautifully peaceful and quiet. It was like stained glass when the light filtered through the trees. Hushed, peaceful, almost sacred.

I was not injured during my fifteen months there. I was not hit, even though guys close to me were. I escaped. I was very lucky. I could easily have been killed. But I didn't want to come home. I liked living in the woods. Liked having everything I needed on my back, in my rucksack. There were no bills to pay. It's a strange thing to say, but it was a comfortable life. There was fear, but I got used to it.

I came home because my mother was going crazy. She was frantic with worry. Lots of parents were that way. Like moms whose sons are in Afghanistan and Iraq now. Dreading the harbingers of death who come to the door. It's not easy for those at home.

I lived on post at Colorado Springs' Fort Carson in an old World War II barracks. I wanted to return to Vietnam. It was the fall of 1968 and I had just turned twenty-two. I was young enough that I felt immortal. That's what makes war possible. Young men believe … (*pause*) Young males between eighteen and twenty-four … you need those six years to make soldiers out of them. They will risk their lives. They are ferocious. Brutality can be cultivated. It's latent in all humans, particularly young men.

I suffer from post-traumatic stress syndrome (PTSD). Even with the Army training, you still can't escape it. You are toughened so you can tolerate the stress of combat better. "Train hard, fight easy" is one expression. And "More sweat now, less blood later." They make you stay up all night and march in the dark. Sleep deprivation because in a combat zone in Vietnam you would go three to four nights with no sleep. You can actually sleep while you're walking. You start to lose it. You start to go nuts. A lot of PTSD is related to that. It comes with extreme fatigue. The inability to find sleep when you come back, because your nerves are shot. I take two pills, one for depression and another for anxiety and irritability. All three of my symptoms are related to PTSD. If I don't take one of the pills for two or three days, I notice my irritability gets bad.

I stayed at Fort Carson briefly after I came back from Vietnam. I was in the service three years altogether. Then I moved to an apartment near the Colorado College campus. I thought, "I may as well go here." I got a scholarship and a job. But I was not your typical student. I worked for the extension service of Colorado State University in an urban 4-H program working with school dropouts. I was obsessed with trying to make a positive contribution.

That's typical of combat veterans. You see so much shit and participate in so much destruction that you want to help society. But this has to be channeled. Only a small percentage of soldiers have the ability to come back and be constructive. The military doesn't help in any way. You are literally turned loose. We were walking time bombs because we hadn't been decompressed.

Lots of things bother you when you come back from war. The complacency, innocence and ignorance of civilians. There I was attending Colorado College a few months after I got out of the Army. I envied the students' naiveté, their sheer enjoyment of life. I couldn't be like them. I felt deficient. Of course, at that time there was no concept of war trauma. Nobody talked about how they felt. I basically had to educate myself about that.

Just about everything was highly traumatic for me when I came back from Vietnam. The first trauma was Vietnam. The second trauma was entering an anti-war campus. There were about forty to fifty vets on campus at the time. We vets banded together. We were grossly misunderstood. The worst for all the vets was the way we were ignored. Treated as though we were invisible. Our experiences meant nothing. It was assumed we were all responsible for atrocities and the nightmare Vietnam had become that everybody hated. That attitude lasted until the mid-eighties. In the nineties the climate started to change.

In 1989, I started to go to a veterans center for help. These centers, mostly in city storefronts, were set up by the VA in the seventies under pressure from Vietnam vets. I started to talk to people and understand that I wasn't the only one who felt the way I did.

Even now I suffer insomnia bouts. I am totally tired but wide awake. It has to do with adrenaline. A lot of young guys, veterans of the present wars, I know are taking ten different medications for anxiety, depression, sleep, suicidal thoughts. One guy told me he didn't know which medication it was but he was becoming impotent.

Most military veterans are not combat veterans, and I think every combat veteran by definition has to have PTSD. There is nothing like it. Combat is the most stressful thing humans have devised and are subjected to. I don't care how tough you are.

PTSD is poorly understood even by professionals. It's not past stress. It is damage to the nerves so you can't handle present stress. The symptoms are very predictable. Depression, irritability, anger, rages. Something is not right in your brain and you can't enjoy life. You have a permanent case of what we used to call the black ass—a really, really bad mood.

Veterans Affairs, the VA, doesn't deal well with vets' trauma and war-related mental problems. The VA has a lot of female therapists. Women often think that war is a male pathology that they can treat and cure. There are especially a lot of feminists who think that patriarchy creates war. If they were in charge . . . (pause) . . . they believe war would not happen.

I am dismayed by the pop culture that has seized on war as a game. Video war games our children play. And there is so much talk about sending women into combat. The arguments against that idea are not about equality. They are about our future, children, nurturing. Wanting to create better than we have. You cannot take women and make warriors out of them and expect society to escape the consequences.

What I'm saying is that the warrior virtues are not what we should teach young people. This is because war is not romantic. It's about death and destruction, and endless sorrow and grief.

In 1979 I started to get sick all the time and nobody knew what was wrong. I was hospitalized in the spring of 1980 with my legs swollen like balloons. It turned out I had blood clots. It took doctors so long to discover what was wrong with me. Doctors are lazy. I don't feel positive about psychologists and psychiatrists either. They stereotype people and think they have all the solutions. However, I appreciate the care I've received from the VA doctors. They do the best they can. But I am still chronically ill. It's due to stress.

My soon-to-be wife came to visit me in the hospital. She claimed her husband beat her. When I was out of the hospital, I moved in with her. I was so lonely and isolated. I worked for the city, the human relations commission. I listened to people complain. I'm good at that, though.

Lots of vets suffer from psychosomatic illnesses. Lots of vets recover. Some don't. I don't understand why. I try very hard to work toward more awareness now. There are a lot of young fellas already set up to experience the same things we did.

When I came back from war I forgot. But ten years later PTSD was triggered by a helicopter overhead. I thought I had put it all behind me but it hit me like the proverbial ton of bricks. I had pushed it all into a deep hole in my mind because society was so put off by Vietnam.

In the mid-nineties I found other vets to talk to. I found another combat vet who understood PTSD. Soldiers themselves know it and have the ability to cure it, but they can't articulate in clinical terms. They can help others if they are empowered. But the professional community sees this type of sharing as a risk of retraumatization. The therapists' big bugaboo. They misunderstand that through soldiers telling their stories there is healing. It breaks isolation down.

I have put together a group in Colorado Springs called Veterans Remember. Veterans Remember is all about coming home. Veterans talk to other veterans, but spouses and families are there to listen and respond. This allows for communication to be established—and this creates home. It's successful, but it is all up to me to put everything together. I get tired. I hold a lot of hands.

It is very easy for me just to stay home. My shelter, my cave, my perimeter. I lock the door and close the blinds. I read and sleep all day, sleep in the day. I don't want to do it. But there is another definition of home: creating a bunker mentality of home. I resist that. I want to get involved, volunteer. It's an uphill battle for me to be a part of something. It's easy to drop out completely. Disappear. But even my three grown kids, sooner or later, will want to know where I am. But how long would it take them?

For a lot of vets there is withdrawal. There are secrets that civilians don't know about, that vets hide, don't admit. The single biggest thing is that combat veterans want to go back to war. This is the big secret. We all want to go back to our wars. Even those who deny it. A lot of us combat vets don't want to admit to PTSD. We don't want to talk about it. Then there are the liars who say they were in combat but weren't really. They make up stories or say they don't want to talk about it. Phonies are common.

On the other hand, I've met draft dodgers my age who went to Canada and who are envious when they see this. (*He points to a small pin on his jacket.*) It's the combat infantryman's badge awarded to those who have been in combat. They get really jealous. They say, "You got to see combat. Life is unfair."

I just read an article in the *Atlantic Monthly* about a reporter who was embedded long-term with combat infantry in Afghanistan. It's the same crap. Afghanistan is the same stupid crap. It seems the army hasn't learned a single thing. It's Vietnam all over again without some of the lessons. American veterans and their lessons are ignored. America has historical amnesia. Vietnam is virtually forgotten.

When I was in the Army, we trained with the British Royal Green Jacket Regiment. Their military insulated them from the brutality of war through pride in their unit. We just don't have that any more. What I noticed about the British Army was that it was a special network. For them it was like the pride of home, a nuclear unit where the commander was the father and the wife of the commander was the mother, often hosting soldiers in the home. They were posting people in the regions where they came from. They were much more intelligent about it. There was much less violently criminal behavior. I was reminded of the U.S. Army of the fifties.

And they were much more cohesive. In American culture it is hard to maintain cohesiveness. Even when I was a professor at UCCS, I couldn't fit in. Sometimes I would pop off and say things. Blow my stack. I tend to be forgiving of people, but people are not forgiving toward me.

I have had to live by myself. It has been a stress to live with anybody the whole time. I was married for nine years. All my experiments with living with other people have failed, even though I miss my kids.

I own a house. Maybe my divorce was not all my fault. I could have been the perfect husband and she would have left. I was number four. Now she is working on number six. She is one of those women not willing to settle for anything less than perfection. I can say truthfully that I did love her, but I was angry at times and hurt her. But so often it had to do with anger at myself. People do not put up with other people's problems. It's hard to keep a marriage together.

Our culture has trended to selfishness. Very few are willing to be patient or communicate. But all these years, all this time, I have been trying to find home. I'll keep trying. I do keep trying.

Doug

Some of the signs in Doug and Dorothy Gale's front yard:

"What is faith worth if it isn't translated into action?" Mahatma Gandhi
"How Is the War Economy Working for You? Veterans for Peace"
"Support Our Troops—In the effort to be healthy and have homes"

Doug Gale opens the storm door of his Pueblo, Colorado, home. He is a slight man with white hair and a white beard and mustache. The back of his green sweatshirt says "Feeding Children Is Our Number One Goal." He has on a "Wage Peace" button.

Doug guides his wife Dorothy into the living room and settles her on the couch. He sits in a chair near her. Dorothy has Alzheimer's, so she won't be participating in the interview actively, but her blue eyes glisten and she seems engaged in what her husband is saying. In the next room, KCME public radio from Manitou Springs, Colorado, plays classical music.

Dorothy and I enjoy music and information from around the world twenty-four hours a day, thanks to the public radio station. It is always on as long as we are in the house. It keeps Dorothy smiling. We turn it on for ninety minutes at night and are usually asleep before it is finished.

Our helper just left. Other than her assistance three times a week, I take care of Dorothy. On the third week of every month we go to the Boulder-Arvada-Golden area, where we visit the children. Our daughter

Susan takes us and brings us back. It keeps Dorothy from forgetting our children.

I was born in the United States, but not the U.S. proper. It is not a state. It is not a province. Can you guess? It's not Puerto Rico. Yes, the District of Columbia.

My dad was in the Navy in the supply corps. After World War I was over, they decommissioned a lot of battleships and sold the armor plating on them, which was unsurpassed. My father said, "We're going to regret it." Guess who bought it? Japan. We were listening on the old Philco radio about the bombing of Pearl Harbor. That December 7, tears rolled down my father's face. It impressed us. We were ready to blame Japan for everything. As a result, I went into the Navy at nineteen.

I had aunts and uncles sprinkled around the country. My mother told me to go and visit them before I went off to war. I visited family in Texas, Florida, Ohio and other places.

Then I went to basic training at Sampson Naval Training Station in the New York Finger Lakes area. It was very cold, 30 to 40 degrees below zero. I was given the job of stoking fires. I was lucky because I stayed warm. When we'd go out to drill, we were given wooden guns. I was never on a firing range. They were making guns at that time—they didn't have enough guns.

I volunteered at Sampson to go into patrol torpedo (PT) boats. They were 77- to 80-foot-long boats with big Packard engines. They could go 35 to 40 knots, about 40 to 46 miles per hour.

In Melville, Rhode Island, they started to take us out to get introduced to the boats. I got to fire a gun for the first time, a 20-millimeter cannon. A plane went by and here I am shooting this cannon. Next they put us on machine guns. We did that for three to four months. It was really ludicrous.

From there we went directly to Tulagi in the Solomon Islands, across the bay from Guadalcanal. We were following as the Marines cleared up to Zamboanga in the Philippines. All this time I was keeping my mother informed, although I couldn't write and say where I was. They censored all letters. I described the lush green islands, so she knew where I was. It made me feel good.

In 1945, one month after Hiroshima, I was with the command squadron at the head of all the PT boats. My boat had been chosen because it was surrounded by armor plate and was deemed more defensible. They picked our PT and said, "You're going back with a Silver Star or a medal or you're not going back at all."

Our job was to patrol the beaches of the Japanese shoreline. The Japanese had landing craft back in the jungles. We'd go after these barges and shoot at them with .50 caliber machine guns and .40 millimeter cannon too. Our boat was special. We worked with a destroyer escort. They would be three or four miles out. We would tell them: "This is where you shoot." They would pick it up on their radar and fire their guns.

One time we reported barges and the skipper told the escort, "Here they are. Go after them." But the destroyer took us for the barges and fired on us. I had fortunately gone up on deck to get air and was sitting on a life raft. We lost half our crew. I was cushioned from the explosion and thrown up in the air.

I had a life jacket on. Most of the force of the explosion took place in the boat underneath me. There were twenty men. I was the only one who wasn't injured. I had just gone up to get fresh air while I was on a break. It was stuffy in the armored compartment down below.

Ten of my fellow sailors died in the explosion. That experience has influenced me to work for peace for the rest of my life. Wars just breed hate. There's nothing good about wars. I think Obama basically feels that way. More power to him. But it is up to us—our patriotic and civic duty—to speak up for peace.

Coming home from the war, when we got to Leyte in the Philippines, we were given a physical. The doctors were examining everyone who came. As I was getting an exam, he asked me how long I had been over here. Two years, I said. I was not very excited about going home. I heard the doctor question a Marine and ask how long he had been over there. Four years without a break, he said.

I made up my mind right there that I didn't ever want to feel sorry for myself. But the real beginning of my feelings about war came when I was on a Liberty ship after the bombings of Hiroshima and Nagasaki. It was so crowded with GIs that I slept on the deck. I got to talk things over with one after another of the men.

Today we bring soldiers right home. It's a shame. Our Veterans for Peace Chapter 129 tries to stay in contact with homeless vets in this area. Many are suffering from PTSD and drug addiction. Our chapter works on all these issues.

When I got out, I bussed across the country. I started in October, just before Halloween. I ended up in Gettysburg, Pennsylvania. On November 1 the bus drivers went on strike, so I was hitchhiking with my sea bag to Philly. People were very kind. A pickup carried me right downtown—$1 taxi fare and I was home. I arrived at six in the morning. Our dog Trixie, a Dalmatian, was there to greet me, and I got Mom and Dad up.

I was able to attend Pueblo Junior College and then graduate from the University of Colorado. I started out in business but became a teacher. I ended up in the town of Pueblo because, as I had passed through here and the Royal Gorge going home, I'd revisited an uncle. He had said, "If you ever come back, you'll have a job." He owned a gas station at 4th and Main. I took that job. I thought Pueblo was paradise at the end of the rainbow.

Getting into college was a process. I went to the admissions office for junior college. I was really, really fortunate. There was this really wonderful lady, Lulu Cuthbertson, who gave the appearance of a stern, strict person, but her eyes were glittering all the while she was talking to me. She looked over my records and said, "You had a couple of problems your last two years of high school." My first two years in high school, I had been on the honor roll at South Charleston High School in West Virginia. My dad was stationed at the depot down there. When we came back up to Lansdowne, Pennsylvania, it was a new high school for me. The first day I went to school and there was this teacher, Mrs. Krist. Her name was Krist, but we called her Christ!

She said to me, "You're Bill Gale's brother? I don't want any trouble out of you like I had with him." I took my books off her desk one time when she asked me not to and I was out of school for a week. That set the tone for the next two years. I graduated with a D average.

But the lady at admissions at Pueblo Junior College said, "Well, that's all done. You're accepted." A great lady. She was certainly one who helped to give me incentives. I never would have gotten to go to college without the GI Bill. I got college paid for, medical benefits, and I got a home. Fortunately, I had no medical problems. Without the college opportunity, I never would have met this young lady. (*He smiles at his wife. She smiles back.*)

Dorothy was born and raised in this house where we are sitting. We were married under the cedar tree. (*He points out the window to a forty-foot tree in the front yard.*) We moved to this house when her parents died and our five children were grown.

I became an elementary school teacher and first taught seventh and eighth graders at the airbase in Baxter east of town. Two hundred and fifty kids, one building for sixth through eighth grades. Across Highway 50, at the air base, they had preschool through fifth grade.

I taught just about everything and became the scoutmaster as well. I got to do it all. As a teacher, I did conservation. All the teachers had meetings and we talked about how important it is that kids love the earth, be stewards. I think Christ said, "Whatever you ask in my name, this I will do."

I worked professionally with the Boy Scouts for six years. I spent summers at scout camp and doing scout activities. That took me away from my wife and children for three months of the year. It was a mutual decision in the family that I would go back into teaching. I stayed as a volunteer in the Boy Scouts.

After Baxter, we moved to the suburbs of Denver and I taught in Adams City. It was out near Rocky Mountain Arsenal. It was a place that had nuclear facilities. Our kids knew about the dangers. They learned about soil, air and water contamination and the dangers of radiation to humans and wildlife.

I was a teacher for twenty-two years. I hope I had a big impact. Some keep in touch—I know where they are. So many were called into the service and were in Vietnam and Iraq. Our Veterans for Peace group wants to be able to get into the schools along with the recruiting office. We want equal time.

I have two brothers, neither of whom saw action in World War II. That's good. Dan was a colonel in the engineers, building roads. He didn't have to carry a gun. Bill was in the Air Corps, but he never had to go. We've lost Bill, but Dan is still active in Veterans for Peace, church and other peace activities.

We believe in the absolute abolition of nuclear weapons, Star Wars, and nuclear power plants. I hope the disaster in (Fukushima) Japan will wake people up.

I walked the country with the Great Peace March for Nuclear Disarmament in 1987. Atheists, agnostics, Jews, Muslims, Christians—every conceivable race, creed and color—joined the march. It started in Irvine, California, and finished in Washington, D.C. I think we made an impression.

My church followed my progress. See this photo? It was taken outside Sterling in northeast Colorado. A dirt road. My group walked twenty to twenty-five miles a day. We were part of an advance party that notified the police of our intention to conduct a peaceful, nonviolent march at the nuclear facility near Sterling. Forty silos are still there! At the time of our march, they were active.

I had so many wonderful experiences with all the people in the Great Peace March. We visited people in their homes, churches and work. Basically we wanted to inform people of some of the problems of nuclear facilities and to let legislators and Congress know they should be working for the U.S. people and not the conglomerates and greedy billionaires.

In '89—it was the first Bush administration—there was talk of a nuclear disarmament agreement, but no real push. With the present-day political climate, we see too few bipartisan efforts and so much divisiveness. And this "Boston" Tea Party! People are duped because they hear the same things over and over. What we citizens have to do is stand up and speak out: "This is not true. Our country is being sold out."

The Xcel Energy and Concrete plants east of Pueblo are all mercury-producing plants. The munitions depot is storing napalm gas, mustard gas and deteriorating nuclear missile weapons. The Sierra Club and other groups continue to try to get them to dispose of them in the proper way.

My nephew is responsible for a paper entitled "Consequences of the Abandonment of the Alpine Mine in Gilman, Colorado," where there were PCB capacitors, the passive electrical components that store energy. When not disposed of properly their breakdown results in contamination of the soil, air, water, plants, animals and humans.

Companies just go off and leave these toxic wastes. "That's OK," they say. "We don't live there." The Xcel plant, for example. Where does the electricity go? Oklahoma. We're not getting electricity. All we get is mercury contamination that continues to poison all God's creations. When the wind blows from the east, it is carried out here.

We've walked and camped for causes. We'll be doing it again because they want to build a nuclear plant near here. Here's an issue of the *Christian Science Monitor*. The headline says, "Japan's Long Road Back: Why Nuclear Power Will Continue." I share magazines like this with my wife every day. I try to read to her every day, which benefits both of us.

We belong to the United Church of Christ. It welcomes everybody. I've never had a problem with anybody. People see Dorothy and me and see our open door. We try to say hello to everybody.

A Puerto Rican family we know is Zen Buddhist. We always feel perfectly welcome at their house. It's hard for me to sit the way they sit, but we are always accepted. We think Zen Buddhism is a wonderful religion. The Baha'i Faith, they're a great group too. They accept everyone. There are some Muslim people here. We've gotten to meet some. I haven't had any contact with any religions I can't appreciate.

Our granddaughter Katie married a young man who is Hebrew. We've gone to the synagogue here in Pueblo and feel welcomed. We get invitations to come visit people, which we do. In turn, we invite them.

Dorothy and I are refusing all pharmaceuticals. Our doctor told us he's not going to give us any meds or vaccinations unless our temperature rises too high. Let the body fight it. We don't have aches or pains. We don't have it all up here. (He points to his head and he and Dorothy laugh.)

Doug fixes lunch. He takes a large slice of quiche that one of his daughters has made from the freezer and puts it in the microwave. He adds tomatoes he has found in the lower part of the fridge. He pours glasses of unpasteurized milk from a dairy outside town. They are going to eat outside in the yard. It is the first sunny day after a hard Colorado winter. Doug helps Dorothy down the porch stairs and goes back for the food tray, which he places on the stump of a recently cut tree. They sit in metal chairs next to it. There is only one plate on the tray.

Doug: Dorothy and I will be using the same plate. (*Doug takes one bite, and then feeds his wife the next. She leans toward him to receive it.*)

This is the cedar tree we were married under in 1949. It has grown a lot taller. Ruth, a woman I protested with at the Nevada test site—introduced me to the world peace prayer. There are times when people say it around the world, so it is a continuous chain of people praying. We say it before every noon meal:

Lead us from death to life,
From falsehood to truth;
Lead us from despair to hope,
From fear to trust.
Lead us from hate to love.
From war to peace.
Let peace fill our hearts,
Our world, our universe.

Michael

Michael drinks a cup of coffee at the Barnes & Noble extension of Starbucks in eastside Colorado Springs. His dark hair is spiked. His tie says that he works at a job where they want you to look professional.

I was born in Odessa, Texas, but I never lived there. I grew up partly in Indiana, San Antonio and Dallas with my mom and two siblings. I never knew my biological father.

I was an average high school student. Mainly, I didn't get why I was supposed to be studying, where it was going to lead me. Throughout high school, it was like, Why? I was not a party animal. I was hard to motivate. I needed to have a reason why. Other than what they told you, which was that it would put you on the bottom rung of society if you didn't graduate.

I went to the University of Texas in Arlington. The relationship with my mom was kind of rocky. I was not a troublemaker, but I needed to make my own way. Finding money for school was hard. I went for two and a half years. I went and got loans and a part-time job that I worked at almost the whole time. It was difficult. Finally, I just got to the point where I thought, "I can't keep putting myself in more debt."

I started living with my mom and stepdad and things were getting even rockier. When I was twenty-one, I had a falling out with them. At that point I thought it was a good idea to join the military. She didn't want it.

I had made straight A's at first in college. At one point I had two jobs. I worked for FedEx for three weeks. It was so bad I thought I'd rather be in the military. I signed a contract with the Air Force on my birthday in January 2006. At the end of March I went to boot camp at Lackland Air Force Base in San Antonio.

I went to tech school to learn networking and computing for three months. I had to wait for a month to be deployed. I was given a lot of busy-work, running around cleaning things, basically. In September of 2006 I managed to get assigned to the base of my choice, Ramstein Air Base in Germany. It was nice. I was kind of in culture shock, but I had a couple of years of German in high school and two classes in college. I got out and traveled. Not right away, but when my girlfriend moved to Germany from Thailand we traveled. I wasn't motivated to go out at first when I was there. I wanted to see the sights but it felt kind of lame doing it by myself.

My girlfriend and I—she's my fiancée now—got to know each other through a pen pal program. The first couple of years I was there, she stayed in Thailand. I visited her in Thailand when I was on leave and she moved to Germany in 2007 to be closer and to study for her master's at the University of Kassel's international master's degree program. It's three or four hours from the base. I took the train there every weekend.

I was deployed the first time to an Air Force base in Afghanistan. The first year I was deployed was not a big worry because I was in the communications base shop. Our job was to keep lines of communication open at all times, especially when convoys took people outside the wire.

It was good, tax-free pay. Lots of people volunteered for this type of deployment because it was better than waiting for a slotted position, one that you were forced to take. The higher-ups liked to fill the slots on the base because it looked bad to other senior leadership if they weren't filled. So there we were twiddling our thumbs. Being apart from my fiancée the first time was pretty bad. The deployment itself was fine. I played the guitar. I just considered it to be temporary duty at another location. Not a big deal. You could go off base. But you did get this feeling of purposelessness to the whole thing.

When I came back to Germany, I readjusted to my fiancée. We had issues. She made me promise I wouldn't leave again. I couldn't do that. It was not in my hands. It was a constant topic of conversation. Then it was the elephant in the room that you don't want to bring up.

We did get readjusted, though. We traveled a lot.

Then I was put into a different squadron. The same base, a different mission. Contingency operations. They were a bunch of gung-ho, mission types, looking at deployment every year. It was an all-encompassing squadron—from communications to convoys. They were really deployment oriented. We did exercises all the time. We'd just go off for two weeks to field training grounds.

It was kind of stressful. You couldn't plan your life. Stuff would come up randomly. I did get a lot of traveling done. My girlfriend and I worked around it, but it would not be easy for married people. It was still tough even without that aspect. The constant potential for deployment created a stress on our relationship.

In the summer of 2009, I discovered I would be going to Afghanistan—Kandahar Air Force Base. Operation Enduring Freedom. Definitely a combat zone, even though I would be strictly working on the base. I didn't want to break it to her. I had a guilty conscience. I knew it would make her stressed out as soon as she learned. After about a week, I told her.

I had been going to school to get my bachelor's degree in information systems security and I was scheduled to graduate in June. "You guys are jackin' me up," I told them. "I've already been—just last summer." I had already been deployed and I was a senior in the shop, a semi-expert. Anytime they need something from the shop, they go to that guy. There were airmen who had just finished technical school. I argued with leadership, "Why aren't they sending these guys?" I didn't win, obviously.

 It was a lot more stressful on me this second time because my grandfather had just died. I didn't want to go for that reason. It kept me more depressed because he was more of a father to me. That deployment was worse for the relationship with my girlfriend. Five months. It was not like I was in the Army getting in firefights. But it was not playing right for her mental stability. Fire shells came randomly into the base. Most of the time they never hit anybody. It was al-Qaeda or whoever, working with the smaller terrorist groups. It was a major Taliban stronghold.

At Kandahar I was doing the same thing I had been doing in Germany—networking, server-related stuff. The server provided services to the computers we networked to. E-mail. Everyday business stuff. We built our own site on base like we always do. We built tents, routed power. We brought equipment to build our own servers, but the base we were connecting to said no way. It was a security thing. They said, "You have to connect to us."

I felt as useless as the last deployment. We were kind of out of the picture. Just kind of sitting around waiting for stuff to break. That's how deployment works. You're bored. You don't care if somebody attacks. Whatever.

Some people have more nervous personalities. Those guys were sent home. You've got to find something to do. Come with a personal goal because otherwise you go nuts. There is nowhere to go. A lot of people worked seven days a week. I took online courses and worked toward a degree in my major. But there were no testing locations in Afghanistan.

Seeing some things there put things in perspective. The normal American is disconnected from seeing what is really going on there. There were a lot of minefields everywhere. It was dangerous to walk. We have sophisticated equipment to clear the minefields. But they used Afghanis with metal detectors. With bulletproof vests. I don't know what good those vests were supposed to do. They were like those X-ray blankets from the dentist's office.

The mines are pretty low velocity, but if it goes past a certain point it can blow off your arms. Our military has full bodysuits for explosives disposal work, but it is still dangerous.

At the front gate, the Afghanis would come every morning to find work. At the security checkpoint they had a huge cage to separate them from the people outside. They were packed in like sardines. Then the site supervisors would go in and grab guys. They would have Afghan guys all over them because they wanted to work. The kids would come to the fence to beg for bottles of water.

The non-U.S. personnel who worked on the base were usually Filipino, Indians, Pakistanis—people the military could move there cheaply and get clearance for. There were some Afghanis doing construction. But using them for the mine clearing—I had a problem with that. I also felt it was a misuse of labor, especially when we had machines to do the same job. But why spend our manpower to run the machines, that was our military's mindset.

In October of 2009, I came back to Germany. My fiancée finished her schooling in February of 2010. I stayed a while on a visa extension, then I wanted to go back and see my family. I hadn't been back for a year. I went every Christmas until Grandpa died. Then there were family issues I didn't want to deal with. I didn't go this past Christmas.

I stayed with my parents a while. I graduated in August of 2010. I had accomplished what I wanted to do educationally. It helped me get a job as quick as I did. In the beginning of November I found this job at the Space Command doing information security work as a contractor—not a government employee.

I'm twenty-six now. This job is not my ultimate goal. I want to do more policy writing, reviews on stuff in question. "How secure is this?" "We've got these problems, how do we fix them and what should our policies be now?"

I have ideas about war and U.S. involvement. Intervention shouldn't be used at all unless it is absolutely necessary. I'm of a mind that if you send people's sons and daughters in mortal combat to fight, you have to have a good reason. We can't take on the whole world. I don't go with the pre-emptive intervention. Don't go to war unless we are invaded.

The allegiances that obligate us to go to warfare are more dangerous in less obvious ways.

I believe in dissent in the interest of making sure the U.S. is doing the right thing. Darfur was mass genocide. There are injustices all around the world but you don't see us intervening. But if there is oil involved or if it's a strategic area, it's an issue.

It's funny when you get that type of epiphany. Suddenly something doesn't make sense. I'm not extremely conservative, but I grew up in the middle of conservative ideas and hawkish attitudes. The first two years in the service it was kind of my attitude.

I'm at the point in my life where I am trying to establish myself so I have a secure future. A transitioning point. My fiancée wants to stay in Thailand, so now I have to find a job there. You know how Asian families are. Much more closely knit. Her family is half Chinese. There you know every Chinese family in your region. They can help you.

I don't have any attachment to American culture. I don't mind a wedding there or finding a life in Thailand. That's fine. I do worry about finding a job. They are trying to restrict foreign entry for jobs. They keep a quota. They would probably rather hire a Thai person. It would be cheaper, and they would speak Thai.

It's possible I could work for the World Health Organization, or an organization like that. Or a foreign company.

I've been to Thailand three times and I'm about to go the fourth time next week. The only trouble with working as a foreigner is that all the jobs are pretty much in Bangkok. It's crowded. Among the top five in the world. The traffic is horrendous. The city is so kind of dirty and noisy.

Colorado Springs is OK. It would be nice to have a bigger downtown. The first time I saw it, I said, "Oh, this is the downtown?" The base in Germany was good—an hour away from Luxembourg. An hour and a half from the border of France.

It's hard to mesh with people here. They are a bit younger. They are considerably younger in mindset. They like to get smashed till they can't move. I didn't ever relate to that.

I'm independent. I don't go out much. Normally I go home to my apartment at night. Just do stuff on my computer and stay there.

Tom

Tom went back to his native Queens directly after combat in Vietnam in 1969, then moved to a small western city. He has been active in veterans' concerns almost since his return.

New York City was not a good place to figure out life after the war. I just wanted to get lost when I came home. Four or five months later there was Kent State. I thought, "I have to get involved. We're shooting our own people now?"

I still suffer from post-traumatic stress disorder. I feel so bonded to the Iraq guys coming home. We really got screwed coming back from Vietnam. From the public calling us baby killers to the older people saying, "What the hell? Can't you win this war?" We were not welcome in the DAV (*Disabled American Veterans*). Everybody was pissed. We were caught in the middle. There was nasty stuff in airports, people spitting on us. Especially in San Francisco.

I had all these crazy memories, visions of war. I had two days in San Francisco after I came back from Vietnam, and then I was dumped. I remember being at the Presidio and thinking I would call Mom. I didn't. I didn't know if I could talk to her. I took the redeye to JFK, and at 4 o'clock I was ringing the doorbell. "Who's out there?" they said. I surprised them.

The civilians back home didn't want to face the reality of war. With our war, there was a division in the American population. They'd see on TV a GI putting a lighter to a villager's home. The first thing I did when I returned was to grow my hair. I didn't want to look like a goddam GI.

I can relate to being homeless. When I came back, even though I had great parents, I would walk around the city barefoot, smoking grass. I had no idea where I wanted to go. Dad was beautiful. Mom didn't know what to think. I had some joints in the house. They had no idea what I was doing.

I got busted. I drove with guys I knew to Woodstock. We had a nickel of hash, a nickel of pot, uppers, downers. We got stopped in a little town.

In New York City it would have been nothing, but in a little town … we had to get a lawyer. Dad said to go see the family lawyer. I told him what it was like over there. Fuckin' shit. He said, "You'd better talk to your dad."

Dad was in construction. I finally was able to tell him about Vietnam. We had a wonderful relationship. He passed on. I miss my rock. I didn't know my dad before the war. Mom was the dominant one.

I got married to someone I was hanging out with in the park. I was not into that before. I was going to college before I was drafted. To Long Island University. I hadn't kept up my grades. I went to night school and was doing better but I wasn't carrying enough of a load.

If I had forgotten about the first certified letter, I would have been saved. But the antiwar movement was not as strong as when I came back. Four months after Tet all they wanted was infantry.

I admire men who went to Canada to avoid the draft. They never knew if they were coming home to their families again. They stood up. They had a conscience. Look at Muhammad Ali. He was a big hero. He paid the price for his convictions. I never saw a conscientious objector as afraid. You get into combat, that's when you're afraid.

Yes, I served in front of the flag, but I was pushed.

At boot camp, it was "Run harder and faster. Get in good physical shape." We had a tough drill sergeant. They really yell out at you like you see on TV: "I can't heeeaaaarrrr you!" After a while I figured I would just mouth the words. I said to myself: "I ain't doin' this stupid stuff." But I know what was going through my brain. It was to kill. There was a lot of brainwashing to kill. But the problem is, when you come home, they don't take it out of you.

I didn't learn anything about the jungle. Two months in boot camp focused on the mental training to follow orders. They tried to re-create Vietnam in one week. You were so tired all the time. Up at five, to bed at eleven. You were always half-asleep. Lectures. How is it you get lectures to learn about the jungle?

I was twenty-one when I went to Vietnam. I spent fourteen months there. Combat. First we were at Bien Hoa Air Force Base outside Saigon. Like Camp Liberty in Iraq. A safe place. Everyone was drinking 10 cent canned beer. Budweiser was proud to support the troops. They had a club-house. A few guys were heads. We listened to our Doors tapes, those reel-to-reels at that time. We had comfortable barracks. But we were pretty sure that when we went out we were going to see some shit.

For six months of combat, I was in point position, the first guy at the head of one of two columns leading the way through the jungle. The position was a process of elimination. The guy before me got blown away. The guy before him was blown away. I was just marking time before I was blown away. As point man you have the weight of all the other lives. You can get someone else killed. You walk down the trail looking for signs of things, or meet with people under fire. There were helicopters over us sometimes. There were trip wires, booby traps. For the six months I was point man, no one in the squad was wounded. I wasn't wounded even though there were bullets coming at me.

I have been in the town where I moved from New York for over thirty years. I recently retired from the postal service. I walked the downtown area daily.

When I first moved here, I started grinding my teeth at night. There was nobody to talk to about PTSD. People were not concerned about the guys coming home. Then we became the image of the mentally disturbed vet. Like in *Kojak*, Travis Bickle in *Taxi Driver*, the guys in *The Deer Hunter*. Those were bad as far as portraying Vietnam vets.

D-Day stuff, *Private Ryan*. I can't watch that stuff. I drift back. The lights come up. People start talking. I'm still there. I'm done. And war is still going on. I can't put it all behind me when new wars are going on. I hear in the news that two helicopters have been shot down. I know about that.

In the eighties when *Rambo* came out—I mean I don't want anyone watching those movies. Kids love guns. Rambo could do anything. In reality, we didn't do diddley in Vietnam.

Platoon with Oliver Stone was the first one to put a real war on the screen. It pleased me so much. Charlie Sheen, at the end, says that it's the obligation to build ourselves again and teach others what we know. I've been doing that. From the time I joined Vietnam Veterans Against the War after Kent State.

I've read books to understand how other people feel about the Vietnam War and about the history of the Vietnam struggle. I belong to a Veterans for Peace chapter. It's a national organization to help educate the public about the true costs of war and to influence legislation.

I hate to see things that are happening in Iraq and Afghanistan. I listen to guys coming back. There is grudging recognition on the nearby base that we have to address their problems. They are understaffed as far as medical needs. They are better trained to recognize symptoms, though. But the first way they deal with any of the disorders is they give you anti-psychotic drugs.

In my unit, we came home and said, "Gee, I'm not feeling myself. I need to go see a psychiatrist." If somebody found out, you were a dumbass, a shitbag. Until a few years ago, there was a stigma. They have therapists embedded in each unit over there now. Before, if your buddies found out you were getting help, you were thought to be unreliable.

Iraq vets are a bit more accepted. They still have to fight at the VA, though. TBI (*traumatic brain injury*). We had Agent Orange. Had to take the chemical companies to court. Finally, in the eighties they started recognizing PTSD and opening veterans outreach centers. It still can be a boondoggle as far as red tape.

Vets should get treatment immediately. Except I know a person who went to the VA and was told that the budget wouldn't allow for any more PTSD cases. There was an overload. The military budget needs an increase to help vets. The VA workers are 100 percent wonderful Americans, but the VA itself is an old system. Slow to change. Under-funded.

You never know when PTSD symptoms are going to strike. A vet I know, a musician, was on stage when an amp blew. He hit the ground.

I want to tell somebody about the horrors. (*Pause*) I can't say the word. (*Pause*) Immolated. Like a Buddhist monk. Gasoline. Something you don't want to see or smell or put in a body bag. If I looked at pictures of it, I would get sick. It's part of my memory I've got to go through.

I don't care for barbecues. It's too much of a reminder.

I'm part of the Wounded Warrior Project. We help injured vets get help and stay connected to one another. We back legislative issues and help advocate for vets. There are more community-oriented civilian organizations set up to help. I don't know what would have happened if I had been able to get help for PTSD after I came back, but I try to let go of my own bitterness.

I was in the VA system, trying to get help with substance abuse. But what has been most healing for me has been running. In 1979 I participated in the "Run for the Roses" race in Boulder, Colorado. I started running. I started feeling a little better. I started finding myself. I'm not a baby killer.

I'm not the loser I was told I was. I was facing the same kind of challenges I did over there.

But my wife and I separated. "You need help," she told me. "I do," I said. I knew it. I started running so much I got Achilles tendinitis. I had to say five Hail Marys on my Achilles before running. My podiatrist said to go see a yoga teacher. I went to a few teachers. Then I found Iyengar yoga. I resisted the teacher. I had all these goddam walls around my heart. I didn't let her in. I couldn't say, "I love you."

I lost a friend in Vietnam who was shot in the back. You said you love someone, then you lost them. The guys who stand with you, you love them. Shoulder to shoulder when the shit hits.

So the yoga teacher worked on the walls around my heart. I started to get in touch with my emotions. Crying. I had been taking my emotions and stuffing 'em. In yoga I was learning who I was. When I started to go to the vet center, unfortunately my wife was still at the point where she didn't want to be with me. Now they give the family help, how to deal with us when we get distant. My wife and I never talked. She never knew what medals I won, what action I'd seen. Longtime friends, twenty-five years, don't even know I have a Bronze Star.

I started to tell my wife I loved her. It still didn't go down but we separated on fairly good terms.

Now I teach yoga to other vets, and I have been running for thirty years. I run marathons around the country. I'm qualifying right now for the Boston Marathon. I've run that before. Years ago, when I first ran in the New York Marathon, my father watched the race. But I got the dry heaves. Heat exhaustion. I was doing it for the family, but I wasn't ready.

I started an annual veterans run in my city in 2005. It benefits a homeless veterans' living environment for vets in treatment. I got good people to help me. We had three hundred people the first year at the park. A lot of them were vets. A lot of old vets came up to me and said, "Thank you. It's about time."

I've trained for triathlons too. Now I want to learn how to swim. I do fine in a pool but in open water I had a 'Nam experience. My first triathlon I had to swim across a lake. It was dirty, like a black lagoon. I never swam in a lake before the race. I jumped in and hyperventilated. It was like being in a VC bunker, black as a coalmine. I got pissed. I didn't want to let it bother me. I bought a wetsuit. I was determined not to let it get to me.

That's why I'm taking swimming lessons.

After one local race, I saw massage therapists had set up tables for the runners. I met a massage teacher and decided to learn how to do it. I learned anatomy. I saw where you stretched, from the base, from the muscles. Now I do individual massages and yoga for trades. I have donated massages for causes. I'm really on the road to healing.

I went to Nicaragua in 1988 with a Veterans Peace Action Team, when Nicaragua was a war zone. We vaccinated over 1,000 Nicaraguans and were building state-of-the-art latrines. Our group was in a tiny town in Jinotega province. Jacinto Hernandez, the co-op we were working with, consisted of fifty families growing coffee and corn and raising cattle. But that was some of the most dangerous farmland in Nicaragua.

The women and children definitely outnumbered the men. Whole farms would patrol the villages by night. The children would help. Their education suffered.

There was illness and disease. The children had parasites. There was diarrhea, whooping cough and malaria.

The days I was there working at Jacinto Hernandez was some of the hardest work I've ever done in my life. We only had to break the jungle in Vietnam. Building latrines, we encountered what the people there experience seven days a week.

We were pouring concrete in 95 degree heat. The whole village worked. The oxen hauled rock and sand. The children hauled water. There was no electricity. No cars. No services.

My mother grew up in Ireland. I've been there four times. I traveled on a bike. That's something I was robbed of when I was a young guy. I didn't get to just travel around. I spent a month in Ireland going from pub to pub, talking to people and learning history. That was another journey. I felt my youth was stolen.

I came home from Vietnam with the thousand-yard stare. I have pictures of myself like that. It looks like I am pretending to be a soldier. You can see the slump in my body. All that youth gone. I was an old man.

Now I enjoy the mountains and the parks in the state where I live. I see a lot of nature on the trail. I get on a deer trail. I enjoy seeing everything around me, the signs of nature. It's quiet.

I have a woman friend who is understanding. She is an artist and past girlfriend. I rely on her because I get down on myself so much.

I have become accustomed to living by myself. I have owned a house for thirty-one years. I know the neighborhood.

I still will be a patriot warrior to the end. When I give a speech or read poetry at the college here, I bring a friend to hold my hand so I can come down. After one performance, I told a reporter from the newspaper who had been listening that I feel like I'm back in Vietnam when I read my poetry. The reporter said, "You were there just now."

Email from Tom:
The closing scene in *Platoon*, with Charlie Sheen playing a soldier sitting on a medevac chopper, dust and smoke swirling, leaving the big battle destruction behind. He says:

> I think now, looking back, we did not fight the enemy. We fought ourselves, and the enemy was in us.
>
> The war is over for me now, but it will always be there the rest of my days. But, be that as it may, those of us who did make it have an obligation to build again and to teach others what we know, and to try with what's left of our lives to find a goodness and meaning to this life.

Tom: Back then it was great to realize that reliving the war was normal for us grunts and that I was on that path of speaking out and doing things to make this world a better place. Still am. Always will be.

John

John Walter takes a break from work to meet at the Starbucks on Monument Circle in Indianapolis. He sets up his laptop on an adjacent table so he can refer to his numerous photos of Iraq.

I grew up in Rensselaer, Indiana, north of here about an hour and a half. It's a farming and light industry town of 5,000 people. I wanted to go into the Army. I didn't want to go to college. The Army looked fun.

I started in the National Guard. After graduating I tried to get on active duty. My command was all for it. They said, "Go. You have our blessings. Get out of here." It was a slow process getting out of the guard until 9/11. By May of 2002, I was on active duty. I was nineteen.

I went to Fort Lee, Virginia, for training and became a cook. From there I attempted to go to Army Airborne School, but the paperwork got messed up. I ended up at Fort Carson, Colorado. My unit in Virginia said, "Have them send you to Airborne School."

I brought it up the first day at Fort Carson. They said, "Airborne? Wake up! We're the fucking cavalry." Once I was into my new unit, the thought of the Airborne was "Well, whatever." I was single, living in barracks. My platoon buddies were older guys, so there was always plenty of alcohol. Work hard and drink harder. In 2003, we were considered part of the invasion force, but we were not the initial troops. The infantry led the division. We followed right behind the main forces in the spring of 2003.

I don't know the name of the place where we landed, somewhere outside Karbala. We heard Bush's announcement that the war was over. Now what do we do? We hadn't seen anything.

From there we went out just past Rutba for a few months. It was pretty quiet. There was some drama here and there. One commander got into a little bit of trouble. I'm not saying any more. There were civilian abuses, let's say. It was not public knowledge.

The Syrian Desert was kind of an interesting place. Not during the day. Nineties and 100s and at night chilly. It drops 25 degrees at night, you feel chilly. We went into Rutba. Show-the-flag type of stuff. They had a lot of support troops with cannons do that. That freed up the combat troops to do other things. We were pretty much hanging out. Watching the village. Security.

One day downtown—it's not a big place, but it was the center of town where there were markets and stuff—we heard yelling. We went up to the roof of the police station, where we could see the market. There were people scurrying. We realized it was a meat exchange. A goat had escaped. It didn't want to go to slaughter. It was running around in a circle with thirty people chasing it. It brought all the traffic and people, the entire city, to a standstill.

Here's a map of Iraq. The only thing out there is Rutba. It's the only place to trade and buy goods.

In June of 2003, we went to Ramadi. Ramadi was hot. An Army

camp. Right off the Euphrates. A swamp. The sand fleas were prodigious. (*He shows a photo of a blistered arm.*) The first night, I counted 'em out. From elbow to shoulder I had approximately 200 bites. Both arms. We had mosquito nets. The sand fleas were small enough to get in. We used DEET on the cots and sprayed the nets with permethrin. It was agony the first week or so, then I sealed up the cot as best I could at night. The windows were blown out so that didn't help. My roommate had a big roll of duct tape. I duct-taped the mosquito net to the cot and used a flashlight to look for holes to tape. It took an hour to get ready for bed.

There it was hot even at night. We spent July and August in Ramadi. We recorded one daytime shade temperature of 139. It was 130 to 140 for a whole week. At night it would only dip down to 110–120. No fans. You wanted to sleep with no clothes but the sand fleas prevented you from doing that. I thought, "What do I do?" I was sweating, dumped sweat off my cot. I drank three liters of water an hour.

I was cooking during the day for between 600 and 800 people. One night we had as many as 1,100. People coming in from combat. I'd get up early and cook breakfast, then break for an hour and start working on dinner. The heat? I got used to it, but I didn't like it.

In Ramadi, we lost the first guys from our unit, three or four. We went to Al-Asad onto an airbase where the Marines had a presence. I remember the highest and lowest points. We took over the base, an Iraqi Air Force base. That was the beginning of Al-Asad turning into a big logistical area. From there outposts were maintained. It was more like a hub with spokes. I was sent out to Haditha to cook. (*He flips through photos.*) It was an interesting place. It was on the Euphrates. I had an apartment room that was built into the side of a dam. One side was U.S., the other the Azerbaijan army. We cooked up here on the top of the dam. The platform below was occupied by goofy-ass ducks. It was hours of amusement, watching these dumb ducks. They were elegant flyers but every landing from the reservoir was a modified crash landing. If you've seen an American coot, they looked sort of like that. They would zoom over our heads to the bottom of the dam.

We rotated in and out of Haditha. It was sort of combat, but not a whole lot going on. At that same time, around Thanksgiving of 2003, there was a big operation out of Al-Qa'im near the Syrian border. We surrounded the town and made house-to-house searches for explosives. I was the company commander's driver on a two-week mission. The object was to gather up weapons. I was a private just driving a captain around.

It rained the entire time we were over there. I drove a canvas Humvee, soft shell. After Al Qa'im my division went back to Haditha. Another case of me out there cookin'. Then we were sent to Rawa, a downsized operation. I was promoted to specialist. Our mission (*he makes air quotes*) was originally to secure the command post. One captain made a deal with us, one of the sweetest set of orders I ever received. He said, "You don't have to worry about doing security as long as the command post has hot coffee and soup." I spent all my time just making coffee. Five gallons at a time. Then I'd sit and play cards, listen to music. In another hour and a half, I'd make more coffee.

The whole time out there, I was the only combat injury. I was unloading a truck, a supply of water, and stepped on a rock. I twisted my ankle. It popped. I was on the ground in agony. The sergeant comes out. "Shall I get a medic?" Yeah, you dumbass. He comes back with three medics, an ambulance, a doctor, a PA and the chaplain. It swelled up, was black and blue. The medical officer said, "I could medevac you, which I would rather not do, or we can wait until tomorrow."

I waited it out. I was given chemical cold packs and Motrin. Not long after that I was packing. My first deployment, I think when it comes down to it, I was every kind of bored.

We were flown from Al-Asad with a stop in Frankfurt and Newfoundland in an Air Force cargo plane the entire way home. In Newfoundland it was midnight when we landed. Fricking cold and snowing. Our platoon leader had just been promoted to captain. We were unhooking and laying out on the floor 'cuz those bench seats are uncomfortable. An Air Force guy says, "Get back in your seats."

Our captain looks at the enlisted guy and says, "My guys can stay on the floor."

We had been together for a year for better or worse. We were just laying on each other. A year in a tank crew, you're in pretty close quarters. You don't care if you're laying on some guy's stomach.

Stepping off the plane, I found myself nose to nose with a full colonel and a first sergeant. He was shaking my hand like I was his long-lost son. "Who the hell was that guy?" I said. "He sure was glad to see us." They gave us a cold hamburger and a hot can of Coke, something the USO put together. Couldn't they even put the Coke on ice? Yep, one minute back home.

My truck was in storage, so I couldn't get it until the next day. We got rides to the liquor store. We used a screwdriver and a pair of pliers to open the wine. We finally had to push the cork down into the bottle. I had intended to party all night. I hadn't had alcohol in a year and had just jumped nine time zones. After a drink or two I fell asleep.

I came back to Indiana and saw my family. I drank a lot with my buddies, who were in college. We talked a little about the war, but we just reminisced more. The alcohol was free flowing. We were single. I was a twenty-one-year-old male and that's what I was interested in.

The relationship I had disintegrated. I was not a happy person to be around. There were unfair expectations on both sides. I was an angry person. The stress of deployment. Relationship issues.

I wanted to spend two weeks at my barracks home and tinker around Colorado Springs, so I went back there. What money I had left—I blew a lot—I bought a house with. It's a nice small house. Close enough to downtown that I can walk. For a single guy it was great. And it was close enough to Fort Carson that I could be there in a few minutes.

Leading up to my second deployment, I could see the dynamics of Iraq were changing. I knew I'd be involved in fighting somehow. In the spring of 2005, I went overseas again and spent most of that year at Forward Operational Base Falcon outside Baghdad.

A few times a week there was mortar attack. They were taking potshots at us. One guy was hit by a rocket. We were sitting in the chow hall and the rocket hit the front of the chow hall. It did not detonate but blew apart on impact and killed him and injured two or three others. When they evacuated us, we had to walk around the body of the dead soldier.

In Baghdad, it got closer to home; twenty-one guys from our unit were killed. There were a lot more civilian contractor cooks, so I was more involved in the fighting. One thing I did was funeral detail. It got annoying. Seven funerals in one day. I got angry at guys for dying. I wanted to go use the Internet. I wanted to go to the gym tonight. That's what the attitude turned into.

From Baghdad I was rotated out to checkpoints—two areas we guarded where they wanted to have U.S. presence. You'd sit out there for thirty-six to forty-eight hours. There was a dog out at one checkpoint. We were not supposed to have dogs, but it was overlooked. He was not a mascot. He just was our camp dog, roaming around.

It was nice to be able to pet a dog. I had dogs growing up. Someone put a flea collar on him. We had little bowls for him. One time we gave him a Salisbury steak MRE (*Meals Ready to Eat*). The dog sniffs it, licks at it, turns around and walks off. Thirty minutes later he comes back with a dead rat. I knew that shit tasted bad, but a dog would rather eat a rat?

We had sandwiches to eat. Sometimes ham and cheese. Sometimes cheese and mustard. Sometimes just catsup and mayonnaise. I'd rather eat MREs.

Just before my second deployment, a woman from New York I had met online came to visit me in Colorado Springs. When I went back to Iraq, we wrote letters every day. By December we were writing every day and talking on the phone. Very open communication. Sending pictures back and forth. The webcam chat stuff hadn't hit yet. When I came back, my whole unit was being transferred to Fort Hood in Texas. I had re-enlisted to stay at Fort Carson. Then I got the news. Everyone in my unit was in the same boat. All I wanted to do was stay there. They transferred me to another unit at Fort Carson. My new unit was leaving as I was coming home. The unit was deploying so I was being deployed again. I said, "Whoa, sir. I've only been back two months." They sent me to armor school to learn how to be a small arms repair guy, how to take care of weapons.

I got married. We had three weeks together before I redeployed. Here we are five years later with a four-year-old boy, Jackson. I was deployed again at the end of November 2007. I was gone more than two years. I was a gun truck driver for the supply convoy that took fuel, water and food outside the city. We were the battalion's first responders in the city, with the maintenance element, combat tow truck, medical assets and a medic with an advanced trauma kit. Guys were hit with IEDs, so we would go out and pick them up. They were using us to evacuate the injured.

January 28, 2008, in Mosul—that was the day the war really started for me during the third deployment. A patrol got hit in the Palestine neighborhood of Mosul. Propane tanks filled with explosives. All five guys were scattered three sheets to the wind. We collected remains.

We were ambushed while we were out. We were doing a hands across the desert. Elbow to elbow across a field when we started taking fire from a building. That neighborhood was like a hornet's nest. Every available patrol came to that point. We spent hours out there. I had seen a lot of crazy stuff in Baghdad. I had spent a good amount of time as the commander's gunner and in the gunner's hatch. I was pretty seasoned. You jump out of the turret with a rifle. You are reaching out with the captain holding on to your foot. He is holding on to a bar with the other hand. Sometimes you can't get your gun turned around.

Now I got stuck as a driver. I was not the best gunner in the world. I can do it, but I got relegated to the driver's seat and I stayed there. I saw death. Hostile situations where people were hit with IEDs. With the IED threat, one can hit you as a driver or a gunner. Either you die or you don't.

On the 28th, my wife heard NPR say that five soldiers had been killed in Mosul. She knew there was only one responder team. I did not have the option to call home. It was a big stressor for her.

For us, we said, "Well, we didn't die today. Life goes on." Eight patrols from our company continued to go out almost every night with deliveries of fuel, ammunition, supplies and spare parts to the transportation troops. Stress with constant threat? For sure.

We were going out at sundown and coming back at 4 a.m. We'd sleep four hours. Then we were in a motor pool and we would work on the trucks. You had to be in the motor pool from 8 a.m. to 5 p.m. seven days a week. People constantly complained about it. Most people weren't asking for whole days off, just half a day. Let me go back to the room and hang out. The platoon sergeant resisted this. The stress of being out all night long, away from home, and constant sleep deprivation really got to you.

Over the course of that deployment, I can't say exactly, but I think I went on over 250 patrols. From January of '08 to January of '09. Every other night was the average. I was usually in the lead vehicle. That added a lot of stress as well.

A defining aspect of Mosul: there were a lot of cliques in the platoon. My first two deployments, we didn't have anything but each other. The troops and the sergeants played cards together. You had coffee with the section sergeant. We shared packages from Starbucks. General cohesiveness was stronger. There was no satellite, TV, Internet. It's a lot less cohesive now. The more the amenities, the more difficult life became.

We always passed through the ancient city of Nineveh. (*He scrolls through more photos.*) It was pretty shitty. It smelled bad. You could tell some neighborhoods must have been beautiful. I lived in a shipping container there. Day in, day out, it never seemed like we were doing anything besides building walls. Here's a sandbag area we jumped into if mortars were coming in. You were within easy sniper distance.

I started talking to a few guys in the platoon. I had anxiety attacks throughout the end of my deployment. The chaplain I could sort of talk to. Regardless of what the Army says about mental health, you're not allowed to be sick. This guy in the dark shorts with the cigarette? He had his fair share of issues. He was more unpopular with the commander because he sought help.

My unit's time was up and we were supposed to get out in August of 2008 but were part of a stop-loss until early 2009. When I got back to the States, I started to go seek help. I drank more. It was a gradual increase. My wife grew up in a house with a belligerent alcoholic. I wouldn't get belligerent. I would drink until I went to sleep. I had been out a year and I would put down as many as fifteen a day. Beer usually. It didn't matter. I drank what I had on hand. Then I was working as a factory laborer. I built windows. I was getting up at 4 a.m. I was home by 4:30. Between that time and when I went to bed at 8, I put down an average of four beers a night. It's just what I did. I came home and drank every night. That was my reaction to standing in assembly lines eight hours a day after being in the Army eight years.

I didn't get together with any vets. There was no outreach. There was no "Come to Mo's for a beer at five." None of that. There was no encouragement for it. Guys going somewhere and drinking is not the best thing, but it's not always the worst thing you could do. I don't think anybody thought about getting together.

When I do try to talk to people, their reaction is, "Oh, interesting. What's it like?" They don't really want to hear. In my hometown when I was visiting my parents, I had been sitting in a bar up there and I saw the dad of a high school friend. He was friendly and asked how it was going. He's a Vietnam vet. Actually, the Vietnam vets want to talk about the good old days and the bad old days.

Any place in the U.S. if a guy sees your hat or a pin and he was in the Army, it's the country's best icebreaker. They'll start talking back and forth. You run into that. Lots of guys wear their old battalion pin from way back.

But I don't really talk about my time in Iraq. Talking to people off the streets isn't much good. They want to know what's it like to kill somebody. That's one of the questions I've fielded. Whereas vets from World War II are more apt to talk about that guy they had on KP duty one day. How bad the Army chow was. Camp biscuits and gravy. We can even talk about a motor pool. Half of everybody was in one at one time or other. Part of me wants to be more active in military affairs. Sometimes another part of me just wants to be done with it. I'm out. Best of luck, suckers.

Colorado Springs has some stuff going on. Indianapolis is a big city. There isn't a lot of connection. The only other vets I know here were in Vietnam. I have not run into a single Iraq vet here. Part of it is me in this community—such a big place. In a city this size, I don't know. When you've grown up in a small town, it's discouraging. I like the hotel I have been working for here. I got on with a downtown hotel about a year ago, the Omni Hotel not far from here. I'm a steward and a culinary team shift supervisor. I'm hoping to work at the Broadmoor in Colorado Springs doing the same thing I do here.

I've tried to keep a lot about the war away from my wife. It's unpleasant to talk about anyway. Sometimes I can feel a stress on my chest. A heaviness. I still have back problems. All through my deployments my back hurt. I never sought treatment when I was in the Army. Saying your back hurt was the same as saying you had mental problems. They would say, "You're just stretched out."

I went to the VA for five months. I was given X-rays. The best guess from the doctors at the VA was that I had a cracked vertebra and a herniated disc. It probably happened when I was a gunner in the Humvee. They see those types of injuries when you have a weight on your shoulders. When I started to get treatment, the medical team believed I had chronic back pain. They took a holistic approach. I was involved in a behavior modification study. There were questions like, "When you are in pain, why are you in pain?"

I went every two weeks for almost eight months for physical therapy. I got control of the pain. Then I got sent to mental health. The social worker was a woman. I told her I had seen nasty parts of the world. Of course, I had seen dead bodies. She freaked out.

They got bogged down at the VA. All these people were getting out of the Army and Marines. About a third of my battalion all got out at the same time. Three hundred people in just my unit. In May, June, July and August of '09, there was a mass exodus.

There are a lot of people in and out of the VA. I didn't talk to people. Treat me and get me out of here. My choice is alcohol. It's my favorite. I prefer drinking to pills. One of my buddies prefers pills. He loved all the pills the VA gave him. That was one thing my doctor mentioned, that I was one of the few patients not just looking for more Vicodin. Most pills interfere with my drinking.

It's not glamorous being an alcoholic. I still drink every day and I want to. Sometimes I just have a beer or a glass of wine. When I started getting better—proper—treatment for my back, I cut back.

An essay John Walter shared with the Colorado Springs group Veterans Remember in February 2011:

My War

On the 14th of February 2009 I got off an airplane at Peterson Air Force Base. That was the last time I got off an airplane. I was home. I was home from Iraq, and finished with my third deployment. I spent nearly eight years of my life in the Army, and over three years of that time was spent in ground combat in Iraq. After that much life and death experience, I know of no man or woman who can take off the uniform and start a new life. I thought I could at first, and was excited and eager to do just that, walk away and leave.

So here I am two years later, not a day has gone by when I haven't thought of the war. My War. Iraq truly was my war. I was in the invasion of 2003. I watched Baghdad melt down with insurgent violence and civil war in 2005, and saw some of the fighting of 2008 while in Mosul. 2009 brought us the Status of Forces Agreement and the slow march towards troop withdrawal began.

My social worker at the Veterans Administration referred me to counseling and recommended medication for PTSD. I turned down the medication, and chose to see the shrink. Neither the social worker, nor the shrink were veterans or had ever served in any service, peace or wartime. In my opinion that is part of the problem. When asked if I ever thought of my wartime experiences, I said every day. When she asked why, I told her what it's like smelling burnt bodies, picking up remains of fellow soldiers. What it's like to be in a firefight. Her eyes bugged out and she told me she was sorry and recommended a prescription for me. No thanks on the pills.

You asked, lady. I told. As horrible as war is, many of us vets are not looking for pills, or sympathy, or money, or whatever. I believe most of us want the rest of America to know what we did, right or wrong, bad or good, and just be behind us, support our actions, and listen, truly listen, to what we have to say.

I cannot be overly upset at the team in place at the VA. They are trying hard. They are overloaded, underpaid, understaffed, and themselves "shell shocked" at the masses of new vets coming their way. Many of the new vets they see are young enough to be their children and, in some cases, their grandchildren. Then the contempt: contempt at the VA staff that is my age, the kids that went to college right after high school, that didn't go to war like me. I look at them with a degree of contempt. Should I look at them like that? No. I chose my life and knew full well what I was in for when I re-enlisted in 2004. How am I supposed to talk to someone about my feelings, problems and medical concerns that graduated high school the same year or later than I? How do I combat my own personal feelings, and how do we as a country move forward and take care of all the veterans from all wars past, present and future? As we discuss how to help soldiers and vets, part of the dialogue should be how we improve mental health and wellness without throwing pills at the problem. As much as medical science aids all of us in life, I feel chemical solutions often only cover the problem. While it is a longer road treating the mind without chemicals, it is a road in my opinion that opens more doors, creates more opportunities, and is less physically detrimental in the long run. Along my journey, helping me the most are all of those vets out there that do not, and are not hiding who they were and who they are. As we move forward, let us remember some of the best support comes from within our own ranks.

John Walter, 3rd Armored Cavalry, 2002–2006;
1-8 Infantry, 4th Infantry Division 2006–2009

3 Last Stop

"Being young is beautiful but being old is comfortable."
Will Rogers, Cowboy Philosopher

Jim

Jim Belilove is a resident of Fairfield, Iowa, and a co-developer of the SunnyBrook Assisted Living homes in six Iowa locations. He originally came to Fairfield because it was the town where the Maharishi Mahesh Yogi set up his American school for Transcendental Meditation.

When I first came here, I felt like a fish out of water. I moved from California to Fairfield, Iowa, twenty-eight years ago. Through karmic complications I ended up here. That was the language of meditators in 1973. I'm actually a cosmopolitan person. I was marooned here. But I am happy now. I got married after I got here and raised a daughter.

I started a business called Creative Edge, making architectural specialties. I fabricate things out of stone and metal, typically for casinos and large office buildings. My other business has been building and running SunnyBrook Assisted Living homes. They are all in towns of 10,000 to 20,000.

It's all because of my mother-in-law. I was the typical adult child who said, "There is no suitable place for my aging relative." This led me to SunnyBrook and to my becoming a partner in that business. Truly, the typical story is of hardy Iowans. People in the previous generation don't like to ask for help. They think they can endure just about anything.

The adult children, usually in their fifties, feel the parents are not coping very well. They try to help them. The parents are not living the way they should be—in one room of their house. They can't get out to shop. They don't eat right. Their house becomes a kind of prison.

Sometimes the kids try to take care of them in their own houses. But often that doesn't work because most of them are working or parenting and their parents end up sitting in the house by themselves. It's even more isolating. Plus the kids don't have the skills necessary to care for them. They can't get up three or four times a night to help them. That's why our homes exist and are successful.

The process of moving into one of the homes can be a lengthy one. It is often precipitated by someone falling down, or one of the couple dies and that becomes the precipitating event. We obviously don't rush them. One of our most compassionate leaders will get with family members. But one of the most common things we hear after they do move in is "I should have moved a lot sooner."

We believe people will live at least a couple of years longer here. They have good friends. They eat regularly and well. They don't have to take care of old houses. But it's not always an easy sell. People can be stubborn. They say, "I can't leave this home. I was born in this home and raised my kids here."

We do a newsletter every month to highlight the residents. There are extraordinary stories. People live to be eighty to a hundred years old in Iowa, and every one has a story.

Residents of an Iowa assisted living facility sit in the living room and share stories of why they made the move to their new home.

Gertrude

I've been here for three and a half years. My family made me come. I have arthritis affecting my back and legs. I'm not walking well. We were talking about it. All of a sudden, I'm here. I lived in another town. This has been wonderful. I had just wanted to stay home. I had friends there.

We were farmers, then we moved to this town fifteen minutes away. We stayed in that house twenty-one years. I worked at a shoe store. I went from a big house to an apartment. The house had a nice big yard. I grew three tomato plants every year. I didn't can them. I gave them to neighbors.

Dan

I came here because I am on oxygen and it was hard to get around. I'm from here and have lived here for forty years. I came to assisted living three and a half years ago. It was mostly the kids' decision. I lived alone with my wife for four and a half years. I have four grandchildren and twelve great-grandchildren. They came out and talked to us. They thought it was a great place. I made the final decision, kind of. I could have put my foot down if I had wanted.

I was a custodian for the railroad for eleven years. I was a farmer for most of my life.

I was born in southwestern Iowa over by Lancaster. At school I met a girl. We were married fifty-two years before my wife passed away. She died of cancer. It was just one of those things.

Agnes

I got married out of high school. We went to Chicago for nine years. We came back here because of the kids. We didn't want them to go to school in Chicago. We checked all the places here in town.

I worked at the college when it was here and knew a lot of students. There were 6,000 at that time. I worked at a variety store and the telephone company in the front office.

My husband passed away twenty years ago. I've been here almost two years. I spent a long time by myself.

Virginia

I own the place but they don't believe me. I moved in March. I decided to stay happy here. At least I'm not at home cooking.

My son called and asked if I was better off than being by myself. I would have been alone. Here I try to get out for Trivia every day.

I'll be ninety-eight my next birthday. When my son comes to visit, he jumps up to wait on me. I have three sons. My husband was a mechanical engineer, a graduate of the University of Nebraska. I was a stay-at-home mom in Florida, South Carolina and Iowa.

If my husband were alive in two months it would have been seventy years. We never had a fight. We ironed problems out, our disagreements.

I had fallen on my face. My face was black from the bruises when I came here. I was new and when people couldn't remember my name, they just called me "the lady with the black face."

Bonnie

Bonnie is a resident of an assisted living home in the rural Upper Midwest. As she walks from the common area to her room, she can see orderly rows of soybeans just outside a glass door.

I lived in Denver, Colorado, almost all my adult life. My older daughter and my only granddaughter live on the edge of town. I'm a foreigner here. Meal after meal people talk about the people they know and what is going on with them.

My younger daughter needed my help a few years back when she got sick. I put my furniture in storage and got on a plane to New Mexico. But then with arthritis I got to where I couldn't lift heavy skillets or boiling pots of water. I gave up. I couldn't make or change a bed. I moved to this facility. I gave up a lot. Everybody here did. We sold our worldly goods. Here I order and administer my own medications. I get help making and changing the bed.

Many of the rooms are wonderful. They are bedroom suites that are huge compared to mine. I have the smallest room here. It's because I am trying to save money. I kept my filing cabinet. I kept my desk and my beloved computer, without which I'd be lost. It has a calendar that tells me when my library books are due. I have a long narrow table with all my family pictures. A TV.

There is an infinitesimal closet. The maintenance man hung a double rack for me. All my winter clothes are packed and stored in my daughter's basement. So are my heritage records from my great grandfather. I have a single bed, a cabinet, one recliner and one seat. I'm not a reclining person. I don't know why I bought a recliner. I have yet to recline.

I left a gorgeous room here with a good view out. It cost more. I'm saving probably $350 a month by moving to this room. I have my retirement and my husband's. I was a school secretary and he was a grade school teacher. It's not much. I have what I saved when I sold our house and the realtors were crying for property. It was prime real estate. The money is invested. I get an income check every month. I'm doing what's possible without tapping into my resources.

Weekends I love. I don't have to be organized and go from one thing to another. I don't need to be amused. I read a great deal. I'm on my computer a great deal. I have friends to call.

Betty

Betty Patterson is attending an anniversary celebration for SunnyBrook Assisted Living in Fort Madison, Iowa. She does not live in the facility but has come for the entertainment. A musician has just played the guitar and sung a jazz version of "Kisses Sweeter Than Wine," a more traditional rendering of "God Bless the Child That's Got His Own," and several Irish tunes.

This is the second time I've come here for an event.

My husband was in the Coast Guard. He retired after twenty years. I was born and educated in the house I still live in. My husband said, "I'm gonna buy that house. My twenty years in the Coast Guard is all over." Mom and Dad built the house. It's a hundred years old. My kids didn't grow up in the house, though.

I have four children, three of them girls. One grandson and four granddaughters, one adopted. I have three great-grandsons. We had to move around a lot when the kids were growing up. We lived in three places in Michigan, and in Virginia. The kids come to visit here now and say, "Mom, I slept so good last night."

My grandkids love it. I don't know what it is about it. It's just old. But the grandkids say, "Well, Grandma, we like old houses."

There are four bedrooms upstairs and one down. There is a front room, a dining room and a kitchen. My husband and I lived downstairs. There's a full bath. The bath needs remodeling. It's expensive, and I don't want a bunch of men running around working on it. It just needs a little repair. It's not too bad.

My birthday was nice. I had a full refrigerator with watermelon and iced tea. People came to visit. One man said he was going out and trim that tree outside. I thought, "Oh, no." It was so hot out there.

I used to do outside work. Now I have somebody do it. I do my own laundry, but I have somebody hang it. I get Meals on Wheels.

I love Walmart, but I have to watch what I buy.

It's an old square wood-built house. It was the first on the block when my parents built it. My sister lives next door. My brother built that house after he got out of the army. Mom always had me for dinner when my husband was overseas. We were a very close family.

The doctor said to me, "Stay away from steps. Don't fall." I have a railing going down to the full basement. I do my own laundry. I don't want anybody else in the house doing things.

I had a pacemaker put in because I fell down so many times. I hit my face on the microwave. I called my sister to take me to the hospital. My blood pressure was high. My blood sugar was high. They took me in an Air Evac to Mercy Hospital in Iowa City.

The doctor said, "You can go home and fall down all the time, or have a pacemaker." Next morning they put the pacemaker in.

He says, "You gotta keep going. You can't quit." These doctors just expect you to live forever.

My husband had a brain tumor. He was in the hospital in Iowa City. I didn't know a thing about the tumor. He was a very smart man. He could fix anything. I'm sure he knew what was wrong with him. He wouldn't tell me.

I love it here. I grew up in this neighborhood. Of course, it's all new people now. Everybody thinks I'm nuts living in a big house like this, but I'll stay as long as I can.

Sue Fine

Hospice volunteers are federally mandated as part of a hospice team for each dying person. According to the U.S. Code of Federal Regulations governing hospices, a team must consist of a minimum of a medical doctor, a nurse, a social worker, and a pastoral or other counselor. There is a separate section of the code that addresses the mandated volunteers, who must be provided with "appropriate orientation" and "must be used in administrative or direct patient care roles."

Hospice organizations need to comply with these rules or they will lose funding and certification. Hospice care is a free service provided by Medicaid, paid for by U.S. taxpayers.

The number of individuals and families taking advantage of hospice care grew by 162 percent from 2000 to 2010. At Crossroads Hospice in Kansas City, Missouri, construction crews hang white plastic over an expansion for the crowded office of 220 employees. Sue Fine is the on-staff volunteer coordinator.

Our numbers are growing in hospice care. It is a matter of education. The criteria? There are about one or two hundred reasons to be on hospice. It used to be we got mostly cancer patients. Now we have a lot of heart patients. What makes you qualify is the declining ability to take care of yourself.

Once diagnosed, you can choose the hospice of your choice. But usually people think of hospice toward the very end. There is emotional bereavement support for the family, but the dying person hasn't had the benefit of the support of the team.

Our philosophy is to focus on the dying person's life. How are you going to spend your days with us?

There is this idea: "No one can take care of Mom like I can." We all like to think we know what is best for our loved one. But caregivers get worn down. We work with people so they can take a respite or go on a vacation.

A third of the population is between twenty-five and sixty-five years old. There are a lot of baby boomers. There are so many more stress-related illnesses that there are a lot of younger patients. A lot of heart patients. People are all running around like chickens without a head and sooner or later it is going to catch up with them.

Hospice policy is to tell patients that they are going on hospice. We have to say "hospice." A person could be dead in two weeks, or five or six years, but we have to tell them they are on hospice.

There are misconceptions about dying people. They don't all go through the five stages of Kübler-Ross—denial and isolation, anger, bargaining, depression, and acceptance.

I would be angry. Right now I would have a hard time getting past anger. I still want to be an X-ray technician. I'm sixty-four. I have no time to die right now. I have too many things to do. I was nineteen years old just a few years ago.

I would bet that the longest stages for most people who are dying are denial and anger. But about 98 percent have acceptance at their death. Very few are not peaceful. Death is harder when you are not at peace.

I have been with veterans. By the end of their lives, they are not thinking "I killed, I maimed at war." They have come to terms with their deeds.

A lot of people hang on for some reason. We counsel the family that they can tell the person it is OK to go. It rids the dying person of the subconscious worry that loved ones can't get along without them. When family members give reassurances you can almost see the dying person's shoulders relax.

Sometimes people die minutes after the family leaves the room. The patient may not want them to see them as they breathe their last breath.

When patients who are going to stay at home are diagnosed, you may see them withdraw. They may even narrow down family members and friends they want to see. This is another gift both to the dying and from them to us. Their withdrawal is part of getting ready to die. They are smart enough to know and get us ready.

I'm glad I had the hospice experience when my father was dying. With Dad it woke me up. I asked the hospice team: "Are you this good with all patients?" And when I was there with the night staff, I saw it all in action.

I spent a lot of time in my father's nursing home room before his death. When hospice told me they thought he was getting close to death, I spent the night in the nursing home in a recliner. I slept between my father in his hospital bed and my mother in an empty patient bed.

As children on our farm in Carrollton, Missouri, my three siblings and I were never allowed to sleep with our parents. I was sixty-three and I was getting to sleep between Mom and Dad. I had a journal and I wrote: "I had to be sixty-three years old to get to do this. My other siblings never did."

I like working with Alzheimer's patients. Dad had dementia or Alzheimer's. He went through the early, middle and late stages. At first Mom tried to cover it up. People so often don't understand that there is a human in there. Even if people tell the same story over and over, there is still a person in there to be appreciated.

It is always hard when a person with Alzheimer's doesn't recognize a family member, but Dad or Mom may be living back as a teen. They have not gotten married yet, much less had kids.

If you want to help an Alzheimer's patient, sow a seed. Make them successful. Don't ask them what day it is or who is president or what they ate at lunch. Just say something like "I saw roast beef and mashed potatoes as I came through the dining room. Looks good."

Don't say, "Hi Daddy, this is Susie."

He doesn't know his daughter. He doesn't have a daughter. I used to say "Hi, Roy Frederick Kelb" and ask him what his mom was doing today. We talked about his brothers. He remembered people from his childhood.

When you leave, never say you will be back tomorrow. You might say that you have to go home and give a reason. Something the person can relate to. They don't know tomorrow or time. In the last stage, we thought Dad knew Mom's voice so she would say, "I've gotta go home and fix dinner for the kids."

We kids were all grown and moved away, of course. We had to educate the family as to what to say so he would feel good, not inadequate or frustrated.

I am so thankful to work for hospice. They taught us to make a person with dementia successful. That's what it is all about, giving them confidence. It's not about how my little feelings are hurt. You have to get over that. You have to dwell with them where they are if you are going to relate to them.

It's hard to deal with sometimes. My father was always kind and docile. We were never allowed to say "Shut up." But he lashed out and said, "Shut up" to a nurse. It turns out he was septic because no one at the facility had taken him to the bathroom for three days.

I have moved thirty times in forty-five years. My husband and I fixed up every house and yard. Every place we've been we wanted to leave it better. I came from a farming family. All of us have a sense of responsibility. Dad pounded that into our heads.

I worked in my forties as a teacher in Nigeria through a church organization. I was recruited to work here from another hospice organization. Before that, I was in charge of blood drives for the American Red Cross. Every six weeks organizations would come and serve a full meal after a blood drive. We had linen tablecloths and posted the menu so people could look forward to a treat after donating.

It's important to give time to help other people. Find your niche. Red Cross, the homeless shelter in town, Big Brothers, Big Sisters, be a part of Youth Friends. Find the volunteering spot that is right for you. People are surprised how much they benefit, how much they get back in return.

4 Culture Shift

Kamal

Kamal is a manager in a Midwestern retirement community.

When I was young, my topmost dream was to come to the United States. I had a pen that said it was made in the USA. I didn't use it. I just put it in my top pocket for show.

I first came to the U.S. as an exchange student in Illinois. After graduation, I went back to Sri Lanka with a taste in my mouth for returning. I returned in 1986, sort of like smuggling myself out of my country on a tourist visa.

My family dynamic was that I had a brother who was a huge cricket star in Sri Lanka. I was in the shadow of my brother. I came pursuing the American Dream. My father was a big-ass alcoholic. He was not nice to Mom. Every night she went to bed in tears. I hated this. At sundown everyone would get depressed because they knew that my dad was going to come home drunk. It made me sad. I wanted to do something. I couldn't overpower him, so I became the family clown. I went to see movies. I started coming home and acting out funny characters in Bollywood movies.

The first English-speaking movie I went to, I fell in love with the U.S. I was in third grade, nine years old. It was a Western movie with Clint Eastwood as the star. He came into town, pulled his gun, got these women. I thought, "Wow!"

I kept working toward my goal of coming to America. In the paper they said they were seeking foreign exchange students who could go to Canada, New Zealand, Australia or the United States. It was really a tough process. One hundred thousand kids came down to fourteen. I was driven. Focused.

When I got the last interview, you had to take a family member, but I had to take the train and my mom didn't know how to get there. I had to take my dad, but it was not good because he was an alcoholic. Walking from the train, every two minutes or every block, he would say, "Son, wait here." By the fifth block I figured it out. He got so drunk he could hardly stand up.

Everyone else was there with their proud parent. I was practically holding Dad up. The panel sat him down. Dad's first question was "Tell me how much this is going to cost me." I wanted to deck him with my elbow. That was my closest weapon. I thought they would kick the drunk guy and the kid out of the interview.

When I got home, I cried to my mother. I gave up on the whole thing. Then the letter came that said I was to go to the United States. Then I felt guilty leaving the family. But when I came here I loved everything about this country. I loved the airport. I loved the cars. I loved the houses. I loved the food. I loved the people.

After my years as an exchange student, I went back to my country to study hotel and restaurant management with the thought that I could get a job in that field in the U.S. I went to school and worked in the field as a busboy at the Hotel Oberoi Sri Lanka, one of the five-star hotels, number one in the country.

I went to school in the mornings and worked at night, determined to save enough money to come back here. I did that for four years. I was a waiter, restaurant captain, banquet captain. I got a four-year degree and had four years' experience in the hotel and restaurant industry.

That was the lowest point. I went to school from 8 a.m. to 4 p.m. Back to work until 2 a.m. At 8 a.m., I was putting on the same pair of socks. It was pretty damned close to *Slumdog Millionaire* what I lived like. The same type of boarding room with four people and a tiny cabinet to put your stuff in. I wake up and my socks have holes in them. Somebody is coming and eating my socks. I'm going to lock my socks up, I thought. But the creature did the same thing to me. The creature was so addicted to my socks, guess what he ate next. My toes. A huge rat. I finally started wearing socks and shoes to bed.

I probably have fifty pairs of socks now that I only have to wash once a month.

In 1983 when the civil war started, the hotel got bombed. A bomb left in a suitcase. A good friend died.

That pushed me to want to come to the United States even more. I went to the U.S. Embassy but was turned down. Sri Lanka is a poor country. I was denied a visa for six months. Denied three times.

But all the people who worked in the embassy came to the hotel nightclub where I worked. I built a relationship with them. I got to know them. I learned all about them, where they parked their cars, what they drank. After six months they couldn't turn me down because I knew who they were.

I packed my suitcases. I was out of there. After the plane ticket I bought, I had $10 left. The friend who was picking me up at the airport in Chicago thought I was coming as a tourist. I only had three months to stay.

I went back to the small town in Illinois and found another Midwestern town where I hit the jackpot. One way to stay in the country was to go to school, so I returned to college. A schoolteacher I knew found me a job as a dishwasher. The place wanted my social security number. I said, "What is that?" The people had just bought the hotel. They liked my work. All I wanted was to stay in this country. Just to wash dishes and eat food there. I was so happy with that job. I was so happy at school. I decided, "I am going to own this restaurant one day."

When I came here, I was by myself and had to rely on everybody. A neighbor took me to the grocery store. A co-worker took me to wash dishes. I remember a pastor who picked me up and took me to church. It took six months for him to realize that I was a Buddhist.

One day at the hotel, the kitchen ran out of mayonnaise. I looked at my boss and said, "Dude, you've got the oil and the eggs. Let's go." I made the mayonnaise. The next day I was promoted to cook.

In 1986 I was the dishwasher. I said to myself, "I'm not going to wash dishes for the rest of my life." In 1987 I became cook. In 1989 I became chef. In 1990 I became a U.S. citizen. In 1990 I married my line cook. By 1994, I had become the restaurant manager, the same year my daughter was born. By the year 2000, I owned the restaurant, a casual dining venue with American food.

In my restaurant, most of my clients were regulars. After the tsunami, I did a fundraiser at the restaurant that raised $80,000, which three people took back to rebuild in Sri Lanka.

After about ten years, the marriage failed. But I can't blame her. I was so driven about education. Studying always. After the restaurant, I said, "Oh my God, I'm done. Let's party." I started to be bad. I didn't have a goal any more.

Then I had an opportunity to get into the health care business and work with older people. I have made friends with all the residents of this retirement community. I know their stories and they know mine. I think in life it is important to dream big and build relationships. When I meet someone for the first time, I want to connect. The best way to connect is to get that person to smile and laugh. If you get a person comfortable around you, they start to trust you and you become friends. Once you have surrounded yourself with friends, these are the people who can make your dreams come true.

Now I am driven to give motivational speeches. I went to hear one. I thought, "I have got a better story than that." So far I've got the pens, paper clips, T-shirts and $100 for a talk. I'm working my way up. Eventually I'll be a motivational speaker.

My whole life has been relationship, relationship, relationship. I want to tell people to start building relationships. Start with a neighbor. Start with the mailman. Start with the newsboy, the garbage guy. Those are the people who made my dreams come true.

People who can't pay bills come to me and ask me if I can go to the bank to help them. If a person helps me or is a friend, and then asks me for help—oh my God—I will jump over the roof for them. Any time you take a chance in life, what have you got to lose? This is the wallet I came with. Here is the original $10 bill I came with. It has started to fall apart a bit but I have taped it. I saved it because, even if I only have it and have to go back to Sri Lanka today, I will break even.

I see my daughter, who lives with my ex-wife, three times a week. She's an awesome kid. A 4.0 average. There is complete advocacy for education on my side. She will be a senior next year and already we have the college forms done. I am advocating for a scholarship.

The teachers in my country make so much money. What is happening to this country? I compare the knowledge of my nephews to kids here. In Sri Lanka they go from seven to one thirty, lunch till two, and then are not home until five. Then they do homework. Now some are even starting at five in the morning. The teachers come to the house before school to tutor. Each house has a room dedicated as a teacher's room. Ninety percent of the people have this.

If anybody can improve, it will be us in the United States. I got my daughter a Kindle for her birthday. No other country could have come up with this.

My mother still takes a teaching role with our family's children in Sri Lanka. Each TV has educational channels. She watches the channels and writes down questions. She learns too. She feeds the kids and is a referee on the sidelines. How can you duplicate that kind of bond? It is so comfortable. I would not want to put my mom in a nursing home. She is the center of everything in the kids' lives.

My father passed away about four years ago. About fifteen years ago he turned himself around. The family had time to heal from the bad years. I never had a chance to do that with him. I went to visit when he was sick, and my mother said I had to bring home her favorite Betty Crocker mix. Then she told me not to tell my father he had cancer or "he'll give up on life." There was no nursing home. My nephews were feeding him—a grandfather with kids feeding him. The first agenda was to stop Dad's pain. I smuggled something through airport security, but he refused to take it. "This pain is my karma," he said.

You want to go to your next life with karma surpluses, not deficits.

He had radiation treatment every day, an hour's drive. Two hours of agonizing waiting. One hour's drive home. The doctors and nurses were never on time. "Don't make people mad," said my mother. "Help your father."

The next plan came when I met a nurse whose house was destroyed by the tsunami. I gave her money to rebuild. He never had to wait again.

After fifty years of marriage, it was the first public display of affection between my parents. My mother held his hand to help him. They always had separate bedrooms. She moved into his room. They were truly making up for lost time. There was a *Bridges of Madison County* scene like when Clint Eastwood's character says, "I know you had your own dreams. I'm sorry."

It was all planned how he wanted his last days. My sister took the most care. My dad knew the last time I saw him. I didn't, but his eyes gave me his last goodbye. I tried to make it back again to Sri Lanka before he died. For four days, my travel was delayed. There is a white flag put up when there is a death in the family. I dreaded seeing that. The funeral service had already started.

I like my job, but I still find it odd that older people in America come to group living situations. I'm a Buddhist. We take care of old people at home.

This is a great country, but there is a lot I gave up to achieve this. Money does not bring happiness. Maybe some day when I am old, I'll go back and live in a room in my sister's house. Mom will be gone by then. My sister and I will live together and take care of one another.

But my nephews, for them I'm their hero. "No," they say. "You stay there in America."

Serah

Since this interview, Serah Njuhi has moved to Seattle for better work opportunities.

I am from Kenya, Kabesi around Nairobi, a little area, a suburb. I was born and grew up there. It was kind of a poor place when I was growing up.

I was the secondborn. I went to a little school first through seventh grades there. In high school my dad passed away. We were left with my mom—six sisters and one brother. My youngest sister and brother were very young. It was a big struggle. We had ups and downs. Ups and downs.

We would go to wash clothes or dig a garden at other people's places. I started selling eggs when I was twelve. I would buy them at the market and go sell them in Nairobi to get more money.

We all went to high school. No shoes. One set of clothes to go to school. We wore a uniform. We had nothing to change into. It was hard. I call it hard, but we survived. I'm happy.

One sister had a boyfriend from another tribe. In Kenya there are lots of tribes. He was a physical therapist in a hospital in Nairobi. The man fell in love with my sister. He was given an opportunity for a green card to come here to the U.S. They got married in Springfield, Missouri, and had one child. Then they called my older sister to visit. The second sister. Then she married a white guy here.

Mom couldn't come on the airplane for the wedding. She said to me,

"You go to your sister's wedding." I never dreamed I would be here. I stayed and stayed. Oh well, I started to get friends. "But I can go to another place," I thought.

I had friends in Kansas. They said, "Come and live here."

I went. Oh, I like Kansas. Shawnee, Kansas.

My two sisters in the United States were nurses. They told me, "This is the job you do."

I went to OTC (*Ozark Technical Community College*) in Springfield and started working there. A certified nursing assistant (*CNA*). I only placed an application at Shawnee Gardens Rehabilitation Center in Shawnee. I loved it. It was nice. I was there three years.

I got a green card. I called for my daughter. I had two kids. My daughter and son were very young when I left Kenya. First I called my daughter and applied for her. She was getting big. She was in tenth or ninth grade.

She finished school in Springfield. I have seen wonders from above. She was an LPN. Isn't that something? She became an RN at Kansas City Kansas Community College.

People all want to see miracles happen. But don't wait! The miracle is what you go through.

My son is now thirteen. He loves football. I can't get him out of there. How did he learn football in Kenya? He is a football player. Football is soccer in Kenya. I was thinking he was playing soccer. He said, "Mommmmm, it's American football."

I have to learn. Praise the Lord. He said, "Mom, you are going to end up in Hollywood. I'm gonna play until you end up in Hollywood."

We went and we went and we went to play football. We would drive over to practice every day. We would go for practice a lot. Mmmm-hmmmm. When a kid likes something you don't say no. It's better than doing other stuff.

Oooo, he is huge. He made me do football crouches. If he tackles you it is like he hits you with a shovel and you fall on the ground. I told him, "Don't joke with me. My back is not that good."

I took him to see a Kansas City Chiefs game. He said, "Mom, that is the best thing you have ever done for me."

I met a boyfriend when I went to Kansas. We got together. We have a little boy. A miracle boy. I am supposed to be sitting down and eating, not having babies now. I used to walk with my daughter. People did not think I could be pregnant and have a big daughter. I hid it until I was six months.

I'm forty-five. My boyfriend is still in Kansas. All the sisters are together now. First one moved to Georgia, then another one from Springfield. He will come to Georgia, too. I will settle, get a house and a job. It will be good. It is so different from Kansas. Mmmmm. I'm fifty–fifty. I haven't seen something very good here yet.

Kansas I like because I have a lot of friends there from Kenya and friends I met there. I had a favorite patient in Shawnee. Her name was Tracy. When I met Tracy we would close her door and laugh and laugh and laugh. I love Tracy. I was her aide. I said, "One day you will heal up and leave me."

I got mad because she would just get out of bed by herself. I said, "Call me when you get out of bed." She had pain but I couldn't believe what she would do. She is a really strong woman, and lovable.

I started looking for a job. I am looking in hospitals, nursing homes here in Georgia. We drove around looking, me and my sister.

When they say they'll call you for the job—hmm-mmm. It's kinda hard to find a job. Sometimes I wish I had stayed there in Shawnee. I want to go back again.

The kids are already in school. When we came here they had already started practice. My son has to wait a year. I felt very bad for him. "There is nothing we can do," I told him. "Let's wait for next time."

My sister's husband was killed in Kenya. My sister was one of the teachers. People paid for her to go to California. She left with her three kids. When they came to California, my sister stayed seeking asylum. There is torture now going on in Kenya. From California, they had to move to Phoenix. She had three kids and there were no jobs so we all help with the kids.

I'm a Seventh Day Adventist. I grew up in that church. It's the only church I know. I like it. We go here, one church close by.

Sometimes you keep quiet with troubles. People are so distant sometimes. God will help and we'll get a job.

I miss Kenya, but let me tell you, you people should be happy here. America is great. I love it here. You can just read and read. There is so much opportunity for it. Thousands of kids in Africa can't. They don't think about what they will read, but what they will eat.

I appreciate being here. Every time I feel down, I think I have a lot to be thankful about.

Dolma

In the heart of the Haight-Ashbury district of San Francisco, Ugyen Dolma runs Tibet Styles, her shop of all-Tibetan rugs, folk arts, handicrafts and jewelry. She lets customers unfurl peace flags before they buy them, interpreting symbols and colors for them and making sure they have the size they want. Early in the morning at 1707 Haight, she says Tibetan prayers as she readies her store.

Ninety-three percent of my family are in Tibet. The rest are in India. I don't see them. My favorite uncle became sick and died. I hadn't seen him since I married thirty years ago. I had twelve aunts and uncles—five now who are very old and poor. I support them with a few dollars every month.

I was born in Namru. My surname is Pontsang. I was born into one of the richest families, the highest. My grandfather was the ruler of thirteen districts for many years. Mom was the oldest in her family. We had hundreds of horses and sheep in the yard. A beautiful lake, horses, sheep and love. We suddenly lost everything when China came and took over our country, our beautiful Tibet.

When I was seven, in 1959, my grandfather wanted me to follow him out of Tibet, to follow His Holiness the Dalai Lama wherever he went. My grandfather was smart, so smart. We got out just in time before China took over. We hid in the mountains where it was so cold. All the Tibetans ran into the mountains. I was on a mare tied with my aunt.

In the caves of the mountains we survived, but half my family was so stressed out they died. My grandmother, mother and father who didn't come with us and said they would stay and "go tomorrow," died. They were tortured and killed by the Chinese. My uncles still in Tibet who were young, from eighteen to twenty-five, and my aunt who is a nun, were hurt. But my uncles would always come to the mountains to bring us bread and see if we were alive. There was so much stress. Everyone was dehydrated and tired. Nobody had their full family.

We spent three years on the border in the mountains. I really feel I am a survivor. We lost lots of people, but the rest of us are so strong and bonded.

When we came to Nepal we were very poor. My other grandmother had one kilo of jewels in a crown that she sold. My grandfather and grandmother were so stressed that they died, my grandfather on the border of Nepal.

When we reached Nepal, I felt so relieved because I was no longer in danger for my life. I didn't know the language or the culture, but it was warm weather. Suddenly life was a journey. But a beautiful journey with loving uncles and aunts.

When we settled in Nepal, my uncle said to me, "You don't know how to speak Nepali or English. You have to study."

The first thing I said, my first English words were "China took over my family." The truth will come out.

I had to go get cow dung and water. That was my duty. I learned ABCs with the help of teachers. My younger brother and my uncle taught me as well. I read by the light from a streetlight.

There was not much dress to wear, but we kept clean and took care with education. We survived on whatever we got to eat.

I wanted to be a nun's assistant to help sick people, but they said no, you have to be sixteen. I was only fifteen. My uncle said at dinner—he was so smart—"There is not enough food here and not enough education and we are so far from His Holiness the Dalai Lama. We must go to India."

Everyone said Nepal was not good for money. We got in trains and hid and went straight to India. The first thing was to bring the children close to His Holiness, whatever we had to do. By His Holiness' blessing, I was able to go to Masuri to school. I finished high school with a scholarship and went to Punjab University and got a BA and master's degree in geography. It was the best time of my life. I was never behind in my studies. I did extra work in geography.

The Dalai Lama's niece sent me to do a secretarial course in Delhi. I was able to come to the Tibetan Government in Exile. My surviving grandfather worked for the health department and His Holiness brought me to the health department where I worked as a secretary and a head cashier for fourteen years. The responsibility was great. I was in charge of money for fifty-three hospital payrolls. I had such honesty and did such a good job. I never missed one penny.

I was the only woman to work for the health department in the Government in Exile at that time. It was hard for women to come up. They were kept like in Tibetan society. Women are lower. The Dalai Lama says we need equal rights. Then my boss only gave one month's maternity leave. The Dalai Lama said women were to have full payment, all insurance paid. And maternity leave for three months.

With my job I had responsibilities, and then I became a mother. I came to the United States for the children. I was one of the thousand Tibetans given a visa to come to the United States in 1990. The Dalai Lama recognized my honesty and my sincerity. I came alone. There was not much sponsorship or help here at that time. I was culture shocked, almost sick.

In Washington, D.C., I cried every day. The Dalai Lama came to visit the city. I was a housekeeper—in the lower ranks. He went by the hotel where I was standing outside and pointed his finger at me. "Be happy," he said to me. The Dalai Lama is everything to me: my mother, my father, my guru. We are so lucky to have his leadership in the world. That is why every step, I follow him. If I look at a picture of him, my pain goes away.

I became a nurse's assistant and oral surgeon's assistant at George Washington University, but I was not happy. I was separated from my family. My children were only ten, six and two when I left them to come here. I missed my children.

My husband back in India told me, "You are not having an easy time in America. I should have gone."

My daughter said, "No more crying. I want to go to an American school."

And she did. She has just graduated from college and will go on to graduate school. When my daughter came to the United States, she went to a very good private school. As soon as I got citizenship, my children came here. Unfortunately, I had no time to enjoy my children when they were growing up. When they have their own children, they will realize this. I sacrificed for my children, but I was blessed. The children are now grown and so beautiful and responsible. I was alone raising my children, but our home was always based on the culture of Tibet: warm, sweet and honest.

I moved to Minnesota after three years because the children's aunt was there. In Minnesota I worked twenty hours a week at the county, which paid for my family's insurance. The rest of the time I worked at the family business, a Tibetan store.

I may have had more money but there was no time to be with the children. I looked at my face and saw that I was always exhausted. I saw more opportunity for my intelligent children in California and I didn't like the weather in Minnesota. I prayed and the answer was that I come to San Francisco.

My prayer is that my beautiful three children will be of benefit for others and have good marriages. Love is the most important thing. I would like to see them marry someone in the Tibetan culture if possible. It would be easier for them to share the culture. But if they get love from a person from another culture, I accept that. But not for money. What is the use of being married to someone rich, if there is no love?

I say to them all the time, "You bring such joy in my life. I have no regrets if you kids make mistakes. You can do your own lives. I hope, though, that now you can do things to help those who are less fortunate."

And to my Tibetan family, I tell you, "Thank you so much, my uncles and aunts in India. Hopefully one day I will see you again. I did my best. I didn't even rest one day. I have not forgotten you, not until I close my eyes."

The sad thing in my life is that the Tibetan younger generation is not getting to be strong in Buddhism. Teachings are needed. They don't even have a chance to ask questions about the culture. Every day they are working and studying. I am scared that what they know about their culture has dimmed. If they don't get it now, they never will.

When my daughter and sons came to America they only spoke Punjabi. They learned English here. They now know how to read, write and speak Tibetan. You have to know where you come from. Language is a big part of it. People who are half Americanized, half Tibetanized, they are nowhere. They are confused. They don't accept either culture.

All the people say the Dalai Lama is wonderful. They listen to the simple and beautiful things he has to say. They take his advice, but they don't support him.

Tibetan culture is something unique. We have such a beautiful world leader who works for religious freedom. There are no other leaders to help. No one supports the cause to end suffering in Tibet. He asked China for our religious freedom. Hopefully some other leaders will help us out. That is why I am doing prayers for them.

Now the youth in Tibet are suiciding. The Dalai Lama said stop. But they are desperate individuals. How many years they have been tortured. Young kids are dying here, too. We have to stop that. Our prayers are strong.

Until I die, I will keep telling people my words are truth. They say Tibet is a part of China, but it is not. Some Chinese-American ladies came in and bought a lot of incense. They saw how badly Tibetans are treated when they visited there. One of their sons put prayer flags in his room. In school, he wrote about how the Chinese mistreat Tibetans. They told him it wasn't the truth.

In Portland, there is a Tibetan community. My aunt in Portland guides me every day in the path of Buddhism. For seven years, I have gone to the World Peace Prayer in Portland. It is always on the Dalai Lama's birthday, July 6.

I wear Tibetan dress. It not expensive and it expresses where I came from. I eat Tibetan food.

I'm single now. The fight is still going on to live in America. I have lived in San Francisco for ten years with the grace of His Holiness the Dalai Lama. I have no regrets. I have been here with my shop, Tibet Styles. Nowadays it's not an easy business because there is so little business from tourism. But I just keep on. I have a smile on my face. And for women who are raising a family, single mothers like me, I give them a hug and do a prayer for them.

I give 100 percent from my heart. Some days are challenging. Money is not important. Love is first, His Holiness taught me. I share everything— with the homeless outside the door. They call me Mama and put flowers in my hair.

I have expenses even though the kids are grown. As a mother, I wanted the best for them. Living on Haight Street is very expensive and the rent is very high. I am still working here in the store every day. I'm almost sixty. In hard times, I always think it is the ancestors and His Holiness who keep me going.

I take joy in my health. I tell my children and other people, "Be happy, happy, enjoy. Life is precious."

5 Standing Their Ground

Jack

This interview was conducted driving through the Navajo and Hopi Nations in Jack Courtney's 4x4 Dodge truck, while he was visiting people he knows in both nations. Although the boundaries for each tribe's land have been the subject of much dispute, Navajos occupy roughly 27,000 square miles of Arizona, Utah and New Mexico. The Hopi Reservation sits on about 1.5 million acres of mesa land inside the Arizona Navajo Reservation.

The truck passes through a rolling sandy land dotted and dashed with sage like a desert Morse Code. In other areas, rock outcroppings jut from the ground. Ribbons of the Painted Desert running through both reservations offer a more colorful backdrop.

My grandfather, Antonio Martinez, moved from Mexico to Ash Fork (*Arizona*) in 1887. There are people who have been there since the 1930s who think they run the town now, but we're one of the oldest families.

My great-grandfather was a railroad man along the Yuma Valley Railway in Yuma Territory. Grandfather Antonio Martinez worked for the Santa Fe Railroad between Ash Fork and Flagstaff all of his forty-seven years. My father, Lonnie Courtney, met my mother, Dora—a Martinez—at a dance in Ash Fork when they both were teenagers. My dad and I both worked on the Santa Fe Railroad. That makes four generations. One of my sons, Josh Courtney, works for the Union Pacific out of Texas. That makes the fifth generation of railroad workers. It was a hard job but a good job.

See that exit? Garland Prairie. It was named after a division engineer. My father and he were friends. Tex Garland hired me.

I grew up in Ash Fork. When I wanted to get some money together, I came up to Williams and got a job at the original Denny's. I got a paycheck and thought I was something important. I was promoted from busboy to dishwasher. I hated it. Too noisy.

I was offered a job in an engineering department for the Santa Fe but they said I would have to move to Winslow, so I said no. I don't like that town. I have a horror of that town to this day. I was offered a job on bridges and buildings. I still had to move to Winslow, where I became a student foreman. My foreman there was too mean. Tom Garcia. He never promoted anyone in thirty years. He would say, "How are you gut-eating Indians doing this morning?" Yeh. He was the nastiest man I ever met.

An assistant foreman took me under his wing. I went to Winona. I learned the old-fashioned way anything to do with rails, broken rail changes. We were putting in a new spur for a Purina plant in Flagstaff. I took care of a section on that track. I became a surface-gang specialist. I knew elevations and spirals. Kinda like beats driving spikes all day. Since Winona, I've been everywhere and done every kind of railroad maintenance job.

So, this nasty guy would give an order and you would follow it. He told me on a Friday, "Meet me in the toolhouse after work." He wanted to go drink and chase girls. You never questioned his authority. He never came to the toolhouse. I waited there until Monday morning. Then I went to claim overtime. I went upstairs to Garland and told him the story and he said, "I'm going to promote you. Congratulations. Tom Garcia finally promoted someone."

So I became a full-blown foreman. I was extra gang foreman from Albuquerque to Needles, Phoenix, up to Ash Fork. Lodge 2417. I was well respected. An inspector came one time and told a machine operator that for as much surface as these machines were covering, they were in good shape and extremely clean. The guy said, "That's not me. That's my foreman."

We got a new division engineer. I don't know what the problem was, but he kept giving me demerits. The railroad goes by demerits. If you get sixty, you are laid off six months. He wanted to know how I checked the track center. Had unauthorized equipment to see how far the tracks were apart. It was one thing after another. One day my truck broke down so I couldn't use the radio. It was a Friday and the men had taken off for Gallup and Grants. They drove their personal vehicles so they could go home by way of Williams, Arizona. I walked fourteen miles until seven p.m. I had forgotten to release the track to let the trains run through.

There was nothing I could do. I had fifty demerits.

The roadmaster went out. He asked me to sign a slip afterwards. Charlie. He was a good guy, the nicest roadmaster on the railroad. Had been on vacation so he said he didn't know exactly what had been happening, but he told me, "That guy is going to get you whether you sign or not. Just finish out your work. Just don't quit in the middle of the week."

I worked until the close of the week and was suspended. Three months later, I went to Winslow to claim my job, as I was entitled to do. They said, "We don't know what you're talking about. Go see your union."

I said, "You are going to regret the day you did this to me." The whole time off I had read the union book. About the money I should have gotten. The lunch hours I should have been getting. I thought about running for union chairman of my local, since I knew the agreements thanks to my suspension. The chairman had been in that position for seventeen years. He was a company man. He settled things with the company over a game of golf or lunch.

The first election meeting I ever went to, people got wind that I was running. An old guy stood up. A Navajo with pull. He nominated me. I beat the guy who had been there seventeen years right off the bat. They had a revote against two of the chairman's buddies. I should have won on the first vote count. I had more votes than he or his buddies combined. They didn't want me in, but I ended up winning.

They said, "Jack is kind of a hothead." They didn't know that I had studied the union book like a bible. They had never read the financial account at the meetings, ever. I made sure they did that for the rank and file from then on.

The local voted to send me to Maryland to the George Meany Center for Labor Studies. I rubbed shoulders at George Meany with people from all types of unions. People from the Transportation Union, a guy named Blackie from the Las Vegas Teamsters. I didn't know who they were and I didn't consider them to be a big deal. I spent considerable time there learning negotiating. How to use tact. So you don't blow your lid.

I asked the rank and file before I left if they wanted me to go as is or should I wear a suit. "A suit," they said. I went in a suit I paid for out of my own pocket. A medicine man made me a watchband to take with me. It had rope encompassing the band in a full circle. He said that it represented our tied hands. There were pebbles. "These are the tears we've shed." And the inlaid leafs on it were wings to freedom.

He said that if I was ever broke, I could sell it and come back here. I still have it. It has the Santa Fe Railroad emblem in turquoise.

I was chairman of the largest local railroad maintenance union in the country in the Brotherhood of Maintenance of Way. Over 570 members. That covers anybody who touches the tracks. Back east the unions from Alabama and Georgia only had 30 or 40 members.

In Arizona and New Mexico, mostly Native Americans work for the railroad. It's mostly Hispanics in California. In the South, it was predominantly black people. I said, "I'll vote for you and vice versa." I'd give them 500 votes and they got what they wanted, and they would vote for us.

At that time the outfit cars had twelve to eighteen guys trying to sleep on the siding right next to the tracks. We couldn't sleep. It was hot and noisy. There were no air conditioners and only two stoves and two showers. We waited to cook and shower. The poop from the toilet would fall on the ground and smell. The railroad didn't care because next week they would be moving the car to work on another part of the tracks.

We got rid of outfit cars. They started to put workers up two to a room at Motel 6 or whatever and gave them $30 per diem. There still was no gas allowance, though, to drive into a town for the night.

I went back to working on the track again. The president, vice president, secretary and treasurer of the union were again all Caucasian. They were representing twenty Hispanics and a few white guys. The rest were Native Americans. I told the Navajo workers, "I know you have your hands full to fight them. But talk to your guys. Don't let the 3 percent tell you what to do."

A Navajo guy made president. Tommy Billie. He was from Tuba City.

Shortly after that I was injured. An air compressor hose got loose. Even though I turned my back when I saw it snaking around, the end of it whacked me and broke my back. I have a total of seventeen breaks in my body. I have two rods running the length of my back. Disability. I was thirty-eight.

I went to a union lawyer in Los Angeles named Pfeister to do my case. It turned out he had worked with the railroad instead of against it and would have made $50,000 to $60,000. He made a $150,000 offer to me under FELA (*Federal Employers Liability Act*). I was entitled to past, present and future income and he wanted a third of what they were offering. I flew to L.A. They made an offer two times but it wouldn't even have paid for all I had lost. Four years had passed. What about my future? Then the lawyer said, "You are not totally disabled. You could always sell pencils."

That was a rude awakening. They had been faithfully sending guys to Pfeister. The guys trusted him. He had told me at the pretrial conference when I said one of the things I wanted was railroad retirement: "No jury in the country can guarantee you that. If we were to take this to trial, we might get zero."

I stood up and pulled my pockets inside out. There was nothing in them. I told him, "Last time I checked, zero from zero is zero. But I am not firing you. I'm going to sue you for incompetence and then I'm going to sue the union for allowing an SOB like you into the union halls to lie to us."

I eventually got the biggest settlement of any railroad maintenance worker at that time. Just under $1 million. The person who first helped me was Shirley Flynn. Her uncle defended Miranda, as in Miranda Rights. Shirley knew a lot about law.

At a deposition hearing I was asked questions like, "Do you ever go to the movies." I answered, "No. It's too uncomfortable. I tried to sit through a movie but only once."

The settlement arbitration judge set the trial immediately. It had to be within three months, or settle the case. The good part of the whole story is that just before Christmas, I was willing to sign a contract to get $150,000 up front. The railroad disability check I would get would kick in in two years—$1,000 a month for the rest of my life for injuries.

I said no. First, the railroad will have me killed. They say they'll pay you for life and then come out and run you over. I figured that when my boys would turn eighteen they would get nothing. Not if I died.

On the railroad you get three percent raises every year. I told them, "I guess I won't accept the contract."

The phones were cut with a storm. I had thought about calling back and telling them, "I'll take it." I had been starving for four and a half years. Thank goodness I couldn't call. When I talked to the claim agent representative the next day, he said, "You're a lucky man. They agreed to what you wanted because you didn't call."

I have one annuity and one railroad retirement check. Three percent raise on the total each year.

I went to a national convention. They used to say any member in good standing could represent a union. They changed the rules to say that no retiree may hold office. The Santa Fe didn't like me. I can never hold office again.

The next ten miles you'll see a drastic change. They took millions of tons of uranium out of the Reservation. Coal and uranium. That's what they have taken from the Navajos.

You think there is no one out here, but then you'll see a house with maybe five others around it. It's a Navajo clan. They keep the whole lineage through the female. They don't marry into the same clan.

See? You are entering the Navajo Nation. They run it as their own nation.

Lots of sand. This is nothing. You ought to go up to Page. That sand, when the wind gets blowing, will scrape the paint right off your car.

Hopi people live together in small villages with members of their clan. The Navajo people live in towns or out on the land in these one-family or extended-family groups. You'll see the Navajo hogans. They always face east. Some of the new-style houses face east, too.

My friend Rebecca was paid to be a teacher at the Hopi high school. They gave her a house near the school. We used to go to dances when she worked at Hopi High School at Keams Canyon. We were allowed in because she was accepted. The town where I'm going, Shungopovi, we were invited to the dances in the plaza at the private back part of town. Dances that no other non-natives could go to. Sometimes they post a sign at the entry to town that says no non-Native people are allowed—in the winter quiet season or during dances.

The Hopis are runners. They like to stay in shape. It's nothing to see Hopis running along the road. Rebecca trained to run a footrace for a Hopi celebration and ran seven miles around the mesas with them.

Rebecca had a bipolar thing. I knew something was coming on. We went to ten to fifteen different hospitals. She killed herself in the middle of my ranch. I had just rented a nice house in Mesa for her. She was teaching at Gilbert Chandler Community College and she had finished her PhD in English at the university in Tempe. All but her dissertation. It was going to be on modern communication, or lack thereof, as it pertains to texting. She had terrible depression for years. Somewhere along the line, she just gave up.

I'm going to show you the school where Rebecca used to work. They have to bus the kids from way out. There are about forty buses. Regular-size school buses.

It's the cleanest school you've ever seen. There is not so much as a gum wrapper on the grounds.

They have two playing fields. The Hopi Bruins. Football games are a big event. There isn't much to do out here on weekends, so, even if you aren't a big fan and the Bruins aren't winning much, you'll be in the stadium cheering anyway.

The railroad couldn't hold a job over me so I was like a loose canon. I am still a lifetime member of the union. I'm still on the seniority roster. As an investigator I can go to any FELA railroad. I have a card that says "We sue railroads" and "We file lawsuits under FELA."

I went to work for Shirley Flynn, who did independent contract work for a law firm called Youngdahl and Youngdahl. It's a firm specializing in handling railroad injury cases. There were not that many FELA lawyers in the country. The first year I signed more than sixty cases. I worked for cheap. I made Jay so much money. They gave Shirley Flynn a bonus at the end of the year, but we should have asked for a percentage of the settlements. I was young and stupid. The first year I brought in millions in settlements.

Most of the railroad maintenance workers in this union are Navajo or other Native Americans. The railroad's policy has been, "He's hurt? Send that Indian home and get a fresh one." They will promise anything, but once they get you out of your hogan and off the Reservation, they do anything they want.

I saw a Navajo guy killed in Grants. They found his wife in the middle of nowhere and made her sign papers because they told her he was just in the hospital, in the emergency room. He was already dead. She signed her life away. I got that overturned.

I was working on a Kingman section of the railroad when I broke my back, about twelve miles from the town. They took me by ambulance to Kingman, then realized my injuries were more severe than they could handle there. They took me by helicopter to Flagstaff.

The roadmaster never called my girlfriend to let her know I had been injured. It was the helicopter pilot, whose wife worked with my girlfriend, who called. That is the policy. The roadmasters are taught to never let on how badly you are hurt. They try to get you to walk to the truck. That way, the injuries won't seem so bad.

With me, I couldn't get up. I was lying two feet from an anthill and ants were all over me. The foreman was so upset because he couldn't keep them away. The guys told about the ants in the report. I didn't say anything. They were the ones who said how bad it was.

I'm going to stop and smoke. I've been smoking since I was six. I stole cigarettes from my grandma.

See that dirt road? It goes to Bird Springs. About fifteen miles that way there are 200 people in a village. They have no well. There is no water service. They haul water in fifty-five-gallon drums.

Otherwise nobody lives around here but livestock. The grama grass and buffalo grass are native to the area. The cows eat it. About 10 percent of the livestock are sheep. The Navajos were traditionally sheepherders. The Hopi, runners and gardeners.

There's a truck at that intersection. It's parked to carpool. The wives wait there Friday evenings if their husbands are coming home for the weekend. Now that the Burlington Northern and the Santa Fe have merged, they are taking Navajo on Sundays to God knows where. As far east as Kansas. They might not get home but every other weekend.

One of the places where people are still exploited is the Navajo Nation. It's a shame. Most of the Navajo railroad workers are good hard workers.

In my fourteen years as an investigator for different law firms, I've gotten 300 settlements in favor of railroad workers, most of them Navajo. That's why a lot of people know me and I'm welcome to come into their homes.

I ride in Run for the Wall, a motorcycle ride to the Vietnam Veterans Memorial in D.C. Anyone who was a vet or is related to a vet or knows a vet can ride in the event. I served in the Navy. I'm a Vietnam vet. You can ride in honor of Vietnam veterans or any other veterans. Our motto is, "We ride for those who can't."

I own a ranch in Ash Fork. I have a big barn where I keep all my photos of my days at George Meany. My brother raises the cattle mostly. I try to travel and enjoy life.

Maryanna

Maryanna Christie is president of the Antelope Trails Vendors Organization, a group that provides employment opportunities for Arizona-based Navajo Gap Chapter House members so they don't have to travel off the reservation to work. A chapter house is an administrative and communal meeting place where residents of an area give input to their Navajo Nation Council delegates and decide matters affecting the chapter. The largely female Antelope Trails group makes and sells jewelry and other items by the side of heavily traveled roads in Northern Arizona.

I believe Antelope Trails vendors started about seventeen or eighteen years ago. The roadside stands were just pullouts on the side of the road. But they were so sporadic. We established selling sites, the biggest at an area known as The Cut, twenty miles south of Page. It's where the road for Highway 89 was cut through a big bluff.

We also have selling sites in Marble Canyon, scenic areas like on the way to the Cliff Dwellers Rock House and in Kaibab National Forest. We established the program and the sites because some vendors were getting so much money and we felt it was silly that we were competing against one another—like the elders against me, for example. So we put our vendors into groups. One is for people fifty-five or older that you can be in, but you don't have to be just because you are over fifty-five. You have a choice.

The second group is girls who do not have a lot of silver. They sell other hand-strung things. The third is for people who are starting to accumulate silver. You can make a major profit with silver. The fourth are the girls with tons of silver—really high-end.

We go out every day, seven to ten people at The Cut. Four to nine of us at Marble Canyon. Two to three tables at the other sites. The hours and number of people vary depending on the time of year. If the economy was better, we would have more people out. When the economy went down, we saw we couldn't sustain ourselves, so we dropped the amount of people per site. Members rent table space from the program. Vendors pay $20 to $25 for sites in the summer. It's better than in Flagstaff. You pay $65 a day there. And we don't have to drive to Flagstaff. It's approximately fifteen to twenty miles for each person to drive to their sites, although some people drive as little as two miles.

The profits from the table rentals are used to cover operation expenses and all the rest of the money goes back into the community. We just gave twenty-five scholarships today from money we earned. We helped four families with medical emergencies and funeral expenses this past month.

We bring in $110,000 a year on the average. We make a little less five months of the year than the rest of the time. We stockpile scholarship money for when we need to pay the fall and winter scholarship requests. We give scholarships for college, universities and trade schools.

When there was a massive snowstorm a few years ago, our program brought hay out to people's animals. Any kind of emergency, we respond to it. If people have an odd request, they bring it to the board. If we hear of a house burning down, we immediately give relief money. Sometimes it is just a random person we are helping. I've had people say, "I didn't even know you knew about my mother passing."

I was previously on the board. For fourteen years, the group was managed by two ladies. After so many years I said, "I want to know where my money is going." That was the beginning of the end for them. There was $120,000 a year coming in then, but no money was going into the community. When they wouldn't tell us, I overthrew the government. Now financial paperwork is available.

We hold a lottery once a month. The calendar for when the vendors go out is set up by color. The days are blocked out that are available for you. We try to make it as easy as possible for the vendors.

If there is a bad weather day, and none of the vendors want to go out that day, you don't have to go. But it has to be a unanimous decision. If one person decides to sell all day long and nobody else wants to, it ruins it for everybody else because they lose that day.

We have about 170 vendors. If the Arizona Department of Transportation were to shut us down, it would be an economic disaster. There would be no more scholarships. So many people are bringing us scholarship applications. We pay more out than the Chapter House. Our program is the best economic help in our area.

The board members are compensated. It is a big job. You have to travel, and with these gas prices! The board members get $300 to $400 a month in the summer. The first month I was in office, I put 850 miles on my truck. Now that I know what I'm doing, that's gone down.

It's my last year as president. I've had two terms in office. I brought honesty and integrity back into the program. The bottom line was I wanted to know where my money was going.

Other people will maintain the organization. If not, I may have to take it on again.

The Bennett Freeze

A federally mandated freeze on building any new structures, performing road repairs and improvements to infrastructure, or making any repairs to existing homes was enacted in 1966 on a portion of the Navajo Nation. The freeze affected 1.5 million acres of land that was part of a Navajo–Hopi land dispute and kept 8,000 Navajos who called that land home from fixing existing buildings and roads when they fell into disrepair, and from constructing anything new in the area, for forty-six years. Many moved away when their houses became unlivable. Others have suffered through lack of electricity, water, phone services and other necessities.

Robert Bennett, Bureau of Indian Affairs director at the time the freeze was enacted, issued the order to "freeze" all development after the Hopi Tribe filed suit to add that land to the area affected by another dispute. The Bennett Freeze regulations did not lift until May of 2012, when President Barack Obama signed a bill repealing the law.

In reporting on the repeal, *The Navajo Times* in a May 14, 2009, article said, "Life stood still under the Bennett Freeze area as Navajo families watched as other areas of the reservation received improvements...."

The article notes that an agreement had been reached in 2000 settling the legal aspects of the land dispute between the two tribes. But the Navajo newspaper quotes Navajo–Hopi Land Commissioner Roman Bitsuie as saying, "Congress needed to pass a law that officially ended the freeze so that federal funds would be forthcoming to make up for all the years of deprivation."

While Navajos in what is now the former Bennett Freeze will be able to rebuild homes and infrastructure, improve schools and provide health care facilities, the newspaper speculated that recovery will cost billions of dollars and take decades to accomplish.

Claudia

It's mid-March and a chill wind blows through the Navajo Nation. In the town of Page, Arizona, Claudia sits at a Burger King booth with a cup of tea. She has decided not to sell her jewelry outside today at The Cut, the roadside area where State Highway 89 slashes through the bluffs.

I live about thirty-seven miles south of here, near Cedar Ridge. I was born there and I live there. My mother was born and lived there.

My family had some sheep and goats and some cornfields. But mostly they raised sheep. Mostly that was their income and their food. Back in 1953, it was a time before there was any school around and there was no transportation to get around. My parents traveled by wagon and horse. I went away to school when I was thirteen. The government started to go around to homes in a Jeep. They signed us kids up without our parents knowing, until we were about to leave. We left in mid-August by bus. They took us to Chemawa Indian School in Oregon. There were ten to thirteen busloads from all over the Reservation, all the way from New Mexico.

We had to stay there until the middle of May every year. We missed our parents.

There were twelve of us children in my family. Nine girls and three boys. My oldest sister is eighty-two and she never went to school. Another one is about eighty and she didn't either. They were too old when the people came to take me to school. All the others went for one to three years.

The three boys in my family went to the Tuba Building School. It was the only place they had. In Page they built a school in 1958, but I had already been taken away to school in 1953.

I made friends at the school. I had some relatives over there. One year they sent my younger sister. She didn't know anything. She was in a different dormitory, but she was always crying and lonely so they put me back in with her all year.

I had to learn everything there. Cooking. Learn how to sew. I learned little by little and worked. They took us to Salem. They used to drop us off at people's houses where we had to wash and iron. The pay was not much. Four dollars a day. For me it was really important to save because my parents had no money. I had to pay my own way. I worked after school at the dormitory cleaning. That's how I would buy clothes. I sewed clothes for myself at home economics, too.

They gave me five years to go to school. I didn't even know how to read, spell or count. I always tell my grandkids about it. They don't understand. They start school at three years old. They go to Page or preschool at Gap. Kids are able to go to school here now. The bus runs every day.

I'm the fourth from the last. The older ones helped with the weaving and taking care of the sheep. My two brothers were the oldest. One is ninety-something. The other is ninety-two or something like that. The two boys chopped wood. In those days there was no water anywhere. We had to get it from water holes. Here and there. In the winter we melted snow and boiled it and put it in fifty-gallon water barrels. Now I have running water and live in a trailer, an old trailer.

We are part of the Bennett Freeze. The Bennett Freeze line is a little ways away. Not too far. We are maybe two or three miles into it. They gave us water. We have a water line. It runs Gap to Navajo Springs toward Marble Canyon. And we have electricity.

None of the grandkids saw how we used to live. Sometimes I say to them, "I never saw fast food. Our transportation was wagon, donkey and horse." They look at me funny, like, "Is she telling us the truth or what?"

I make jewelry with beads. Necklaces, bracelets, earrings. The same with cedar beads. You know, the berries of the cedar tree. Inside are the brown seeds. We work with the chipmunks, actually. The chipmunk usually makes a hole on one side of the seed. You make another hole on the other side and string the beads. In 1969, I started making holes through the beads. Back then I sold at trading posts, anywhere. I took jewelry to Flagstaff and around that time they used to buy from me at Cameron and Gap. They don't do that any more.

I'm part of the Antelope Trails (*Vendors Organization*). I have been since 1997. I've gone to Utah and Nevada for shows. All over. California. I used to go two to three times a year. I went to powwows to sell. Pendleton, Oregon, where they make the blankets. I used to go to the powwows at Fort Hall, Idaho. It's a big one.

Back in the days, the trading posts took a percentage of what you sold. In 1969, I started selling cedar bead jewelry by the roadside or trading post, then at The Cut. In 1970, one day a man came where we were all selling and had all different kinds of shells. "Do you use this?" he asked. "No," we said. "We don't know how."

But we bought a little. Then he asked what we really needed or could use, so I asked for glass beads. Maybe it was the next week, he came by and he brought glass beads and needles. He kept asking what we wanted different. One day he came with hishi shells and turquoise and other stones. So it just goes on.

The Antelope Trails sells mostly around Gap. We are about 200 people. Mostly women, a few men. There are four groups. The elderly has its own group that I am in. The second is some jewelry. The third does silver and pottery and more stuff like dream catchers. The fourth does sterling jewelry and pottery. They have credit card machines, too. Those little computer ones you just slide the card through.

We don't go out when it is too cold. I went out today and asked another woman if she was going to sell out there. She is. Not me. I told her, "I'm not going to stay." Too cold and windy. If nobody sets up, you get the day back. You call the officer if it's too cold or you have snow, rain, windy. Too hot? You have to go. You just have to deal with it. If you have an appointment with a hospital, you get the day back if you call before twenty-four hours. So they could find a replacement and somebody else could go.

Women have been selling on the road or at The Cut for I don't know how long. We used to get chased away by ADOT (the Arizona Department of Transportation). They said we didn't have the right to sell there. They still didn't want us to sell there back in the '70s. Then we just went on the roadside, along in shacks until '89. In '90 a lady was going around asking if we could sell at The Cut, see if we could open it up. A man who worked for ADOT, Tom, started asking if he could help. He went to a Phoenix meeting and asked support for us selling at The Cut. Finally they said OK, we could sell there, and at Marble Canyon. That was 1995.

When I couldn't be by the road, I went to California in the winter to sell at the flea markets in San Diego, Pasadena, Riverside, Ontario, Palm Springs, Palmdale and to Yuma, Arizona. I stayed in a motel. That was in the '90s.

Then that man came from Phoenix with lots of shells. "What will we do with this?" we used to say to each other. But he just kept bringing supplies, everything we needed. Even to Ziploc bags. He would tell us what's new.

I use different stones. What people want to buy is always different.

Sometimes they buy cedar beads. Sometimes silver and other stones. Other times they go for the pottery. You never know.

My husband and I have been married like about forty years. At that time I was working in Page as a maid in a motel. He was just going through. He grew up on the other side of Gap. I am from the Red Bottom Clan. My father is Dear (*People Running into*) Water. My husband is Towering House Clan.

I have thirteen grandkids, mostly boys. I had four boys and two girls. One works at the plant in Page. One lives in Bitter Springs. One in Phoenix. One is working in Houston. I have a daughter who lives next door. My youngest daughter lives in Mesquite, Nevada. Because of jobs, that's why they are scattered.

When I came home from school I would learn native ways. With my own children, not all of them took to it. They went to work here and there. Just one daughter nearby. The way I see it, they have earned their own living and it's good for them and their kids.

Their kids don't speak Navajo. Only one girl and boy close to me understand some. They know about Navajo ways.

My daughter in Mesquite got some Navajo words on a cassette or a CD. She had it on her iPod. I went there two or three weeks ago. The kids were listening to it. I was surprised. They could say things and what it means. I didn't ask where she got it, but she is doing it.

My husband used to work construction, like on the roads, and here at the plant—building it, then as an operator. He used to work at the sawmill in Flagstaff. He learned how to silversmith. I was on the road all the time, so he made silver jewelry in his spare time. He did whatever he wanted to do—bolos, rings, pendants. But no more. He can't really see. Sometimes he had a hard time with the solder.

My daughter went to school for welding and traveled all over the east. New York. She was away from home a lot. She was not married. She met a man over there, a welder. She met him in New York or New Jersey, I can't remember. He was Navajo, too, from around Shiprock. They came home. She is not wanting to go to work as a welder now. He is still working as a welder, except this month he had surgery. He traveled around doing welding jobs. They called him for different places and different states.

I keep telling her she should try jewelry. She knows how to weld. I say to my daughter and her husband, "Both of you should try. It would be easy to learn if you are a welder. Then you don't have to travel for a job."

But the price of silver just went up and up. That's another reason why my husband stopped.

During the last few years, with the economy, the business kind of went down, especially in the winter. There is hardly anybody around. I wonder how business will be this summer. I keep saying that.

But we do get people from England, Chinese, all over are coming. France, Russia, Sweden, Australia. Alaska, Canada, Utah coming from Bryce Canyon, coming or going. Just name it. We meet them.

Louise

Louise Yellowman sits in a mobile home made into an office and meeting space in Tuba City, Arizona, on the Navajo Nation. In the next room her son is conducting a meeting of the Forgotten People, a grass-roots Navajo group that is launching a protest against a pending U.S. Senate bill that would rob their area of water and give the Navajo Nation no recourse to complain about future transgressions that might occur under the water agreement.

I was on the Coconino County Board of Supervisors. I started in 1980, to 2008. Twenty-eight years. I hold the record in the state for holding that office. A Navajo woman.

Let's go back. I'm originally from Lupton, Arizona, about ten to twelve miles from Lupton. That's where I was raised. I was born in New Mexico.

I grew up with my grandparents, just Grandma, Grandpa, all the aunts and uncles. It was up in the mountains there, just beautiful. Grandmas, grandpas coming to visit us all the time. We always had somebody to swap their horse and their wagon. We didn't have any vehicles except an old jalopy. Grandma couldn't wait to get in and go to Gallup to get groceries. It took two days for them to go.

I would stay home with the sheep and horses. I was about five years old. Five years old I was at home taking care of livestock. By myself. Grandma says, "Build a fire." Middle of the night, build a fire. So that's how I grew up.

A little pony went around crying. That made me sad because sometimes they took the wagon to the trading post, Three Hogan. The mother horse would pull the two-team horse wagon for two to three days and the little pony left behind would cry. Pretty soon he quieted down and I would take the sheep out and just take care of all that livestock. Yeah, that's how I grew up there.

Grandpa went to about fifth grade in school. Grandma never went to school. Grandpa went to the Apache Reservation to school. He could write like a high schooler. It was amazing, because he only went to fifth grade.

So, one time Grandpa said to Grandma, "School."

I was about nine years old when Grandpa said, "We'd better take you to school in Houck." There was a little Catholic school. The father had been there for so long. I had an aunt who was a nurse. She was always so neat and clean. She became kind of my role model. I wanted to be a nurse like her. She said, "The only way you're going to be a nurse is to go to school."

So I begged my grandmother. One day my grandfather said, "We'll walk to Houck." We lived farther than ten miles. We moved around. This time we were with the sheep way, way, waaaay up high. Winter camps, which were a little farther than summer camps. Actually, it was about fifteen miles.

At three o'clock in the morning Grandpa and I left there. He worked at that Three Hogan Trading Post, where he was a silversmith. We would walk in the snow, deep, and come down.

I would take the Houck bus that would take me down to the school twenty miles. It was Route 66 then. The school was named for that saint who is going to be canonized. She's a Native American woman. Katherine Tekakwitha.

I would walk back twelve to fourteen miles. I would get home about 3:30 so I would help Grandma do the chores with the livestock. Then Grandpa would come back late at night. So that's how we worked. I think I did it for at least four or five months.

Then they asked Grandpa to enter a movie. All those movies at that time were made around Lupton. They have a beautiful formation of rocks. Right in that area in the Lupton Trading Post, they made some movies. Grandpa and other Navajo men joined. It was *Ambush* with Robert Taylor.

Grandpa was really happy to get on his horse and go there. He wasn't there a full week when they told all these movie stars, about twelve of them sitting on horses, that they were going to shoot a gun and one of them would fall off. They weren't told which one, so when a gun fired they all fell off. Grandpa landed on something and broke his hip.

They sent him to Albuquerque to the hospital. Grandma says, "No more school," that I couldn't walk by myself.

So there goes school for me for such a long time. But my aunt keeps coming and she just never lets up. She keeps talking about school, education. Grandma is kind of hesitant.

Finally Grandpa came back from the hospital. He couldn't walk for a long time. What happened was I took care of the sheep. I did the plowing. Then I planted with Grandpa. Corn, squash. Until I was about fourteen, right in there. My aunt insisted that I go back to school. Grandma said, "Go enroll her. Let her go to one of these off *(the Reservation)* schools."

One day Grandma said, "You're going to Intermountain Indian School in Brigham City, Utah. In the mountains," she said. Oh gosh, I was thinking about the bears.

It's about thirty miles north of Salt Lake City. That's where a lot of us showed up. When I got there, I was so lonesome. I sat on my suitcase for two weeks. Imagine a fourteen-year-old girl. Oh, my God, I wanted to go home. But finally I got around and then I loved that school. It was one of the best opportunities. It was like the gate was opened for a lot of us. That's where I met my husband, Frank. We just both enjoyed that school. I became a nurse's aide in five years. We took vocational training. So that's what happened.

Frank, I didn't really know him until he was graduating. I guess he got there about '50. I got there in '52. Graduated in '57. He graduated in '55. He went on to Jackson, Wyoming, where he became a mechanic. He loved that. He talks about it all the time. Some of his friends went up there. They're still there. They own their own business now. Lot of welders. Frank went into the service in '58. He eventually made the trailer park here his business.

I wanted to go back to school. I was helping one of the nurses at St. Benedict's Hospital, the order, the Sisters of St. Benedict at Ogden, Utah. One day I cleaned somebody's third-degree burn and I got a certificate. The lady was Miss Lena, my boss, who gave it to me. She said, "You did a good job."

I worked with her that summer and she said, "You ought to go back to nursing school. I'm going to take you down to the sisters," she said, "and see if they can enroll you in their nursing." She took me down there and the first thing they asked is, "Where is your diploma?"

The next thing is, "What courses did you take? Chemistry?" All these hard courses. I told them I didn't take any of those. They said, "We can't take you."

But Miss Lena didn't give up. She said, "Go back next week to your school at Intermountain. Ask if they can help you and see if you can get your diploma."

I took the bus down there and contacted three of the administrators, the principal. They all said, "We don't even know how great you will be, Louise. In high school they would make fun of you. You're old. Why don't you just stay with your job and maybe some day you'll meet a nice young man and start a family."

I just couldn't believe it. I went back to the little Catholic church there, St. Henry, and the father who used to be our instructor. I thought of him and I went there and the church was open but nobody was there. I walked in there and awww, I started crying. I wanted to go back to school so bad to get to be a nurse. What happened then is that Father came out and said, "What is your problem, Louise? Why are you crying?"

And I told him. He said: "OK, let's just pray."

So we prayed about ten minutes. Then he said, "You know, Louise, I will be going southwest."

I thought: Where is southwest? I thought of Saudi Arabia. I said, "Where is that?"

"It's in your country," he says. "Phoenix, I'll be going to Santa Fe!"

"Oh," I said.

"You'll hear from me in two weeks," he said.

In two weeks he called me. "OK, Louise. What kind of courses did you take at school? What kind of things do you know?"

I said I took some English courses, some writing, math, a little bit of reading.

He gave me eight subjects to learn in two weeks. "Go to your nearest library and start reading. Start studying. Get a tutor."

So I went back to Miss Lena. She said, "No problem. I'll take you over there and get you set up." I was there day and night and the father said I'd hear from him in two to three weeks. He called back and said my hometown St. Michael's Indian School wanted me to come and take a test.

Aaaah. Another two weeks of study. In two weeks I packed up and went and I took the test. My God. I took a test and they accepted me as a ninth grader. I went ninth, tenth, eleventh.

When I was a senior, Frank was in the Air Force. He kept coming to see me. Pretty soon I was engaged. Then I went to San Francisco. I found out that it was a beautiful place and we decided we would get married. My husband and I lived in San Francisco when he was in the Air Force and he went on active duty up there. He had a sister that lived there, too. That's where we lived for about five years. I babysat for my sister Susie. She just passed away. Younger sister to my husband.

But I didn't stop. I went on. I went on and graduated from Mission Dolores High School in San Francisco. That was the best thing I did for myself was to get a diploma. I opened the door.

Frank decided we'd better just go home. He was working for Planters Peanuts, right there by Giants Stadium. We lived there in Bernal Heights. It was culture shock, but it was a beautiful place.

I was kind of frightened when I first got there, but one day I saw a cross waaay over there. I made my own map and I went to that. It was St. Boniface. It was Sunday and there was a choir singing. There people were kneeling down. I just kneeled down and here was Father Emilio from Houck.

He asked, "What are you doing here?"

"I followed my boyfriend. I'm babysitting for his sister."

That's when I told him that the boyfriend and I were going to get married. He said, "Oh, Louise, I guess that's what you've decided, but continue your education."

He introduced me to the church there, the fathers. My husband had to take some lessons there. So that's how we started our marriage.

I got my degree in '61. Then I was just a housewife. Did some house-cleaning. I had four children. Got married in '60. First son '61, then '62, '63, '64. The fourth one born here. We had headed back because my husband, well, I found he was very open-space oriented. He doesn't like to be in a city. We went all over. We decided to move back and, of course, we both needed jobs.

We drove and took our stuff back to my home in Lupton. In Lupton, my husband couldn't get a job. We were up in the mountains. The livestock were still there, but they were like pets to me. I couldn't sell them.

Grandma and Grandpa were still there. Everybody. I was so happy to be back, but I couldn't get a job. So we traveled and ended up over at Gap on the Navajo Nation. That's near Cedar Ridge where my husband's family is from. We met the family. And we came into a thousand sheep. Lotta sheep, goats, cattle. We took care of that for a while, and then I went into this chapter house and Frank's uncle was running the chapter meeting. He recognized me and said, "She's our in-law, Louise."

He said, "We lost our preschool budget last year. We are looking for a teacher, anybody to help us start the school. You were a leader at Intermountain School. You can help us. Would you help us?"

At the Gap Chapter, they all stood up for me. One of my sisters-in-law babysat and away we went to get the money. We had four days, but we actually just made it. Friends, a cousin's sister, friends of a brother-in-law, bus driver, another community member, we all had to be trained. But we did start a Head Start.

It was wonderful. That was my job for a long, long time.

My husband did homeschooling for a heavy equipment certificate and I helped him. He did his tests. Went to California, Bear Mountain, where you get this training, and he got a job with the dam at the Salt River Project, then the railroad.

Anyway, so he and I got jobs, but we didn't have a home. We managed to get one. We put up a tent at Cedar Ridge. There was hardly anybody there. Just us and another family. Just the tent.

I taught in Gap from 1965 to 1970. I didn't have a lot of training, but there I was, a teacher, a mother and a cook. Lots of work had to happen but we got thirty students. They spoke nothing but Navajo, the ones from Gap. Perfect Navajo. My four kids are the only ones who spoke English, except for some traders' kids and some Hopi kids. But by six months, my kids started speaking Navajo. We taught in English and Navajo.

My son is in there speaking Navajo right now in the meeting. He learned, and the girls. That was really something.

In 1970, I decided to go to college full time. I went into town to Northern Arizona University (NAU) to do night classes. I was accepted as a sophomore.

I got a little trailer. I exchanged a squash blossom necklace for a little three-room trailer. Somebody liked my squash blossom. I took the trailer to Flag, to one of the horse stables. They had a little outlet there called Silver Saddle. That's where we were until we bought a new trailer.

I went full time and got my BS degree in education in '73. The first offer I got was for a public school. I moved here and was hired by the Tuba City Public School in 1974. In '75 I got my master's from NAU, again in education. I kept educating myself. That was the best thing I did for me.

As a teacher I started in kindergarten and then bilingual education in kindergarten. And I moved up with my group to first and the same group to second grade. In 1974 I had my fourth daughter, my fifth child. I was teaching bilingual education and my stomach was out like this. Five kids. The kindergartners would take a nap and they were so cranky. I wanted to just walk out. I look back at how strong I was. I was ready to have a baby. My daughter was born the 28th of September. I thought, "Well, I'm OK." I had a lot of energy. At the time I was almost thirty-seven.

At the same time they had asked me to join a group called Community Action Committee. If you see a problem or issue, solve it. That type of thing. That was how I got involved in the county and the Navajo Tribe. I became the Gap Chapter secretary in 1967 and carried it on until 1980. There was a big storm at that time. I got to know some people at the trading post who were able to help us plow the road. People saw how capable I was of getting somewhere.

While I was a secretary I was able to bring water to our area. Yes, we lived on the Bennett Freeze. One of the things we asked for was water, water. Somebody brought it down to the foot of the Gap. Just pumped water there. There was nothing going out. One day I was telling a woman in a powerful position this situation. I was writing to her. She was able to get us $388,000 for the water to Cedar Ridge. Yes, it was Bennett Freeze, but then another bill came out of Washington. They gave Navajos four chances. They gave the Hopis four chances. They said if they started a project and if the Hopis didn't interfere and the Navajos didn't interfere in theirs, everyone could continue their projects. It was like: walk softly like a cat.

So that came, in 1976. Lo and behold, this money came. With the help of many men in the community writing the resolution and sending it different directions, we were able to get that money to work. We put the pipe in the ground, but the water wouldn't go through. Because we needed to pump the water.

We rounded up everybody, in the trailers, all the missionaries, all the people and, lo and behold, there were substations where they could pump the water to Cedar Ridge. So the water went as far as Cedar Ridge, and then to the trading post and then the electricity came to the trading post, to Gap. Luckily the Gap trading post had this old generator, even though the oil was leaking, but that's what we always borrowed for preschool. Put the line through.

We built a house. We'll be there this summer. Frank started in the fifties before the Bennett Freeze, but he never really finished it. You couldn't really finish a project and say it was yours. It was just sitting there. But we have finished it now. Since I retired, we put on a metal roof and did the inside.

One of the friends of my in-laws had become an electrical engineer in California and started his own company in Fremont. He had two people working for him. One night they came to Gap to look for us. They couldn't find us. It was so pitch black, they said.

We had a little tiny hogan. They couldn't find anything. When they did find us, they were standing there and they looked up. "What are those over there, that line above us?"

I said, "That's the electricity."

Frank was ironing my pleated skirt with one of those old cast iron type irons when my in-laws' friends showed up. They said, "Well, what is Frank doing ironing with that old iron?"

Right then my sister's husband's friends said electricity could be brought down. They said they could do that in a couple of weeks.

In 1980, a group of people from Flagstaff came and asked me to think about becoming a member of the Board of Supervisors because the board had been three members and now there would be five. I got nervous, of course.

I reached out to the little leagues that bring some of their money here and to the Parks and Recreation. People didn't really know what the county was all about. The first time I didn't have anyone to run against. I was the first Navajo to try for representation on the board. The first Native American and a woman.

I got elected. Now what? I was really amazed how much paperwork there was. All of a sudden I've got so much on my plate.

One of the things was to take care of the uranium tailings piled up here. From 1980 to '88 we worked to put that thing away. We covered the uranium tailings up. We had to deal with Congress to turn their heads around with whatever means to get their attention. We had news conferences. The county really helped. The sheriff, Joe Richards was the sheriff. He definitely helped. We hosted the biggest news media and press conference. I guess word of it blew all over Europe—England, France—people got so interested. They were hunting me down over here. One of the channels made a tape of me. People started coming to me.

We brought all the health people to help us, university people from Northern Arizona University came. So much testing. Goats and sheep were drinking that plume of water and they were dying from it. Oh my gosh, so many were affected. So many people who were victims, testing positive for breast cancer, leg cancer. You know, there's a lot of cancer. I even have one myself.

Contaminated. About twenty houses near here were contaminated. People were telling us that their homes were glowing at night. A plume of water was glowing at night. Kids were playing in there. Our own leaders came to test it. It took forever, but they did it, and we had to educate everybody in every school. Oh my God. People didn't know what it was, we didn't know what to call it. The dirt. The tailings blew all over.

After we got the tailings covered, we started a uranium victims' group and started having meetings every month. We started a case to get relief. We took it to Window Rock to the tribal council. Ahhh, these are our leaders. They actually didn't see the problem. I don't know. And today it is still going on, like with water issues now. The legislation that Congress is trying to get through to take water rights from us.

So we came that close to getting people compensated. We got $150,000 for the tribe. We got a lawyer. It takes a lawyer to win these cases. It is so hard to push in there. Ordinary people cannot see their way to be compensated. The government has so many ridiculous rules and regulations.

It became so clear that the children in Gap needed their own school. All they had was preschool. When I started teaching kindergarten I saw that people were making fun of the kids who came from Gap to Tuba City. Teachers, teacher's aides. Saying, "Oh, their hair is not clean, they smell like smoke and potatoes, mutton. They don't do their homework."

They were putting them down. I told them I lived there. "I taught these kids. We don't have electricity. We don't have running water. We don't have anything like that."

While I was secretary for District 3 and up here in Tuba City teaching, I thought to myself, "This is a good opportunity to start a school in Gap, their own school." I wrote six sentences about how the kids ride on the bus twelve hours a day. They don't have enough time to do their homework because they have to help with chores. They don't sleep enough. They're on the bus at six o'clock in the morning. I was talking about my kids, too, because they went from Gap to here, right?

I drafted a resolution for my chapter. When it was approved there, I turned around and gave it to the public schools, to the school board I worked for. Luckily, the superintendent who hired me did a feasibility study at Gap and Cameron, and they built two schools, which we have today. Beautiful. You have to see them. I'm so proud of them.

Before, the people never knew who they were voting for, particularly the elderly people. All these politicians come. Oh, my God. And, you know, they don't live here. They're from outside. And the people here have no idea who they are voting for. They just punch a name in. I thought I had better make it easy for them. After that, I found out who was running and who was going to be good for us, then we would work for those people.

It was good that I joined the county. I paved the way. One of the things we needed was county referral offices. There was eighty-eight acres here owned by the Babbitts, you know, five brothers way back who made their territory up in Flagstaff and they had trading posts. One in Cedar Ridge and on the Hopi Reservation too.

Inside their eighty-eight acres was a piece of county land. It was like an island. I thought we needed that place for the referral office to have things like Navajo voter registration and a Department of Motor Vehicles office. The state told us that the office was a duplicate. "You're the arm of the state," they said.

"Well," I said, "it's needed." So old Senator Hubbard, he represented this district and he lobbied. We all lobbied. The director of ADOT came down with others. They spent the day and said, "Wow." They lobbied the state to give us money. We got that there, and that was a plus for us.

When I started, I really didn't know county government. I knew about Navajo government. But I didn't know about the state government or Washington government. All these governments we have to work with to get anything done. I was able to get things. I brought the library in with a lot of help. We got that from the Bureau of Indian Affairs. I had to go to Washington. Work with the Congress. Senator DeConcini at that time.

I was able to get some roads out here. We have lots of roads, highways with a lot of accidents. We got bus roads through the county. It rained and rained so much in Gap. We built a road. It cost over a million dollars. Just a mile and a half.

They redistricted in 1992. I had more under me—Page and all the way to the state line. The people of Page woke up one morning and there I was their supervisor. It shocked a lot of councilmen. I had a hard time proving myself to them. Some people inside Page accepted me, but the political, elected officials, they had a hard time accepting me. It was hard for about a year there; I just spent time getting my name out, telling them, educating them, that I'm a good Navajo woman, a teacher. Just to be accepted.

I worked setting up a newspaper. It's now the *Navajo-Hopi Observer*. In Page, we developed another one. We were able to do a lot of good in Page, like the Powell Medical Center. The state gave us money. We built a clinic there for the people. That's a heavily used clinic. Then we were able to put the seventy-two-hours jail up there and an alternative school. Like me, I had a second chance to go to school. A lot of our young people were dropping out from school for one reason or another. I thought how they could go on for their degree, their diploma. A diploma is so important. It opens the door for you. You can be whoever you want to be.

I became full time on the Board of Supervisors in '99. All this time I had been teaching, and starting the schools, like Gap. We took breakfast over there. Every year they wanted to give us up, cut our budget or just close the school. We believed in that school. Parents could be involved. A lot of people could go back like I did. You don't know until you go to the university and look back. The window. It's like that Grand Staircase at the Grand Canyon. Beautiful.

People were dumping trash all over. Navajo and Hopi people. Right on the side of the road. Trash. College students came to visit, even some of my own kids brought their friends and they would say, "Mom, it's so awful to see this trash. Maybe you can do something."

What can we do? We didn't know. So I started looking for money. I said, "We are going to have a state-of-the-art transfer station."

We sure did. It's right there. I was so stubborn. I was mean. I wouldn't vote for the sales tax unless I got us a million for that transfer station. There was a lady who was an angel. She was in charge over in Fort Defiance. Her name was Christie. We invited her to eighteen chapters. She said, "The Indian Health Services has $100,000, Louise. We can start there. And start building your forces."

I went to the county and said I needed help. They took me down to Sedona and that was the state-of-the-art transfer station. I said I wanted one in Tuba City and each community would get trash bins. If we do that for the Grand Canyon, we can do the same thing for the Reservation. That was my word to them.

They said, "Louise, you've been on the board so long. It's about time we help you."

That was the board members. I thought that was very nice. Then they said, "It's going to be like anything else, Louise. We can't waiver anything. People are going to have to pay for their trash."

Then I thought, "These people don't know how to pay for their trash. I thought I'd better head over to Window Rock." Luckily, by chance again, I have an uncle, Tom Shirley. He was the sanitation director in Window Rock. And my nephew, Mervin Smith, was helping him. So we said to the tribe, "We need somebody to pay the tipping fee (*gate fee for the waste delivery facility*)." We got it. That satisfied the county, our paying for the trash to be picked up. Outside they pay to pick up trash. Let's educate these Navajos, Hopis, Paiutes. This is where you start dumping trash, but the Navajo tribe is going to pay the tipping fee.

We didn't have any landfill. We had to go all the way to Flagstaff. Right now we haul tons and tons of trash.

Kelsey Begaye was once president of the Navajos. He's from here and we really lobbied for him. He told me to host an economic development summit. I got NAU and all three counties—Apache County, Navajo County and Coconino. The counties said, "You come up with two things that will help the Navajo Nation. I thought, "What? Whoa!" Sales tax. I could not believe how much sales tax goes into the (*Arizona*) border towns. Millions. If we could just start with a one-cent sales tax."

We rebuilt the juvenile detention. We built a two-story-high health department. Another general office building. And we remodeled our courthouse. All three counties helped us. My number one thing was sales tax. Guess how much we have now. Six cents here. Millions and millions. This chapter has been getting millions now, but they haven't fixed potholes yet.

The last was the park. Louise Yellowman Park. You probably saw it. Parks are for kids. They were chased off every piece of pavement. I said, "I'm going to build you a state-of-the-art park."

And they love it. That's the heaviest-used park. I left with that in 2008 when I retired. They helped me, those students, those little kids. They wanted their area where they could play. I got a lot of compliments.

I got an Athena Award in 2006. The Athena Award is presented by the Women's Chamber of Commerce in Flagstaff, but women's organizations all over the United States give it. When they gave it to me they said I worked in two worlds perfectly. It's beautiful. I thought it was really an accomplishment.

My husband and I built this trailer court now. We just celebrated our fifty years. Our golden anniversary. It was so beautiful the way my kids put together that fifty-year anniversary. They wrote it in the *Navajo-Hopi Observer*.

My husband got sick in 2004. He became diabetic. He lost a foot in 2007. He's in a wheelchair now. He's doing good. And then at the same time, he was a very hardworking man. We literally built this ourselves. A trailer court with fifty spaces. It took a lot of plumbing. A lot of maintenance. So basically these last two or three years, I have had my own business, I guess.

You know, while I was in office I worked with the Clintons, Hilary and Bill Clinton. Bill Clinton has been inviting me to meet with him and be on one of his projects, but because my husband is sick I have not been able to meet with him. He does a lot of projects. He told me I could work on diabetes or HIV, whatever I could do. "We'll fly you to New York," Bill Clinton said. That's what he's been doing with women who have worked so hard to make things happen. He said, "You are one of those."

I just felt bad I haven't made that trip. But my husband goes to dialysis three times a week. I'm a nurse now. It's a very good thing I'm not afraid to give him a shot. I am here with him. So, that's my job now, with him.

Melanie

Melanie agreed to be interviewed after she talked on a Taos, New Mexico, radiothon about services offered by the local shelter for abused women. She knows firsthand how important the organization Citizens Against Violence is to the small community. She never mentions the name of her ex-husband, but always refers to him as "he" or "my ex."

I am a native of Taos Pueblo. I have a Zuni father; I'm half and half. My mom's from Taos Pueblo. We have a pretty large family on both sides. I'm a mother of three boys—twenty, seventeen, and seven. All boys. The oldest will be twenty-one in December, and that's freaking me out.

Their biological father is from Zuni Pueblo. We met when I was fifteen. He was about nineteen, and my mom and dad did not like him. So naturally I wanted to be with him. Yes, naturally. So we started going out. It was a long-distance relationship. We were writing constantly. And then, when I had the opportunity, I ran away to go meet him in Albuquerque, hang out for maybe a week, until my mom and dad found me.

By that time I was seventeen. Then I got pregnant with my oldest son and I moved to Zuni Pueblo. I dropped out of high school to go through the pregnancy and then I went back a year later and graduated in '93.

After I graduated, I moved back to Zuni Pueblo so I could attend UNM (*University of New Mexico*) in Gallup and I started going to school. He was there. He was working too and going to school as well. And then I had my son and we would come up here to Taos and visit. My parents were a little better with it because they had a grandson, their first grandson.

I was doing really good in school. I was going for my associate degree in nursing. But I got pregnant again, my middle son, and so I didn't go back and finish that. I had two young kids, like barely two and a half years apart.

And he was happy with that. It kept me in one place. I was pretty much isolated there. I have a lot of family down there in Zuni, but I wasn't allowed to go visit them. One time I made the mistake of asking him if I could go hang out with my cousin when I should have just told him I was going to do that, and he told me no. That pretty much set the grounds for our relationship. He was pretty controlling. He isolated me a lot, and he was really controlling with his parents too.

He had a pretty good job as a nurse and he would help contribute to the whole household. He thought that gave him authority. He was their oldest son. Tribal customs just put a lot of emphasis on the oldest child. I myself am an older child of my siblings. I have more responsibility and, yeah, more authority.

So there was something going on up here at the Pueblo in Taos. I think my brother was finishing his religious training. So we came up, and I was pregnant with my middle one then, and we were like already not in a good relationship.

During that time his dad passed away. He died from alcoholism. I think he was about forty-two, forty-three. Really young. He didn't get along with his dad that good, but he was having a difficult time. Well, his dad died on his birthday. So we went back down to Zuni about two and a half weeks later, and I had my middle son. Things were OK. Of course, he would have his tantrums. When our middle son started getting bigger he would favor him more. My middle son looks exactly like him. A carbon copy of him.

It was the same way with him and his dad. He looked nothing like his dad, and so his dad always questioned whether he was his. My older son looks more like me, and then he had the audacity to say, "Well, maybe he's not mine."

And then he says, "Well, maybe they're both not mine."

And then I told him, "Unfortunately, yes—I'd rather have anybody else but you be their dad."

Then I would tell him, "Yeah, they're not."

Oh God, he just took that and ran. He used that totally as a weapon. "Well, you said they're not mine." That was just always the argument. And, of course, I'm a single mom stranded. I didn't know how to drive. He didn't let his mom teach me how to drive. I'm at home taking care of the kids. We lived with his mom in the mobile home. We just had one bedroom.

I was messing around all the time, according to him. Oh so, you know, my two kids, like I had all this time to go and mess around with everybody else. He was always worried about my messing around when I would come up here to visit my family. It got to the point where I left him and came back and moved in with my parents up here and started figuring out what it is I wanted to do, how to support my boys.

And so he moved up here. He got a job. He transferred up here to the hospital. We were kind of talking, but he couldn't change. I started reconnecting with my family and high school friends. One time, my cousin, a male, came up to me. We were talking and when he left, my now-ex was like, "Who's that? I bet you're sleeping with him." So it started all over again. And then he started talking about wanting to move away to Denver or Arizona. I knew that he was just going to isolate me more, just take control. He wanted more, and I started thinking, God, even if we move, we're taking him and all that he thinks with us.

Just before my oldest son turned three, he was diagnosed with retinoblastoma, which is cancer of the eye. He ended up favoring the eye.

He's been cancer free since he was that age. But we were in the hospital during all the surgeries. I didn't eat that whole day and I asked my husband to get me something to eat after all the family left. They went all the way to Albuquerque to support us.

I realized I was hungry like maybe two in the morning. And the hospital's in downtown Albuquerque and I knew there might be a Burger King or some place open. So he went out to get me something.

I was just looking at my son asleep and I was wondering what all the rest of his life was going to be and I didn't realize that maybe three hours passed. Then he showed up and I asked him, "Where were you?"

He said, "I just had to take in everything that happened. I went for a walk."

I just took that as OK. Later on I found out that he was with an ex-girlfriend that night.

We were living up here with my mom and dad in a single room. It was like a thirty-by-fifty, not that big. We were getting electricity hooked up— we needed to shower and stuff. We would just walk across a short distance to their house. My mom and dad didn't really want him living with us, but, you know, he was supporting the boys. Even though we lived that close to each other, I didn't always go next door to visit. I would go over when they were gone, because I would have to cover up the bruises. He was physically, emotionally, mentally abusive.

It started with my second. You know, you always think, why don't they just leave? And you do try to leave, but when they're following you everywhere you go, and he'd tell me, "Who's going to want you? You didn't finish college. You have two kids. You don't have a job."

And I told him, "I don't care if anybody wants me. I want *me* for me. So I can take care of these guys here, you know?" A guy is the last thing I wanted. I remember it was my grandma's birthday and he worked me over pretty bad. Then my oldest one, at that time, he must have been three. Yeah, about three and a half. And then my son got in between us and told him, "Don't do that to my mom. Don't hurt her."

And so he left to work, and I was looking at myself in the mirror and I didn't even recognize myself. And I went—I, oh, it was the hardest thing to do is go next door and ask my mom and dad for help, because I didn't know what to do. I knew I was either going to end up dead or I would have more kids with him. Those were the only two options I had.

I would end up dead, or stick with him and have more kids and it would be that much worse—stuck with him. So I went next door. My mom and dad were so shocked.

Of course, my dad wanted to go find him and do the same thing to him.

I had been hearing on the radio and seen a few articles about the CAV (*Citizens Against Violence*). So Mom and Dad drove me over there. It was like the hardest thing to do. You know, the initial shock of seeing so many bruises and right away they did my intake and we were moved in that night.

I had had enough. Like, nothing was going to change. Nothing was going to get better. We moved into the CAV shelter. A lot of things came out. He has a son younger than our oldest and one younger than our little one. So there's siblings in between. And I was the one that was messing around, right?

All that was revealed. We were separated, but we had joint custody. He had visitation rights. The system then, I don't know if it's gotten any better, but when I was going through the divorce process, the lady in that division was no help. She pretty much took the guy's side. It was weird.

And so he never really reported his income for support. I knew I didn't want his money, alimony, child support, because I didn't ever want him coming back and saying, "Well, you took my money. I want my children."

And so I was fine with that. We stayed at the CAV. We didn't leave that place for maybe a month. I got into the six-month stay there and the boys started the counseling they give children there. They are still close to one of the workers. Then I started working at the CAV thrift store. I started readjusting to just living without that heavy weight. We moved out from the CAV. We had our own place, so we were doing good. He wouldn't really visit with the boys because he had a drug problem by then. He was doing cocaine. He was too wasted.

It had probably been over a year we had been divorced and then he started trying to get clean in time to see them. He would come once in a while. I remember one time I knew he was high. I could just see it in his eyes. They were dilated. Cocaine. I remember when he was way high that day, I was like, "I'll go with you and the kids."

I didn't want them to be alone with him. The kids and I went on that roadway down by the university, where they close the road off, and he was there. He was standing on a rock. It's a pretty good fall down. He was all spaced out. The boys are playing. I said, "It's a good thing I'm here."

I was watching him and he was totally faced away from me, and I was thinking, I could go over there and push him off. I was thinking, yeah, because he was all wasted. They would do the autopsy and find all the drugs. It would be an accident. Now I could be done with it. A clean break. I'd just have to do a lot of therapy.

He would hang out with us and then I remember I started to feel weird, like spacey, and then I was thinking, "Oh my God, maybe he's drugging me." Then he started hanging out with these losers that were in town. They're still around, some of them that haven't died. I cut him off being with our boys because he was staying at these people's home and he would expect our boys to go over there and hang out with him. These are drug-dealing houses.

So I told him no, and in the meantime I met my husband that I'm with now. He pretty much knew my situation. I clicked with him. He is older than me, about eleven years older, and I told him from the start. As we were getting more serious, I told him, "I come as a package. I have two boys."

He has girls, two older daughters, and he was so happy to have boys. We moved in. The girls were fourteen and sixteen. They would try to put things over on their dad. Having been at that age one time, I would let him know, "This is what they are really going to do." They thought I was so mean.

We had a mobile home, a little trailer. It was a three-bedroom. We started decorating it because it was like a bachelor house. When we opened up his fridge, all he had was hot dogs, bread and milk.

And it was funny, getting all that together. He would open up the bathroom cabinet and there would be my makeup and womanly products. The boys' names both start with "Z" and they got into Zorro books and cartoons, so there would go a "Z" on everything—his stuff. The trees got carved with "Z"s. That was really kind of a battle in finding the common ground—how to be parents to my boys, for him to be an authority figure and disciplinarian, because there were a few times I had to tell him, "Well, they're my boys."

Then I heard myself say, well, it is his home that we're making together. We did have a talk about it and that's really been the basis for our relationship. Even brutal honesty. We just talk about everything because if you don't, it just won't work.

We knew from our prior relationships what not to bring into ours. It wouldn't ever work if you bring all that baggage. His ex, he didn't marry her, but the mother of his girls, she would come over and try to stir up stuff. I'm so beyond jealousy. We still go to his ex-mother-in-law's. She still invites us to their family functions. She's sort of become the grandma.

About eight years ago, we bought a house together, a modular home that we had set up and are making payments on and painting, decorating. The only thing that I regret about it is when I was pregnant we were looking for a three-bedroom because we figured one of the boys, the oldest, would have left and gone to school. He did, but then he came back and he's still at home. We should have gotten a four-bedroom. The youngest, he's wanting his own room. So we're working on that, saving to have that built.

My husband does flooring. He's a flooring seller by trade—carpet, tile, wood floors. He was doing a lot of those modular homes for a guy out by Rabbit Valley Road. They started talking and he thought, "Well, these are nice houses. I might want one of these."

We knew what we wanted from one of the modular homes. If we had one, we would want these French doors here, clerestories. We went to Espanola. We saw some but they weren't what we wanted. And then the saleslady said, "Well, we have another place in Albuquerque."

So we said, "Well, if we go now, we can go and look around."

I'm probably five months pregnant now and we're looking at houses. I'm trying to walk up the steps. I think the last house they let us in, it had French doors, the clerestory, the bathroom setup. We said, "Oh my God, they built this house for us. We'll take it." We did all the paperwork. The closing was the hardest part. And then they finally delivered one half of our house and it sat there for maybe three weeks in the yard. They delivered the second half and I would walk in it. It was so dusty, the construction dust, and I said, "Oh my God, it's going to be a lot of work to clean."

It took maybe another month. The contractor took a lot of money up front, but he only had time for these other jobs. He was playing catch-up and ours was on the back burner. Then we found out he didn't do all of the licenses properly for our house. That was another delay. They finally started pouring the foundation. They moved one half onto the slab and then, I think finally by November, late October, it was done. They had delivered our home parts in May.

I had my son in August. We had to move the other trailer up to the property. We live where it's family property, divided between his six brothers and sisters. We moved the trailer up to his brother's property and we lived there. It was so hard. Every morning, get up, get your coffee, look out, and see your house there in sections.

We finally moved in. It was funny because all the walls were beige, like manufacturer's spray everywhere. It didn't bother me until maybe a year later when my son was a little bigger and he was able to play. Then I started playing with colors. My husband is colorblind. He would say, "That's a nice color."

I'd look at him and say, "Are you serious?"

Now when people go to our home they say, "Oh, these are such nice colors in your house," because my living room is a really pretty yellow color. The fireplace is red-walled. Then the kitchen is called February gold. More of a golden color. The dining area is sage green. I'm always changing the bathroom color. Last year it was blue. This year it's kind of an earth tone. The only thing we need to change now are the carpets, and it's true, just like how the mechanic never fixes his own car, my husband, well, it takes him a while to do the flooring.

Right now we are self-employed. We have a good truck, a little burrito wagon that we sell food out of. Like frito pies and tacos, hamburgers, hot dogs. Last year we were out at the Rio Grande Gorge Bridge before they tore up the parking lots to do the bridge repair. This year what we mostly do in the morning is make breakfast burritos and sell them. We make them at home together. Then I assemble them and he goes to sell them.

Now my husband's working with a friend of ours doing a remodel, so he does a little bit of everything. He's been taking our middle son with him. My oldest son likes school, so he's going back for the fall semester at college. He's going to get his degree in art. He does jewelry-making, painting, just a wide variety of art. And then my middle one, he's going to get his degree in liberal arts. He's fluent in Russian. They are just unique in their own way.

My youngest son is seven. He's the active one. He's taking tae kwon do. He learned a lot of arts and crafts from the vendors last year at the Gorge Bridge. He likes to do carvings and beading. He just learns a little bit of everything. There'll be days he'll say, "Mom, where's my beads?" and we'll have to get them out. And he recently got taps on his shoes. My middle son plays the drums. My oldest one plays bass guitar and their friends like to come over to our house because I'll be like, "Turn it up!" or "That sounds good!"

I do see my ex, mostly at family funerals down in Zuni, and nothing's changed. Maybe nine years ago, I was working at the casino at guest services and we shut down for a few days because of fires on the pueblo. One of my cousins is a firefighter and the crew was meeting here at the powwow grounds. My cousin heard my name come up and he sauntered around to see who was asking about me and saw my ex. My cousin told him, "Why are you asking about her? What are you going to do to her? We know what you did to her and you're lucky I don't throw you down right now. You're not worth it, even though I would like to pulverize you."

My other cousins, who were also firefighters, said, "Oh yeah? You're the dude, huh?"

I guess they encircled him and told him I was in Denver and married. "If she tells us that you tried to bother her, you'd better just watch out because we're not going to have mercy on you." I guess they set him straight on that. The last time one of them saw him, he told him I was in Canada somewhere. I guess I'm just like a checkers piece, all over the place.

Sometimes I think if he ever did come up, he would be looking for that other Melanie. When I was with him I wore glasses. I didn't wear makeup. My hair was always up and my clothes were two sizes too big, just to deflect any remarks he would have about me.

You couldn't win with him. We never really had any happy times together. We would go on family trips, but he would always manage to ruin them. He would just go into a jealous fit. Sometimes me and the boys, we talk about him. I've never said anything like, "Your dad was a jerk." I mean no really colorful words because he was like that to me and I left before he could be like that to them.

I remember a couple of nights after we checked into the CAV shelter, I was thinking about where I was going and whether I was going to follow through with leaving him and divorcing him. I knew trying to work it out wasn't going to make it. And my boys were asleep. I looked at them. I said, "I do not want them to grow up like that." How could I want them to have to deal with these things? I didn't want them to grow up and continue on with the drinking and drugging, thinking it was OK to be like that to women, or anybody.

Right now, I've been clean and sober for eight years. I haven't smoked pot in nine years. I do participate in the fellowships of AA and NA, and my husband now, he's been clean and sober nineteen years. He sponsors young guys. He does talk with our sons a lot about it.

My oldest son is saving up for a car. I'm apprehensive about it. He's going to be twenty-one. What if he drives off and just continues driving to see the rest of the world? That scares me.

Back in February, my husband was going to work and taking this group of guys to a meeting in town. They were three runaways from one of the treatment places here in town. They were sixteen, eighteen and nineteen. They were staying at the men's shelter. My husband brought them home to feed them and hang out with us. He has a habit of doing that. Even grown men, he'll bring over. You know, we don't just let anybody in. I have good discernment and so does he. We'll feed them and show them other places in town that will help them.

But I looked at those boys and thought, "God, these are like my sons' ages. I don't even know how those parents can sleep at night wondering where their kids are, if they're safe, if they're fed, warm." I would hope my boys are well-rounded enough to take care of themselves. Yeah, I'd rather see them drive off and explore the country than hitchhike or just bum it.

I am not going to be negative or spiteful against my ex with what he did to me. I didn't want to pass it on to my boys, because I remember there would be times when my mom would speak negatively about my biological father and I'd think, "Well, I'm part of him. Does she feel like that about that part of me?"

Consciously knowing that, I tried to break some of those links in the chains that get added to families. It's awesome to know that our youngest one has never seen us drunk or under any influences or even fight.

My relative with fetal alcohol syndrome has kids. My husband called and told me they don't have anything to eat at their house, so he offered to bring them to our house for the night. He came in with the kids yesterday. They're all lively and happy. We have a little swimming pool. Oh, they just couldn't wait to jump in it. They were playing and running around with my son.

Then the little girl comes in and she was sitting by me. She wanted to draw. She was sitting there and drawing. I was asking her what it's like to be at her house. Just making small talk with her. She said, "Well, right now, they're all drunk and fighting."

To ask her a lighter question I said, "What's your favorite music, your song?"

She said, "I don't listen to music."

I said, "What?" This little girl can't even be a child. Just the harsh reality of it. Her parents don't even know what wonderful kids they are.

She found a pair of my heels, not that high. They're boots and she's stomping around in them now. I told her, "You can have those," and she's all happy and lit up. When I go home today, we're going to do her nails. She wants them like mine.

My relative has been in and out of jail. He always says he's going to stay sober for the kids, blah, blah, blah. When you're in those kind of programs or serious about your recovery, you have to do it for yourself. You can't do it for a job, the kids, nothing. You're going to fail every time.

Me and my husband have talked about maybe fostering kids. I did go to a meeting about it. Oh my God, they want so much information. But they do have to pick the right people to do it. A lot of people just do it for the stipend they get.

This little girl, I can see it in her eyes, what she has to see at home.

I had a big old family party for my grandma when she turned ninety. There were certain members of the family I told my husband I didn't want there. I don't like to be fake with people. It's best not to have people around you who are rude. I don't like that energy in my home. I just have to stick to my principles.

Celeste Trujillo

There are three waivers to sign before entering the women's shelter in Taos if you wish to speak with a staff member in the offices. No one is allowed to go back to the area where the women are living. Maintaining anonymity for clients is a strict rule here. The shelter's location can't be anonymous in this town of 7,000 people, but the identity of the women who seek out this shelter is unfailingly guarded.

On the way to the office wing, there is a long table piled high with donated loaves of breads and cakes. Community Against Violence (CAV), the name of the organization that runs the shelter, is rightfully mum about clients but it is constantly in the public eye when it comes to seeking donations and keeping the public aware of victims' needs.

Though the shelter does get local government and federal funding, CAV holds an annual fundraising campaign. People donate clothes and food and there is an annual drive for shelter children's Christmas presents. There is a Mother's Day project. The playground in back of the building was built with community support. The thrift store proceeds all go back into the organization. The popular store had to move into a larger space in the spring of 2010.

That same year, the Taos News reported a wave of assaults on women outside bars. The perpetrators had slipped date rape drugs into the victims' drinks.

This prompted Citizens Against Violence to publicize statistics related to abuse in another front-page story. CAV director Malinda Williams and shelter director Celeste Trujillo said eighty-two rapes had been reported to their organization the previous year. Two reportedly were men. An estimated forty-nine of the eighty-two crimes were against children. Twenty-five percent of the rapes were against children between the ages of thirteen and seventeen. Thirty-five percent were committed against children twelve and under.

Those numbers are not any different than the yearly average. We deal with this on an everyday basis. The drug-facilitated rapes we've been seeing do not surprise me either. It's nothing new. Alcohol is the number one factor in young adult rape. Taos statistics are actually lower. In big cities the number per capita is way higher.

I have been shelter director for four years and an employee in various capacities for seven—shelter advocate, answering the hotline, and taking care of the women in the back. I made sure they were safe, feeding their kids and doing their chores, but talking with them was more important than anything else.

Before that I did client advocacy, helping to find resources for the women, things they need like housing and food stamps. I have seen them through the process of getting restraining orders, supported them at criminal hearings, and went with them to court dates or I went on their behalf. In criminal cases the woman doesn't have to be there. I can just let her know the outcome—if there was a plea bargain, if the defendant received jail time.

The organization has been in existence for over thirty years. Initially it started after a group of murders due to domestic violence. A group of four women said, "What are we going to do?" The answer was to provide shelter services by letting women come into their own homes or putting them up in hotel rooms. Then they grew into a little office on Montoya Street.

CAV now has thirty-two employees, most of them full time. Some counselors are on contract. There is an overflow of clients for staff counselors because two just can't do it all. There are advocates, maintenance people, prevention program staff, batterers intervention program staff, community relationship staff and thrift shop employees.

In 1997, the town of Taos donated space for a shelter with a place for women and children on site and an advocacy center in the front. Five years ago, the shelter built an annex with a safe room for interviewing children who are victims of sexual assault, and for the counseling and financial departments.

In the state of New Mexico, we are one of the only publicly known shelters. Our decision came because it is such a small community and we wanted clients to be able to get to us easily. We weighed the pros and cons of anonymity of location and thought: Why not just be out front?

There are different ways women get to the shelter. They may call the hotline and say they had a domestic dispute with their partner, husband or boyfriend. We can't go to their home but we talk with them about how to be safe. They can call law enforcement and they will pick them up and bring them to the shelter. They can go to a family member's home. We can meet them in a public place, or they can drive their own vehicle to the shelter. A local doctor or agency may refer them when they complain of situations at home.

When a woman first gets to the shelter, she is in crisis. We do not hassle the women with intake papers. All the victims are worried about is their safety, their children's safety, and where they are going to put their head down. We know the paperwork they have to fill out is hard and repetitive. We are required to ask certain questions, but we always tell them if it is too uncomfortable they don't have to answer. We try to not bog them down. We ask the questions on behalf of our funders. Yes, the paperwork has to be done, but in my book paperwork is secondary.

The questions are often personal. They are about their histories, the reasons why they are seeking shelter, if they have been sexually assaulted, the names they were called. Women name the person who has victimized them, even if they are not going to press charges.

We have a twenty-four-bed capacity. It can house all single women or eight families. The rooms are not dormitory style like most shelters. There are individual rooms like a hotel, each with a private bath. The communal rooms are the dining room, kitchen and playroom. Everybody loves it. We are always full. The average length of stay is thirty days, although there is a ninety-day capability with the option of another thirty if they are not strong enough emotionally or financially to leave. This is not usually long enough to get their case through the court system. The longer the stay, the better the outcome in terms of a woman's stability and ability to deal with life issues.

The average is seven to nine times for them to leave an abusive relationship for good. Some will never leave for good. Most are financially connected to their partners. We don't promote that you have to end your relationship. We promote safety within your relationship.

If they come back before the abuse happens again, they are successful. We are not here to judge. We tell them, "Please don't feel you can't come back." Some of them genuinely love their partners and don't want to have to leave them.

If they want to hang out and not move forward, that's OK. But if they want housing or to be referred to counseling and get their children counseling, we do that. We encourage the moms to go to group counseling and meet with an advocate on a daily basis.

If they want housing, we get them connected. We look at local apartments. If they have no job or income, we get them on food stamps and Temporary Aid to Needy Families and Medicaid. We help them write resumes, send them to unemployment agencies, help them read want ads. If they have never had jobs or developed skills, we help them apply for financial aid so they can go back to school. Some just want a respite. That's OK, too. In general, we help empower women to make healthy decisions for themselves.

Most women come from Taos County, but the shelter partners with various agencies around the state and accepts women who need to flee their communities. A woman's partner may have found her and she wants to go where she is not in danger. She might have supportive family in Taos.

Sometimes people come from out of state to stay in the facility. Taos County is a hard place to live, especially when women have these other issues. There are very limited resources and it is all tied to where you are coming from and how resources here compare with those elsewhere. It's harder for many people from out of state because it is so rural here. It's hard even for people from Santa Fe or Albuquerque. Here you can wait a year and a half for housing. It's ridiculous. The public transportation is inadequate and sometimes women do not have the fifty cents. We try to get bus passes, but you really need a car here, particularly to reach outlying areas. Women are often in cultural shock when they first come. We try to tell them in advance so they can make an appropriate decision.

CAV teaches in schools. Preventive programs are geared toward kindergartners and young kids, teaching about safe and healthy touch. With older kids, they focus on oppression and social justice issues. Another program works with teens through the detention system. We meet with resistance. People think sexual violence and abuse doesn't happen in the schools.

People are really uncomfortable with sexual assault. They don't want to acknowledge it. They close the door. They are not dealing with it. Even the police get very uncomfortable when you talk about it. We try to do a lot of training with what we call active bystanders. That is, if you see something going on, it is your duty as a human being to step in and tell people what they are doing is illegal and to stop it. It's not just teens with peer pressure who don't want to stand up and say something. You'd be surprised how many adults don't want to get involved.

Convicted batterers are required to go through a domestic violence program for fifty-two weeks. There is a Women Who Use Force group. For women who hit or strike out, it is usually situational. They are hitting back or they even instigate violence just to get it over with. For batterers, it is continually a conscious choice.

Younger children generally adapt to shelter life. They feel well and safe. They start to play. The older ones do not have as good a time. There are rules. They have to go to bed at a certain time. They don't want their friends to know they are living here. They are embarrassed.

We always try to reinforce with the women that it is not your fault or your guilt to carry. Striving to build confidence is our number one goal. We never break confidentiality. We don't call them at home. We never say who lives here. We hold that sacred. That goes for everybody inside these walls. If staff members see clients outside the shelter, they do not acknowledge them unless they say hello first.

There is anger within the shelter population. Women ask, "Why did I have to leave? He gets to sit at home and do nothing. He doesn't have to change his behavior."

It is so patriarchal. Women are second-class citizens.

It is so typical to blame women, to find a woman at fault for what is happening to her. The more people learn about oppression, the more they are awakened. People here tend to think that the recent sexual assaults are just done by out-of-towners. There is a natural assumption that no one from Taos would do this. But this is human behavior.

I am thirty-six and was born and raised in Taos. I just had my third child. My mother worked for the shelter. She told me about a job at the shelter, and thought I would be good for this work.

I found my niche. When women walk in I see they have no hope, show no signs of happiness. They may leave two to three days later to a month later, and you see them smiling. You see their kids smiling.

6 House/Home

Linda

Linda Safranski lives in Shawnee, Kansas, a suburb of the greater Kansas City metropolitan area. She is raising three boys on money she earns from cleaning houses.

I was born in Arlington Heights, Illinois, a suburb of Chicago, and grew up in Palatine. I was born in 1962.

My father was a bartender and a part-time restaurant owner. He repaired lawnmowers and bikes, too. My mother was a hairdresser who worked from our house. She was very career-oriented. She sold Shaklee, Avon, Amway. She and my father had talked about buying a resort in Wisconsin, ten cottages and a bar. They had put a bid on it when my mother got pregnant. It's possible the bid fell through as well. They didn't get it.

She had seven miscarriages; one was stillborn. This was in a previous marriage, and she thought she couldn't have children. I was a surprise. She was out on a fishing boat and she got sick. She was thirty-eight years old.

She said, "Oh my God. I'm pregnant."

So she and my father got married. They had been together a couple of years. She lied about the date they got married to her parents. Her parents were very German old school. My grandparents in Wisconsin were from Germany.

My father's parents were from Poland and moved to the Chicago area from Michigan City, Illinois, across the lake from Chicago. My grandparents were actually very wealthy in Poland. They owned a farm and a restaurant, but the Communists came in and they hightailed it here.

My father died when I was six. At forty-four of cancer of the esophagus.

I cried in school every so often. Now I don't remember much about him.

My mom stayed in the same house she had bought in the '40s for $13,000. She was a year older than my dad, so she was forty-five. She owned the house outright. She had bought it with her second husband. She got married to her first husband when she was nineteen and he went to World War II. They got a divorce a year later. She always told me she had married him to get out of the house.

My mom brought me up in a Lutheran school, a private school, through eighth grade. I went to church five times a week. Wednesdays in school, Saturday and Wednesday nights, and Sundays for two hours. Plus I was in the choir.

I started working as a hospital candy striper at fourteen. I was a shampoo girl for a lady across town. I went to a public high school and from high school to college, a junior college called Rainey Harper. I was nineteen and living at home. I wanted to work in two opposite fields. I wanted to be a social worker. I babysat. I loved kids so I was interested in early childhood. But then I also wanted to major in interior design, work at Lord & Taylor and design windows.

I went to college two years. Just as I was starting college, Mom found her ankles were swelling and she was getting sick. Her feet would bloat up.

I had bought a Camaro with Mom as the co-signer. She couldn't believe I wanted such an expensive car. The next day she went into the hospital with cirrhosis of the liver, even though she only drank occasionally. She was in seven comas.

Then I took some jobs, like for a clothing store called Jitterbug and Jewel Food Store. It was union, $8 or $9 an hour, really good considering that minimum wage then was only $3.35 an hour.

Mom's health coasted for about six months to a year. The second semester of the second school year I had to quit college and get a full-time job, office-type work. Her meds were costing $200 a week. She was in and out of the hospital and had no insurance. She had no savings. She worked at first to pay what she could. To keep the hospital off her back, she'd send $10.

We put the house in a land trust after her first coma. The lawyer handled it so well. We took her checkbook away. The house and all she had was paid for. I still had my car payment.

At the end of my mother's life I was praying "Please take her," because it was too much. She was so sick.

I went to Europe after she died. I went to seven countries. To see the world. I remembering planning more trips, but I got diverted.

I inherited my mother's house. The next-door neighbor said she knew of a girl who needed a place to live. I thought, "No, no, no roommates." I tried to make it myself on $250 a month, but I had to let her move in.

My roommate was a hippie. She loved to smoke. She had a roach clip hanging in her car. I drank only once in a while and never smoked. I had been a good teenager that way. I sat her down and told her, "Don't do drugs. Not in my house." I was real blunt. Still, we became the best of friends and she is the godmother of my boys.

I had left the Jewel Food Store before Mom died because I got that office job with a pretty big company in Wheeling. I stayed there a couple of years. I answered an ad with a guy who offered me a job selling powdered mix for ink for old presses. I did marketing research. I made calls asking people, "What do you do with your chemicals?" I was so bored!

I left and worked for a company that sold tanning beds as a sales administrator. I helped set up shows and also did research there as well.

I had been dating a guy from my junior year in high school until the June after my mother died. After taking care of my mother, it was hard because he was a diabetic and an alcoholic. I saved him with orange juice and candy bars quite a few times. But he was my best friend.

I dated a guy a few months who was half French and half German. He was everything I wanted. His dad was in politics. He was five years older than me, in business sales. He broke up with me. I cried for two weeks.

Then I took a job as a receptionist and in accounts receivable. I met a guy through friends who became part of our group. There were six of us and we called ourselves The Big Chill. We all had divorces or had been dumped.

The guys would play darts. I couldn't stand Lonnie. He was a social butterfly going from table to table. We actually hated each other for about a year. He thought I was a priss, and I thought he was a scumbag. I was going to marry a doctor or a lawyer anyway. I took golf lessons so I could meet a doctor or lawyer.

The big downfall with Lonnie was that he could dance and I loved to dance. He could do everything from the two-step to the Polish polka. He and I would dance for hours, then we would go our separate ways. One time he asked, "Do you wanna dance to this one?" and then we ended up staying up all night.

His wife had cheated on him. He had a baby, Martha. The baby was at his house quite a bit. I met her when she was two or three. I fell in love. I never thought it would be a problem, his having a child. I would think, "Oh, maybe Lonnie is not the one I want to marry," but then I would think of little Martha. She was well behaved. Friendly. And there wasn't any family in my life.

We got engaged in February of 1987 and were married in the summer. I was still working. I had Johnnie, my first son, in November.

When I met Lonnie he was a chemist for a coatings company in Chicago. He quit and started a business doing carpet installation. He had his own flooring business installing carpet, tile and linoleum with six guys working for him. He sold his two-bedroom house. In Cary, Illinois, we bought a bigger split-level further out from Chicago. The house payment was $800 a month. It was an hour and a half drive for me to work. I quit. I left my job after Johnnie was born and decided to stay home. We had Martha with us a lot.

We decided to move to Kansas City. Lonnie's parents lived there in Osawatomie. Lonnie and I went there for a vacation one year. We thought it would be great if our kids were brought up with grandparents. And the traffic was terrible in Chicago.

I felt like it was OK and felt supportive of being here. We moved in March of 1990. My son Brian was born in Kansas City, and my son Terry four years later.

I opened a day care that I ran for nine years with fifteen kids. I had it in my house in a subdivision called Maple Falls. We had a four-bedroom, two-story house. It was just beautiful. We bought it for $121,000. The prices for houses were much more reasonable than in Chicago. We sold the twenty-year-old, three-bedroom home in Chicago for $40,000 more than we paid for the bigger house here.

Lonnie was doing carpet. There was a boom in Johnson County, where we lived. I was cleaning a couple of houses to make money for the kids' sports, soccer and baseball.

After we had been here about seven years, his daughter Martha moved in permanently. She was in eighth grade. We didn't want her to go to Shawnee Mission West High School. We heard Northwest was a better school, so we moved five blocks away to a seven-bedroom house with three full baths.

We loved Ashley Park. We loved our neighbors. But we talked about if we could find land, we would not necessarily need a bigger house but a place where we could spread out with the kids, a couple of acres. We wanted to stay in Johnson County because of the schools.

We stumbled across Sylvan Creek Estates. It was a lot of almost five acres and had been on the market for a long time because it was next to a creek. We sat on the idea for a year. It was right next to a flood zone. We watched to see that it did not flood. It was $75,000 on the market. We got it for $70,000. We laughed. We had started bidding on it at $60,000, but who cares?

It took us a couple of years building the house, 3,000 square feet. Four bedrooms with two full baths. We called a few builders to see what they offered. The builder had a great reputation. We checked. We had no problems with insurance. There were never problems with the creek because we built the house far away from the flood plain.

We loved it. There was no noise. We were two minutes from Highway K-7. Lonnie did all the carpet and tile. We saved so much by his doing the work. We did everything right.

Money was getting tight. We had not sold the old house and had mortgages on the land and the new house. Just as we were building the house, I talked Lonnie into selling our camper and some resort property. I felt we were going to be too stretched. We used the money to pay off his van, the boat and some credit card debt.

All we had to worry about was my car payment and the new house payments. After eight months, Lonnie's behavior got strange. We had a friend who was a finance guy who told us we could get our loans refinanced. When it came time to refinance the house, the guy called and said Lonnie had not made the mortgage payment. I said, "What?"

He was in charge of paying it at that time. I went to Lonnie. He said, "I don't have enough money. Maybe we should get a title loan on the van."

I said that was a good idea, because we were almost there as far as meeting our mortgage payments. A week or so later, the guy called again and said that nothing had been done. No payment made. When I asked Lonnie, he said, "I just don't have the money. I just don't have a job. I can't find work. I lost a big client."

I said, "You're kidding. We just built this house. It took us two years to get into."

I didn't understand. There was a building boom. And his behavior was just weird. He would lock himself in the basement all night. I would go down there afterwards and see a propane torch, candles, glass pipes that looked handmade. He didn't smoke. I didn't know what it was. It didn't look like he had been smoking pot.

I heard that he liked to smoke pot before I met him. But he had never touched it when I was with him. He was a great father. He would take the boys out fishing when he got home from work. He never missed one of their games. He was a fun dad. We had a boat. We used to go out fishing and camping together. We had always traveled. We were a regular family.

I came home from taking the boys on a ski trip to Colorado and the dining room set was gone. Lonnie had sold it.

We hadn't been getting along. I would wake up at night and pound on the basement door where he locked himself in. I had a key but he barred it shut. Then he would get a phone call and he would be out the door. I tried following him but I kept losing him.

Then he started staying out all night. He left at eleven and came back at four. He gave up drinking, which I liked at first. He wasn't nice when he drank hard liquor.

He started saying he was going to go stay at this lady's house. He made it sound like she was elderly and had cancer. He was helping her move and she said he could stay on her couch. I totally believed him.

Her nineteen-year-old son came over one day and I asked him some questions. He was slow, but he told me that his mother was only one year older than Lonnie and that she didn't have cancer. That she was on some disability.

I discovered Lonnie was on meth. I had no clues. It was so bizarre for me. I had never known anyone on drugs and what their behavior could be. He got paranoid. One night I was sitting on the couch with my middle son, Brian, and Lonnie came in. We were giggling about something. He flipped the kid up against the wall by the throat. That was one of the first signs. He looked like he was going to kill the kid. Brian was twelve. I said, "Don't ever touch my kids."

If he was in a bad mood, I'd run. We all hoped he would fall asleep soon after he came home. But you don't fall asleep on meth.

He threw me to the wall of the garage one time against some rods that bruised the back of my head. He took a sledgehammer to my car several times. I had to get a restraining order. I wouldn't let him see the kids.

I found out he was living with this lady and she was doing meth, too. I had been so naïve. After I found out, I would sit in church and cry. One time I talked to a lady whose son-in-law was a pilot and was just drug-tested for meth. She said, "We have been in counseling." We both sat and cried. She knew what I was going through because of what was happening with her daughter.

I only had a couple of houses I was cleaning, but I posted ads and picked up more houses. In 2003, I filed for divorce and put the house on the market. But while the boys and I were living there, I had no gas. I couldn't afford it. I boiled water for the boys' baths. Lonnie had decided at one time to hook up a propane bottle to the hot water tank. It blew and there was soot all over the basement. We were without a tank, period.

We had the house on the market and didn't make any payments for one and a half years. The girl who was in the attorney's office for the mortgage company was fantastic. I called her every day the house was on the market. She said, "Just keep me abreast of it."

I could have sold it to a person I worked for but I backed out. The house was appraised for $450,000 and they were offering about $100,000 under that. I didn't want to seem desperate. I eventually had to get rid of it for $370,000. It was headed for foreclosure. When I called the woman at the mortgage company to tell her it had sold, she said, "Oh thank God, Linda. I didn't want to tell you, but it was going to be auctioned off in a couple of weeks."

I walked away with a little more money than Lonnie because he was behind on his child support. I got a whole $20,000 to support three boys. I picked up more houses to clean.

The boys and I moved to a farmhouse, where I tried to hide. I had to guard the boys from the psycho maniac man. We had a six-month contract for $1,200 a month with storage. But the house had snakes moving in and out of the walls. There was a crawl space with a sump pump. It was so damp. It created health problems for the kids, so we moved to a two-bedroom apartment where we were crammed in—three boys, a bird, a dog and me. We stayed there three months, then moved to this house.

I put $10,000 down on this house. I used what money was left from the house sale and borrowed a little from a client. I had networked, and through reading the newspaper I knew there were people out there who did lease-to-own. An old realtor friend called and said, "I know a guy who does mortgages."

He knew a realtor who lives in Olathe who does contract-to-deed. My friend told me, "He's harsh, Linda. He's harsh." I met him. He's just mean. He said, "You fall behind, you're out."

I was looking for a house for $130,000. I looked and looked. The kids would have to change schools for some of them and go through another life crisis. We had just moved three times. But the cheapest I could find was $167,000. It's a nice house. I got my heart set on this one.

I did a contract-to-deed. I still didn't have enough work. I had no child support. "Oh my God," I thought, "I hope it gets better."

But I had wanted a house. The kids wanted a house. We only had to be in an apartment one time. I wanted better for my kids. We used to be in a beautiful big house. What was going through their heads about apartment life? Moving so many times is taking a toll on them, I thought.

A girl I knew through a mortgage company got me into a loan. I owe her a lot for helping me. It was an 8.9 percent rate, which was high, but I got into a loan and got rid of the contract-to-deed guy.

Three years later, I was able to do my first loan modification. I did another later. I can't do any more. I'm done. I'm afraid I will lose my house.

My oldest had a fractured femur from soccer. Then I didn't have enough money for them to do sports. I just couldn't afford it.

I saved every penny for food and clothing. I applied to Social Rehabilitation Services for help, to Catholic Charities for help with utilities and food, to the town of Desoto multi-service center where clients volunteer. Oh man, it was survival. We didn't go to any events. No, we didn't go anywhere.

Johnnie would have a friend over. The kid would order pizza. Johnnie didn't know how to handle it. The kid would have to pay for it. My other two boys would just be there looking at it. The visiting kids didn't know our situation. And the boys didn't have any idea how to dig up money even for a tip.

I couldn't afford shoes. I put duct tape on the bottom of their shoes. I fed the boys rice and beans. My mom left some coins and I cashed those in. I cashed in the boys' savings bonds. You'll do anything you have to.

I started to try to pay for lawyers to get my child support. I did not have money for hot water, much less for an attorney, but what I had learned is that you do not get anywhere without an attorney. It's a game.

In 2008, I was told by a judge to release the kids to someone who does not merit them—to let their dad see them. But he is an addict. His daughter knew he knew the way to get by a drug test. Lonnie was a chemist. How was he ever going to make a break from addiction?

He admits that if I hadn't stuck him in jail for no child support, he wouldn't have made a break from it. He was in for eight months last time. He tried to steal his own van out of an area with a chainlink fence to get it out of hock. He had plea-bargained to get out. He had more months to serve because that was a felony.

He sliced my tires. He sabotaged the kids' computers. It all caught up with him. It took a few years to do that, unfortunately.

I am done fighting with him. I am not going to live with an ulcer, but it's hard not to shoot off my mouth. It took years off my life. What did it do to these kids? It's hard not to say, "You made a hell of a mistake, dude." Lonnie built himself up and had his own business and then lost everything to drugs. I found out he was homeless at one point, living in vacant homes under construction at a lake. That is a whole other world he got into.

Brian, my second son, got in a car accident. I had to get an attorney. It was $500 for him, but I fell behind on taxes and the mortgage. The time period was the same as the mortgage crisis. I was trying to get caught up.

On Labor Day weekend of that year, I missed my payment by a day. I went to talk to them but they threw me into foreclosure.

I consulted with a national mortgage firm that promised to help people facing foreclosure. I told them, "I can't pay. I'm just short." I really was. I was only $150 short, but I just didn't have it. I had $500 from a tax return. I sent copies of my paperwork to the mortgage firm, which was supposed to forward information to my mortgage company and make phone calls on my behalf. I thought they were taking care of it.

Then letters came to the house saying that it was going to be auctioned off in April or May. I thought I could take care of that. I made a phone call to the firm I had hired to help me. They had no records of anything. Nothing in writing. No one had been representing me to my mortgage company.

I called the Better Business Bureau. These people had been in business for sixteen years. I had given them $400 for them to do nothing. They sent $150 back, but I was still gypped out of $250. But I let it go. It was a learning experience. Last month it was all over the news that you shouldn't hire these guys, companies that promise to help you settle your problems when you are threatened with foreclosure. It was a craze where companies were taking advantage of the mortgage crisis.

I saved the house from foreclosure. I would tell the mortgage people, "I don't want to lose this house. I'll do anything to keep it."

My mortgage guy told me, "That is exactly what we want to hear." That makes them want to work with you.

The years we have been in this house have been tough. I have done any work I could, including mowing lawns on the weekend with the boys. I don't have any family to rely on. But I kept saying to myself, "I am not going to fail."

The boys have been through a lot. From stomach problems to mental problems. Broken arms and legs. I had to watch my youngest, Terry, one day so I took him to work. He had an accident where a chainlink fence ripped him. I fainted at the lady's house where I was cleaning. He had to have two layers of stitches.

The boys have been on Medicaid, although we didn't have that at first. I don't have health insurance and have had health problems. Thyroid problems. I broke my wrist. I broke my tailbone. I'm afraid about my work. I can't vacuum with a broken tailbone.

I can't sleep at night. I wake up and think, "This is crazy. How am I going to make the mortgage this month?"

I worry about the expenses when the boys go back to school, gifts for holidays like birthdays and Christmases. One Christmas I gave Terry a piece of paper for five guitar lessons. I told him I called the place and they couldn't get him in for a lesson until February. I had lied. They were pretend gift cards and I was just buying time.

But all the trials are worth it to stay in this house. Why would I go rent an apartment for $850 a month and some change? I have a 2,000-square-foot home. Yeah, I did live through hell for a while trying to keep it.

I owe my sanity to cleaning houses. It is a good stress reliever. And I was going into places where they didn't know my family and I could talk about some stuff. It's better than seeing a psychiatrist. I owe a lot to clients and other people who have helped me get through the rough spots.

I have been through some anguish, but life's a gamble. You fight for something that's worth it. I'm so sentimental about this house I don't think I will ever sell it. Lonnie and I had six houses together in sixteen years, but if you talk about a favorite house? No, none of those. This one means the most to me.

Mike

Mike Loftin is executive director of Homewise, a private non-profit agency that helps moderate-income residents in Santa Fe, New Mexico, become homeowners. He discusses the pervasive American desire to buy a home.

Home ownership is the great American Dream for me. There is a story there. I grew up in Albuquerque. My parents bought a home in the fifties. My mother still lives there. They raised three kids there. When I was fifteen, my dad died. He was forty-seven. He was self-employed at the time and left a bunch of debt, including IRS debt.

My mom worked part-time at Sears in the hosiery department. Then she got a job working as a receptionist for an auto body shop. We didn't really have a pot to pee in, but we had a house that she was still making a payment on, and the payment was way less than what you could rent for.

Because of that debt we lived in fear for a number of years: the IRS could put a lien on the house and take it. She had a good friend and bridge partner whose husband worked for the IRS. I remember him advising her, "Don't do anything. They're probably not paying attention, but don't shine a light on it."

I still remember when he came by—I don't remember how many years later it was—and said, "Look, if you haven't heard anything from them by now, you're home free."

All of us were afraid of losing our home, the one thing that gave us stability. What would happen if that went away? For me, security-wise, that was really important. It probably had a big impact on me.

My mom eventually got a job as a secretary at the University of New Mexico, a much better job with a pension, and some benefits and health insurance. Her life gradually got better. The one thing she didn't have, after thirty years, was a house payment. That's when she started saving for retirement. She paid taxes and insurance and that's it. And even when she had a payment, it was a hundred-something bucks a month, because they had bought in the fifties. The house was around $18,000 or something ridiculous, and interest rates were low back then, too.

In these times, people are sort of horrified at the thought of investing in a home. It's a difficult thing, right? Conventional wisdom or conventional ignorance is unexamined. It just becomes this true thing.

Here at Homewise we started a website called rentsucks.com, where we are using a little more fun kind of advertising. We wanted to get people's attention because they're so stuck in all the bad news. I've seen financial reporters for CNN say stuff like "What's the middle class going to do? You can't get a mortgage any more." Well, that's not true at all, but that's what people hear all the time. *USA Today* did a story a few weeks ago with the headline "Renting, the New American Dream?" In the body of the article they quote a survey that says that 83 percent of people renting want to buy a home.

Well then, renting is *not* the new American dream. It may be necessary. There may be reasons why people do it. But it's not the dream. People want to buy, but there's all this confusion and people say, "Oh, it's too scary."

In retrospect, 2006–2007 was probably one of the worst times to buy a home, but 2012 is probably the best time. Home values are lower than they've been for a long time, and interest rates are the lowest they've been since they invented the thirty-year fixed mortgage. This is a great time to buy a home.

We presented our first white paper to a group of business leaders. The purpose of the white paper was to examine the conventional wisdom on home buying. It includes a slide of a buffalo running in one direction and the herd running in the other direction. Then there's an image of one buffalo sitting in a pasture and maybe thinking a little while.

Economists and others have studied this herd phenomenon, and it's fascinating, right? Most people tend to buy into the stock market when it's way high, and they sell when it's way low, which is exactly what you don't want to do. The old "buy low, sell high" thing works in reverse because the herd is always delayed.

We're trying to look at what's going on, to have this more rational approach and help people look at their options. When you decide not to buy a home, you're deciding to do something else. You're deciding to rent in most cases or stay with your parents or whatever.

So it's not like you're not making a decision. We did some funny marketing stuff to say, "Guys, you're making a decision anyway. Be deliberate about it. Think about what makes sense for you." The most important argument in that white paper is that a housing expense for most people is a given, right? You're going to pay something for housing, and it tends to be your biggest expense. The decision to rent or buy is really the decision about where you put that payment.

Now the arguments that home ownership doesn't make sense are usually from financial advisors and people who prefer to have you invest your money with them in the stock market. They don't make money if you buy a house, but they do if you go into the stock market. It's very self-interested and very destructive. But the thing is, even if there is no appreciation in the market and you spend $1,000 a month on housing, if you put that into a house payment and the house costs you $150,000, at the end of thirty years you have $150,000. Put that money into rent and you have nothing. It's always nothing.

It's really a no-brainer. Somebody came out with a report that looked at a hundred American cities and compared the costs of renting to buying. In ninety-eight cities, it was cheaper to buy than rent. The two exceptions were San Francisco and Honolulu.

The other downside of buying is if you're going to be moving. Then you've got to cover closing costs. If you're thinking of moving in a couple of years, most of the time it doesn't make sense to buy. If you plan on being in the same place you can buy something for less than you can rent it.

This is what we do to help people: Once we get some financial information back from a client, we make an assessment of their credit, their savings and their debt. We meet with them to get an understanding of their situation—what they want, what their objectives are. Then we work with them to create an action plan to achieve it. Some people come in and they're in great shape. They need to find a house in their price range. We analyze their purchasing power and what programs they're eligible for. For example, if you work for the schools, there's a special down-payment program. If you work for the hospital, there's a different one. If you're buying in the county, it's different than in the city. And then there are programs by income. We know the programs really well, and we know what kind of first-time mortgages are available.

The plan we set up typically will have a section on what to do to improve credit, what to do to increase savings, and what to do to reduce debt. Everyone we help to buy a home goes to our homebuyer education class. The class makes the process clear to people and lets them know where they are. If they understand their path, their stress level is a lot lower.

To help people who really have a lot of financial issues, we have a financial fitness class. The class covers how you think about money and why you and your spouse fight over money issues. We tend to develop our relationship to money within our families. The goal is to get people thinking that managing their money is something they can master. For a lot of folks, money is magic. It just kind of happens. So if you understand the reasons why you deal with it the way you do, then you can decide how you want to do it. Sometimes those are really emotional moments. These lightbulbs go off: "Oh, this is what you do." It's really cool. I hate the word "empowering." It's overused, but it's an empowering kind of thing.

There are some who don't make it, even though we put them through the classes, but not a lot. We track people who are over thirty days late. That's a leading indicator of people getting in trouble. Over many years now, our delinquency rate has been lower than the rest of the market. We think that the homebuyer education and homebuyer preparation we do are the key. When stuff happens, our buyers are more resilient and better able to cope.

Where our folks get in trouble is when they lose their job. We service most of our home loans now, so we maintain a relationship with the borrower. If someone's lost their job and it's a temporary thing, we can work with them. But we work with them early. We don't wait until they go 120 days late. In other words, we don't just say, "Oh, here you go. Here's your house." If they fail, we don't want their house.

In the old subprime days, people made it work by upselling you, and then the only way you could afford the home you had fallen in love with was an interest-only mortgage. It was an adjustable-rate mortgage and you're just layering on risk, and that's why a lot of people tanked.

We're conservative that way. We ask, "What are you comfortable with?" You may have to stretch out of your comfort zone. We'd all like to pay $500 a month, but that's not going to happen. We tell some people before they are buyer-ready and just looking, "Save that extra amount of money every month and see if you can do it." If they can do that, then they can handle the payment.

I started working at a neighborhood housing authority. I had been a community organizer in Chicago for a couple of years. There I always bumped up against housing issues. As a community organizer, you're working in neighborhoods. Neighborhoods are pretty much defined as where people choose to live. When you're dealing with people, you're dealing with their housing. I dealt with arson issues in one neighborhood. It was awful. And people who were being displaced Uptown in Chicago. There was a lot of gentrification and development going on there affecting a lot of people. Tenant organizing is really, really hard.

The last place I worked was in a mostly Mexican immigrant community. People moved there as immigrants and, when they had enough money to move out or buy something, they would do that because they considered it a bad neighborhood. So the issue there was: How do you make this neighborhood an option for people? If people didn't stay in the neighborhood, you were never going to make it better. It's just a constant turnover with a lot of gang violence.

We needed a stable community. Everybody thought the answer was to work on gang violence. I said, "Well, 22 percent of the people who live here are owner-occupants. Everybody else rents. It's a transient choice, and they're moving." The mobility rates in churches and schools were ridiculous.

Kids don't get educated if they're moving all the time. All they do is spend their whole time adjusting socially to a new group of people. If people don't know who their neighbors are because they're not around long enough, then they don't know who the guys are who are casing out their houses and ripping them off.

We knew we had to figure out a way to get people to put roots down there. So we started doing homebuyer education. There weren't even any realtors working the neighborhood, right? Everything was done by word of mouth. We did this whole campaign to get people to buy into the community, and within a year or two we had to start building homes to take care of the demand. We really had a big impact. So that neighborhood today has really weathered the foreclosure crisis well. It's one of the most stable neighborhoods. The neighborhoods that people were moving to, to get out of immigrant neighborhoods, are the ones that have crashed. It's really interesting.

We are doing more than helping people buy homes. We don't see home ownership as just a roof over your head. If you do it right, it builds long-term financial security. That is our mission. But it means you've got to get a good loan, not a subprime loan. You've got to buy a house you can actually afford without stretching too far or you're going to lose it.

Historically, if you look at how America grew its middle class after

World War II, there are two big things. One was access to home ownership, and the other was access to higher education—the G.I. Bill. But back then, there was one way to buy a home. You had a certain kind of mortgage. You had a certain foundation—a down payment and credit. The subprime mortgage industry really screwed that up.

We think that financial security is like a three-legged stool: one leg is disposable income or discretionary income. You make more than you spend and more than your debt payments. The second is liquid assets or savings, and the third is long-term assets.

In our case, the long-term asset tends to be the home. A lot of non-profits have got into promoting home ownership. They always think of it as asset building and wealth building, but that's the long-term-asset part. That's only one leg.

You can get that asset through a subprime loan, but doing it that way ignores discretionary income. You're paying more than you need to on your house payment. You want to get that payment as low as possible so people have discretionary income, because that is what goes into the savings account. We really see financial security as an upward spiral: the little things you do build and build and eventually, when you have those three basic things taken care of, you start thinking more about retirement and other kinds of wealth building.

Some people fall off a cliff economically. Oftentimes, it's a downward spiral. They say, "I never save money. When I have to put tires on my car, I borrow on my credit card at 21 percent, and now that's sucking up money, and I'm not saving money. And then you refi—maybe you already own a home. You refinance all your credit card debt into your home, and then eventually there's no give because you are living on borrowing.

The way we think about it is, if we do this the right way, it can be a path. We say you want to have the right home with the right mortgage with the right financial habits and the right knowledge. We're really big on building savings habits. If people put a little bit away every paycheck, at least they're controlling a portion of their budget and they're building and they're thinking about it. It raises awareness. And people really feel good psychologically when they have money in the bank. You're on top of it if you own your own house. Even people who are under water with their existing mortgage still have a positive attitude about home ownership.

Really the issue is, most people are not buying a house for the investment. They're buying it because they want a place to live, something they have control over. That's the big benefit. If it appreciates in value, that's even better, but that's not the essential ingredient. People want stability.

It's hard to know how this is all going to play out. This recession is really different from other ones. Our take on it is that Santa Fe is a very nice place. That has not changed. Lots of people like living here or would like to live here. We think that when the economy recovers, prices are going to start climbing again.

At the height of the market, our job was really hard because in Santa Fe the median price of a house was around $460,000. A lot of folks we work with were priced out of the market. We're working really hard right now to help those folks take advantage of this market.

We're building affordable houses, and the other thing we're doing for the future is buying land. We think land is going to get more expensive, and so we want to stockpile it. We're buying low, but we won't necessarily sell high. You've just got to be comfortable that you can hold it.

We're buying land to build more for loans. We built thirty-something homes last year. We're building two subdivisions right now. We're one of the few building through the recession. Although the vast majority of people who buy homes are buying existing homes, there's still a need to build new affordable homes.

At the end of our last fiscal year, 128 households had bought a home from us. Since I came on board, it's over 2,500 households.

I didn't hear this story until much later, but when my parents moved to Albuquerque they didn't have any money before the kids were born—no savings. The builder who built the home loaned my dad the down payment, which, by the way, was completely illegal. The seller is not supposed to provide that. He just said, "Well, you pay me back when you can."

So the first debt my dad ever paid back was that one, because, I mean, you're not going to let someone down like that. My parents couldn't have done it without his help, but that's what launched them. The reason my mom is financially secure today is because of that house. She could save money.

She's remarried. They don't have a lot of money at all, but she always had a dream to go to Hawaii. They've been four or five times. She had the wherewithal to live a retirement that was not just secure but had some fun in it. Now her husband has Alzheimer's. She just had to check him into assisted living because she couldn't manage to care for him any more, but she has the wherewithal to do that.

So here's a guy for whom the single-family home doesn't work any more. He needs intensive rental housing and that's what happens. At different stages in life, we need different things, and for this country to be strong on this front, we need housing policy that recognizes that whole housing-need spectrum.

I think what we've got to do in this country is reinvent how Americans buy their first home, and if we do that, we could help expand the middle class again. Real wages have declined in this country. We've really got to get back to basics again. Working people need to have hope for a better future. And I think one way to do it is the same old stuff. It's access to education. Our educational system is a mess. That's one pillar of it, and the other is having people be able to own a home and build on that asset. I think the third is health insurance. Lack of health insurance can wipe you out. There's the added pressure of the financial insecurity that comes when people don't have access to health care. I think if we stuck to that stuff, we could be growing again and not be in this funk.

We've had people in our program who have failed, but not a lot. It's usually around job loss—health, divorce and job loss. The divorce situations are tough. Sometimes one of the spouses is buying out the other, and we refinance that and work with them to make the transition better.

One stage in life isn't more important than the other. And home ownership isn't more important than helping homeless people. They're all important. We never know. We can move into any of those places. There are no guarantees in this life.

7 Katrina's Legacy

Kryzra

"If we live by the Spirit, let us also walk by the Spirit."
Galatians 5:25–26

After a brief landfall in Louisiana in August of 2005, Hurricane Katrina's eye-wall passed over towns on the Mississippi coast and barrier islands with sustained winds of 120 miles per hour. Winds persisted for seventeen hours.

According to the Federal Emergency Management Agency (FEMA), Hurricane Katrina decimated every mile of Mississippi coastline. More than 300 were killed and thousands were homeless. More than a million people were affected. Billions of dollars of damage was done to, and by, bridges, barges, boats, piers, houses and cars when they washed inland. Beach towns were almost completely leveled. Ninety percent of the structures within half a mile of the coast were destroyed by the hurricane's direct hit and subsequent twenty-seven-foot storm surge.

In East Biloxi houses were ripped off their foundations and debris and vehicles swept inland, carried as far as six to twelve miles. Six of the thirteen casinos, floating on barges in accordance with Mississippi land-based gambling laws, were washed inland, contributing considerably to the wreckage.

Kryzra Holmes Stallworth is the wife of William Stallworth, executive director of the Hope Center Community Development Agency. In 2009, she talked about delayed relief efforts, the impediments to rebuilding homes and businesses in East Biloxi, and her community's determination to keep the faith.

When you hear about it on the news, it's different from when you live here in East Biloxi. There were no quick relief efforts, as though we really didn't exist and were of no importance on this earth. About 5,000 homes were destroyed, with about 80 percent of the community under water. Transportation was not available because most of the cars in the neighborhood were flooded from the storm.

Immediately after the storm there were no relief efforts from FEMA, NEMA, the Red Cross, or the Salvation Army. It was difficult to understand why there was no immediate assistance with survival efforts. In Third World countries, relief is supplied the next day, but we couldn't get something as simple as water, food and medical supplies.

Since Hurricane Katrina was my first hurricane experience, I had no clue what was next. We did not have food, water, medication, clothes, electricity, fuel for cars or generators, telephones, computers, or shelter from the extremely hot temperatures and the many mosquitoes that constantly swarmed our area. We couldn't contact our families and they couldn't contact us.

Immediately after the storm my husband went out to see if everyone in the community was OK. He came back and told me not to go to our home, because most of the buildings and homes were destroyed. Since many of the business owners had known him for years, he was able to get medication and food for families in the community.

By the third day, I noticed residents began to be in a mode of panic. I believe some of the trauma could have been lessened if there were some type of relief, especially for the elderly and children. Bill asked volunteers to get busy finding water, clothing, and shelter, and canvassing homes.

Although I am not a native of Biloxi, I quickly realized the history of inequality was repeating itself in this neighborhood. Looking back after three and a half years, it's still sad to think about the facts that contributed to the slow recovery for this area—low-income families, people of color and minorities, those with little education. Because of these factors, many families did not receive SBA loans, many had large losses with very little support resources or assistance with housing, child care and transportation.

The old Yankie Stadium on Division Street was used for multiple reasons including medical care. While we were there, representatives from Oxfam had observed the relief efforts and decided they needed to help this community to prevent it from perishing. After assisting the community, they went back and sent a grant in the amount of $10,000. Bill was able to purchase tables, chairs, a computer, generators and other items to assist in the recovery process.

It was a blessing when Oxfam volunteers found Bill that day. We had no other emergency resources. One group of volunteers reported that they contacted Biloxi City Hall and were informed there was no need for volunteers.

Bill's vision was to provide whatever supplies the residents needed to survive the disaster. He didn't give any of us time to think about the problem at hand, but more about helping others and rebuilding the community even better than before the storm. The goal was to take one step at a time, one house at a time, one family at a time. The community would not just be a place for soup lines, but a source of revitalization.

If the government had played a more responsible role, we could have been an inspiration to other states and countries. If there had been some sense of spirit, concern, and responsibility to its citizens, Mississippi could have been viewed differently by other states. Instead, they chose to remain the same—divided by race and neighborhood inequality. As always, they would rather make a negative statement than allow change.

My husband represents Ward 2 on the Biloxi City Council. Although he is a councilman for Ward 2, he had to work hard to find funds to help save this area. His goal was to develop a plan of progress to move East Biloxi forward.

Oxfam gave us the opportunity to visit Washington. We met with several representatives to discuss the conditions in East Biloxi and the lack of resources. They had not been totally informed about the conditions here. After making a few calls, they informed us they would help as much as possible to provide support to the residents. During one of the meetings, I cried after listening to what FEMA had done for other areas. I could only think of children being bitten beyond any person's belief, bodies that were not removed or stored properly, families going without food and water, no means of communication with families in other areas, no proper shelters.

They asked me what was wrong and I gave vivid details of what we left behind. I told them there was only one pole with a notice that had an 800 number on it; I called the number all day, but nobody answered. We found out later that they didn't set up a number in our area because there was not a building available for them to set up in. They assured us that someone would be there regardless of the conditions in the area. They thought FEMA was on the ground, but there was no office here.

It was weeks before FEMA was established in the area. It also took time for skilled individuals and materials to make their way here. Historically, you hear about the top-down philosophy. It was redefined down here. People with low to moderate incomes were just not a part of the planning process. The blind eye of local government.

This is the older area in Biloxi. Many senior citizens and retirees lived on fixed incomes prior to the storm. Many of the residents have lived here all their lives, raised their children here and plan to remain here. They may not have had extravagant homes, but they did the best they could with what they had. Some people were working two and three jobs to make ends meet. The homes might have been lacking in maintenance but the people were doing the best they could.

The Vietnamese were here for the shrimping industry. A lot had their own boats. Others were plant workers or worked in shipping. Some worked at the casinos and a few had their own businesses. The Vietnamese had a hard time during the relief effort because of the language barrier. They came to the food and clothing distributions. There were boxes of canned and boxed food for individuals to pick up, but they wanted to be allowed to open them. They don't believe in waste, so they didn't want to take things they wouldn't use. They didn't believe in taking what they wouldn't eat, either. They did take noodles, for example.

There was a shortage of FEMA trailers for people in East Biloxi. We started getting FEMA trailers once it was in the media that we were not getting assistance. They had been stored somewhere and delayed. I don't know why.

People did whatever they needed to do for survival. Some lived in tents, with relatives, in back yards, vacant cars and vacant buildings. One lady lived in an abandoned shed. She rented it from someone who lived out of state for $700 a month. The homes that couldn't be maintained, people came to buy, then charged high rent. The former homeowners were left out in the rain. It was one of the dilemmas.

Thank God Bill stepped in to help. Thank God He used my husband. Bill focused on what we could do for ourselves to get out of the turmoil. What brought us back together was coordination.

After four or five months, more volunteers started to come. We started organizing the community and the volunteers. Only by the grace of God and people's hearts and our strength to survive did we pull through. Volunteers came from all over the world to help with the rebuilding of the community. All denominations worked together. There were people from all walks of life, from small entrepreneurs and owners of corporations to pastors, teachers and college students. They just wanted to help us get some type of normality.

The majority of the individuals, the volunteers, were from faith-based organizations. We had a church on almost every corner before Katrina. Catholic, Baptist, Methodist, Buddhist. Congregations gave money to rebuild. A church from Portland, Oregon, sent a volunteer group for a year. Volunteers found areas to stay, even here at the center sometimes. Some worked construction, others case management. If it hadn't been for the churches, we wouldn't be here.

There were no other resources coming in. When grants started to come into Biloxi, it was different for this area. They always wanted to give so much less to us in East Biloxi even though we sustained the larger part of the damage.

Bill met architectural students who came to volunteer. They were planning to design houses for people hit by Katrina. They did blueprints and worked with case managers to best match the needs of families. They became part of the Hope Center efforts. They are now called the Mississippi Gulf Coast Community Design Studio. Architecture students from Mississippi State University come to the design studio and help many of the Hope Center's clients develop floor plans.

Homeowners are still waiting for disbursements and insurance. There has been land speculation. After the hurricane, they lifted restrictions on casino development. Now the casinos can build on land and that may take away land for homeowners to rebuild on. Developers are offering to buy out landowners who didn't have enough money to rebuild their homes. This is driving land prices up. And with the new regulations, it costs about $30,000 to $50,000 more to rebuild your home. We have about 13,000 people who still are not able to rebuild.

We fought tooth and nail for a park. We used to have a more developed one. Volunteers planted trees, but they are tiny. My grandson calls it the hot park. He means there is no shade. Our community needs to have a safe place for children to play. The playground is not safe. The yards are not safe. Some people are living six to a trailer. When children are in constant confinement, the stress is not good for them.

City Hall used to refer to us as the red zone. My husband asked if there could be a change in attitude about our community. We started a Neighborhood Watch and developed block captains. That put things in place to have a better relationship with the police department. One of the residents' complaints was that when they called the police, the response was too long in coming because the police considered our calls not worth responding to.

We thought, "What do we do to bridge the gap?" People here have never been given a chance to be part of change. When we came to the table with the police—face to face—they saw hardworking individuals in the middle of situations they couldn't control. It was an eye-opener for the Biloxi Police Department.

First of all we asked the police not to refer to us as the red zone. "We need your help," we told them. The police started to understand that we truly needed help. There is a rapport that was not there before.

Due to the aftermath of Katrina many houses were empty. Drug pushers would give an address to FEMA so they could get money, pretending they were rehabbing the vacant building. FEMA would end up dropping money into the drug dealers' accounts. The dealers would then turn them into crack houses. The areas were not patrolled. Bill fought hard to get security cameras in the neighborhoods where people had started to do drug deals.

We lost everything. We were unable to get a FEMA trailer. Red tape. Too many processes. So we leased a trailer, but we were paying mortgage and insurance on our destroyed home also.

But when I look back on those times, I see what people supporting one another day by day can do. When you put all the mess aside, you'd have to say that we looked at each other with love.

People ask me what I think about that storm. I tell them the positive: I saw hundreds of thousands come from everywhere and everyone left different from when they came here. They went back home and shared the big picture: love, concern and unity coming out of Katrina. Yes, it took us a long time to get any recognition. As African Americans, we've had to endure a lot. It makes us stronger and wiser. We have the sense to survive even more. Families are knit stronger here now. We pull on all that. Persevere. The unity is there. I've seen what my parents had gone through in their era. That's what is happening here. We are not giving up.

When I think about this area, what do I really want to say? There were a lack of plans for us. That Southern strategy they took to a whole 'nother level. Mississippi had a history of not being able to look at people as people unless they were a certain color. But, if you don't consider us to be people of God, or God's children, what do you do? All of us have the same makeup. Underneath we are all the same.

Sometimes I'd wake up and say, "I'm not doing this any more. I'm not going to." After I got over my little minute, I'd find that I couldn't give up. I have a strong belief in the Bible. If you are not of the spirit, you can't understand the spirit. Even in the midst of disaster, He saw our good work. We never focused on what others could do for us or what we couldn't do. Every day get up and help somebody.

If you focus on the negative, your vision tells you, "It's not worth it." If we had thought that way, this would have been a ghost town.

All human beings need love and have dreams. They want good education for their children. After Katrina, we were not seeing skin color. We had compassion for others and what they needed. The hardest thing for people is to put themselves in another's shoes.

I talked to thousands—sent work orders, did orientation. Volunteers went back home and discussed our problems. They talked to people who had not understood what people were going through, what it is to go through devastation. They helped build understanding.

It's an exciting process. It always touched my heart. People in tears hugging each other. I realized the life we lived before and compare it to now. Number one, I am more appreciative. Number two: on we go from here.

While the Hope Center's aim was originally to help with the immediate needs of the community of East Biloxi, it has now evolved into a full-service resource center for residents to use in their planning and rebuilding efforts. Later in 2009, the agency received an Oprah Winfrey Angel Network Grant that, along with other contributions, has helped the center rehab nearly 800 buildings and complete more than 90 new homes.

Through the Veranda Homes program, residents who qualify as low income can build three-bedroom, two-bath homes that are energy efficient. A house valued at $130,000 costs as little as $90,000.

The Hope Center Community Development Agency has focused on repopulating East Biloxi, but is now able to offer support to other coastal communities like Gulfport and Moss Point. The agency is so successful that its methods have become the model for other Mississippi and Louisiana communities.

Angela

Angela Bui and her family run a convenience store and takeout restaurant on the corner of Division and Oak in East Biloxi, about ten blocks from the ocean. Lil' Mama's Kitchen serves freshly made seafood po'boys and other regional favorites. The parking lot is busy with people pumping gas.

I came to the United States when I was five and moved to East Biloxi when I was thirteen.

We took this place over at the end of August. There was ten feet of water after Katrina. It was destroyed. My brother owns the store. He bought it from the previous owner, who decided to sell the business because there were no more houses around here. No one had enough money to rebuild. They had insurance, but it didn't cover it enough to fix the houses.

Before the hurricane, I did nails in town. When Katrina hit we relocated to Virginia for two years and came back in 2007. There was four feet of water in my house. Seven family members had lived there, including my husband.

Volunteers called us from East Biloxi, and we came back briefly two months after the storm. The volunteers helped us remove debris and belongings. Then we went back to Virginia so our children could continue school. There was no school here for them at that time.

There were a lot of Vietnamese here. A lot relocated. Most Vietnamese people were shrimping. That went away. Their boats were destroyed and they had no insurance. Now they are pretty strict about where you can keep your boats. Shrimpers are able to keep boats on the north side of Biloxi.

Business here is not as good as it used to be. It helps that the construction people are here, but there are not as many customers. Life is not the same. We've lived in shelters or tents. It's hard on the kids.

When the family moved to Virginia, there were complaints from the neighbors. There were about seventeen people in the house because we lived with my brother's family. We came in three cars from Mississippi. My brother kept trying to explain that we had no place to go because of the hurricane. We were victims. They didn't care.

Angela's daughter, Amy: We got a donated car. We had a Dodge Caravan. It cost $2,000 to rebuild the engine. That's how we got a ride to Virginia.

Kids were making fun of us because we were driving a donated car. They'd yell, "Go back to where you belong and stop driving that piece of … bad word." In the Neon you had to turn the car on with a screwdriver. But I appreciated it. It took me to school each day.

Angela: When we returned our family stayed in our car while we waited for FEMA to fix our home. There was so much paperwork. We are all Catholic. The church people really helped us.

Joanne Sealy

At a French Quarter bookstore, a coffee table–sized book called Katrina, *put out by the* Times Picayune *newspaper, shows photos of New Orleans in ruins. In one photo, a woman stands on her home's foundation in Lower St. Bernard Parish. She has pitched two tents on the foundation, her ruined possessions around her. The dolly she's using to clear it all away is positioned nearby. Her quote: "I'd rather live in this tent than live somewhere where they feel sorry for me…. This is all that I have. This is all I ever owned."*

Joanne Sealy works at the bookstore. Nearly everyone was touched by Katrina and Katrina's aftermath, she says. People doggedly returned to the city they love, but everyone had a family member, neighbor or friend die or fall sick afterwards from physical injuries or emotional stress. Her own story reinforces this depiction.

I grew up in Arkansas. I like to say I got to New Orleans as quick as I could. My adult life mostly took place in California—Stanford, Berkeley, San Francisco—but I've kept an apartment here for thirty-five years or so.

I officially "retired" here in the 1990s and have worked at Faulkner House Books since then. I moved my parents here a few years before the storm, since my father's Alzheimer's was getting to be too much to manage for my mom. She lived with me since my dad forgot how to walk and eat. The nursing home is about a mile from here, straight up Esplanade, and she would go up there twice a day to feed him.

We had not expected the levees to break and create the flood over most of the city. If we were going to have trouble, we thought it would be from the Mississippi River.

When Hurricane Katrina was impending, my very good friend, Patrick Lee, convinced me to follow him to Houston and stay with his relatives for a day or two until we could return. My mother refused to go with me at first. My dad was eighty-eight and they were married for sixty-five years. The caregiver we hired to stay with my dad—we had gone to the nursing home that evening to volunteer to stay and help but they said everything was under control—never made it there. Instead, she went to the Super-dome.

We left New Orleans about 3 a.m. the night before the storm and made it to Houston. After Katrina, we tried in vain to contact anyone who might be connected to the nursing home. My dad was missing for three weeks. We had someone look for him, and they found him in the St. Gabriel morgue. He was the first out because my very clever niece had managed to locate him. This was sort of delicate maneuvering. I like to think we got him out the Louisiana way. It was a week later that they called us to say he was there in the morgue. By that time we had buried him in the Veterans Cemetery in Little Rock.

We still don't know the details. We heard that the RN from the nursing home, my dad and a lady with a stomach pump were helicoptered to the airport on Thursday after the storm, and that's where we think he died. We've never been able to verify any of this. I talked at one point, the week after the storm, with the RN, who said they had been separated on the landing strip. This I believe. There was a triage team deciding who was "viable."

I have no animosity about this. I'm so glad my mother and I left. Otherwise, I would have had two dead parents instead of one.

My mother and I returned to New Orleans. My mother, who used to be fun and lively, suffered greatly. She started going to a mental health counselor.

A strange thing happened at the bookstore about a year ago. A very manly sort of man came in several days in a row, always buying a poetry book. Very taciturn. The last day he said a few words, mentioned that this was his first time back since Katrina. He was in the military and flew helicopters. He said he didn't understand why people didn't leave, which of course got my dander up and I said a lot weren't able to, case in point, my father. We began a dialogue. He said he had a flight that evacuated a nursing home near the museum, which of course, was my father's.

He recounted an old white man and nurse he took to the airport. I'm sure it was my dad. He was the only white man at the nursing home. The rest of the residents were black.

We were both rather shaken. I later wrote a letter to him, which was returned unopened. I realized then that the responders are as wounded as we are. I choose to think it was my dad. I don't know.

I've never told my mother. She doesn't need to know this detail.

My neighborhood is pretty much intact. The neighbors check on my mom every day. She's ninety-one now. Our gay guy friends take her to church on Sundays. They go to a Methodist church on the edge of the Quarter that feeds the homeless on Sundays. The church is a gas. They have a large GLTG group plus a few drunks, ladies of the evening and others who choose to live here. It's all part of the inclusiveness of the neighborhood and larger New Orleans.

My mother still sees her therapist. We're tough down here but still manage to enjoy our lives. I could live other places, but this is the place I choose.

August

The New Orleans Youth Empowerment Project is on Oretha Castle Haley Boulevard, a street named for a local civil rights activist. The agency is usually known by its acronym, YEP.

Youth Advocacy Director August Collins unlocks the YEP door. In the hallway hangs a Bob Marley poster with a likeness of the reggae singer inside a bright circle of green, yellow and pink. It reads: "Just can't live that negative way—Make way for the positive day." The door will be unlocked again at about four and the program's teenagers will troop in for after-school activities in rooms at the back of the building.

The need to address youth-oriented issues in New Orleans started before Katrina. There's poverty in this area, social and economic issues, underdeveloped or no resources, single parenting, and family dynamics that have continued generation after generation. After Katrina, it all became worse. Families were dispersed and children were separated from parents. Some kids came back to the city to live without any supervision. Since Katrina, there is a lot of crowding—two- to three-family households.

YEP is a first-of-its-kind re-entry program for juvenile offenders in Louisiana. We are offering some of the most vulnerable youth in New Orleans mentoring and tracking, along with assistance returning to their families or guardians from correctional facilities.

The majority who come to YEP are referred from the Office of Juvenile Justice as part of their parole. They have been found guilty of anything from juvenile delinquency and truancy, to assault and battery, to car theft. Most have been incarcerated and now are on parole. Some are out on probation and ordered to come to the program. Some are reintegrating from secure group homes.

We take an individual approach depending on what each young person needs. We provide violence prevention, tutoring, anger management and lots of activities in New Orleans and out of town.

Our idea is to empower youth in potentially desperate situations to create better lives for themselves and their families and to avoid future incarceration. Once the youth come to YEP, we do constant tracking. We have intensive care management. We have a phone conversation with each one, or are face-to-face with them, every day. Staff members pick them up from school and take them to scheduled appointments. Transportation is a large part of the problem. They have no way to consistently meet their obligations. That is part of the perpetuating cycle that contributes to the destruction of the youths today.

Most of the youth live at home or with a legal guardian. Staff members go into the homes to learn about their environment. We work closely with the parents and the guardians.

It's important to understand the home environment. Kids have no control over that. We, as adults, can separate ourselves from an environment we don't want to be in or don't find healthy. But when you are thirteen or fourteen, you have no control over that.

We sit down with the parents. To work hand-in-hand with the youth, we definitely need to have a relationship with the family for what we are trying to accomplish to be successful. We get an overall view of what is going on. We definitely need to understand the family and their values.

In addressing certain issues, we may run into resentment, but for the most part, parents or guardians value our support. There are even some instances where we assist with bills—groceries, money for a utility bill, the phone for a monitoring device. We have helped pay for school uniforms.

We're helping out-of-school youths with an education program too. Our NOPLAY (*New Orleans Providing Literacy to All Youth*) helps kids get their GED and basic literacy instruction.

NOPLAY has professional teachers and community volunteer tutors. We help with anything that might prevent students from attending school. When it's necessary, we provide free transportation, babysitting for young parents, clothing and financial advice.

It's a better system than most GED programs. We assist them with documentation like a social security card, birth certificate, old school records. This allows kids to enroll without going through the normal hurdles. They can enter the program and start learning.

After Katrina, it became a problem getting records because so much documentation was destroyed. To get a GED, a person has to have a state ID, but that can be almost impossible to get if there is no documentation. I helped one kid for a year. He was finally able to take the test after the documentation process dragged on for months.

Why would you want to do anything to deter a kid who has made the decision to get a degree and get his life back on track?

Since the hurricane, there are lots of schools that are not opening back up. Parents are used to their kids going to a certain school. They don't like that their children are bussed across town. There are neighborhood rivalries. Security issues.

The education piece has been way below the standard of what it should be for a long time. Katrina was the nail in the coffin.

There are too many stipulations on parents who can't volunteer time in the schools. It's good that the schools want parents to be involved, but it's easier with kids from dual-parent homes. There is often just one parent who has a full-time job and has no time to be involved no matter how much she wants to be. Maybe she just can't commit to the level of involvement the school requires because of a full-time job or she has other kids at home. In some cases it's just not realistic.

I always did have a genuine interest in development of young people. Even back in my neighborhood I used to get teased by my friends because I had two or three younger cats tagging along with us. Like my little neighbor and a younger cousin. We were fourteen or fifteen and they're about eight, you know, and they wanted to also come to the movies or something.

I worked at Children's Hospital as a shift supervisor in security and that's where I began to see the effectiveness of interacting with young people because in security, there were teenage boys and there was sometimes a lot of oppositional and defiant behavior. You know, roaming the hospital, not being in areas where they're supposed to. I would get them to communicate with me. One of the nurses said, "Oh, they respond well to you. Every time you're here, they always want to see you."

They would come up and visit me and I talked to them about this and that. So, after leaving Children's, I took a job at Lutheran Social Services as a residential counselor. And I immediately moved up, became a shift supervisor, became a program manager. I did a lot of training. I ran a database addressing the needs of the people in state custody in that facility. And that's where I began to work directly with those young people.

You know, you establish those relationships without being judgmental, but always being supportive and caring. Very nurturing, but stern and rigid if necessary. That's where I started having genuine compassion and a desire to not see people taken advantage of. I just want to see young people be successful.

I'm always advocating for leveling the playing field. I think certain things in society shouldn't come to a private setting. The education of a young person, Medicare and health benefits for young people. It shouldn't matter if I make six figures a year and you don't if your child can go to the same school and have an opportunity to receive a quality education.

Those things I began to look at. I began to advocate for the young people. At some points in time, it's put me in situations where I had to challenge institutions or establishments, even ones I worked with. I would challenge them when it came down to addressing the individual needs of the young people.

I worked in an alternative high school setting. I was an intervention specialist. I was a disciplinarian. I'm a licensed barber, so I always did have healthy conversations with my clients.

That's where it was really brought to my attention that I had an effect on young people. There was a lady that came in the shop and she had twin boys. I remember because their dad was murdered when they were a few months old. I cut her sons' hair. She came back three days later and she was waiting on me. My other partner in the barbershop called to me, "Hey man, remember that young lady? You cut her sons' hair. She's here waiting on you. She says she wants to talk to you."

So, I'm thinking something was wrong, you know? But she just said to me with a smile, "I don't know what you told my sons."

I said, "What d'you mean?"

She said, "Well, they have a whole new attitude. I overheard them saying, 'Remember when Mr. Collins the barber said that if you respect people they can't help but respect you?'"

She had left her kids here and they called her when they were ready, you know? So I had an opportunity to talk with both brothers together, trying to get them comfortable before getting in my barber chair, then individually as they were sitting in the chair.

That's when I realized maybe I had a God-given gift or ability to be able to relate to young people in a way that allows them to begin to look at themselves and separate themselves out of their immediate surroundings and focus on making the necessary steps to development.

I'm passionate. I'm committed.

I'm an only child. People like me are labeled as being spoiled, selfish. And I'm totally the opposite. My family lived in the Lower Ninth Ward across the Industrial Canal and my mother moved to the Eighth Ward area when I was about seven. I lived there until I was twenty-something.

The Eighth Ward was mixed. You know, I'm not going to say middle class. I figure we were average. I come from a single-parent home. It was a little different. My mom worked. I had lots of choices and a lot of opportunities and, in some instances, I had a little too much. Being an only child you never had to deal with the stresses of not having or not being able to have.

Probably in my twelve-to-sixteen-year age range, I had a lot of trouble. I felt like not having a father figure and going to a school that strived for parental involvement was a struggle. I went to St. Augustine High School before I was expelled for fighting. I used to struggle with that a lot. I relate to some of the things these young people here have felt.

With the kids, I tell them it boils down to choices, personal sacrifice, just making decisions that are totally right for you. Know what your vision is and how you want to be viewed in society.

I'm an African American male. So I deal with a lot of stereotypes, a lot of biases. But at the end of the day, I can't fault anyone who doesn't know me any better. Just accept me for who I am. God made me this way for a specific reason and purpose and that's just what it is. We all still have the same functions as any other individual. I still bleed. I still get headaches. I still catch the flu.

I don't put emphasis on stereotypes. It's a little challenging when still to this day I get stereotyped. It just proves to me that we still got a lot of work to do in this world, you know?

I have kids of my own now. I have four girls and four boys. I try to be supportive. At some point in time, it's their life. It's their decision. It's their choice. Whether we agree with it or not, you know, and sometimes it's hard to swallow, but I figure if you keep it on the level of respect, it will allow you to accept.

And I feel blessed to have my mom. She's a strong woman. She rode my behind to the end, but she was supportive. I love her. We have a real beautiful relationship.

We've taken kids from YEP on a lot of trips. Swamp tours, movies, the aquarium, museums, restaurants—so they get that experience—Saints games, Hornets games, Zephyrs games. These are just a few. The kids had never been in the Superdome for a game. Some had only experienced it during Katrina.

We have about a seventy/thirty male–female ratio. Here we have pregnancy and post-pregnancy education groups. Males and females participate in parenting and sex education sessions. YEP recently sponsored four baby showers. Some of the girls coming in this afternoon are in the female empowerment group tonight.

I recently took a group to Memphis where they were in the march to the Lorraine Motel and Civil Rights Museum. It was commemorating the fortieth anniversary of Martin Luther King's assassination. We took part in the candlelight vigil outside the museum. We toured the museum the next day and ate barbecue and bowled and played arcade games.

The march and museum gave them a sense of history and the civil rights struggle that has gone before them. It gave them a chance to see how their poor choices and decisions could take away from the struggle today.

A group of kids just returned from a safari camp last weekend in Morreauville. We spent two nights in cabins and went on tours. Zebras, giraffes, geese, antelope, llamas, water buffalos, bison, Asian dwarf goats, emus, wild turkeys and rabbits were roaming the grounds. They could view snakes and alligators. On the same trip, the kids went fishing and drove four-wheelers. It was a first for me too. It was an opportunity for all.

Our jobs are pretty much 24/7. Anything can happen at any time of the day. We may get a call that a kid is not safe or a call from a parent or caretaker saying that a kid is not home on time. Sometimes a youth needs to be transferred to another place because of safety issues. Whenever there are issues, we can pick them up.

Just because they leave YEP and go out into the world or back home doesn't mean we lose track of them. We keep an open line of communication for two years. With a lot of them we have a relationship forever. Some come back just to be here. It's a refuge, the place they feel safe.

By 2012, YEP had expanded to six programs in three New Orleans locations, helping about a thousand young people annually.

Joyce

Sixteen-year-old Joyce is a new client of the Youth Empowerment Project (YEP), New Orleans. Her maroon sweatshirt boasts the Central Wildcats' insignia: "We are central." The sweatshirt is from the school she went to briefly when the court ordered her to leave her family's New Orleans home and live in East Baton Rouge Parish in what is known as a secure group home.

My probation officer recommended I come here. I have only been coming to YEP for about a month. I didn't like it at first because I didn't know any of the people. But now I like the way the people talk, communicate, how they solve problems.

I was born in Germany. My dad was in the service. Mom is German. We moved around to U.S. Army bases in New York, Mississippi, Alabama, everywhere. We came to New Orleans when I was five. We've been here since then, except for when we left during Katrina.

I'm on probation for truancy and disobeying my parents. I just got out of the Louisiana Mentor Facility system. I went to somebody else's home. It's a system where a home takes in children that are troublemakers. I spent seven and a half months in a woman's home near Baton Rouge. They took another girl and me in. It was difficult. It was so hard being away from my family and in a house where no one knew me. No one cared about my feelings or my problems. I made two calls a week to my mom.

The people in the home I went to were different people from what I know. I was rebellious and I didn't do real good for three months. You're brought before the judge every three months. I wanted to come back home, so I was good the last part of the time and got on probation.

Ever since Dad went to Iraq, things haven't been the same. He came back with a diagnosis of depression and post-traumatic stress disorder. Lots of his friends he was over there with came back with that. He's still being treated and he takes medication. It makes me feel sad. I really don't express my feelings. People only see angry if I get upset. I don't express how I'm feeling, so nobody understands.

I go to family counseling, anger management sessions. I work with a social worker and a therapist to give all those theories a try. I have close friends, but my mom doesn't approve of them.

My parents separated before my little sister was born. After three months they got back together because they were having a baby. Dad had to stay in New Orleans during Katrina because he was a police officer. Me, my mother, my older brother and my little sister went to Washington state. We stayed for three and a half months, almost until Christmas. When we got back, there was water in our house from the rain. All the ceilings were drooping. The whole house had to be fixed.

What really angered me was that my bird died. We had no room in the car when we left New Orleans so we had to leave him behind. There were already cats and two dogs in the car and we had to leave one dog behind as it was. I had only had my bird since January before Katrina. I named him Tweetie. He was a parakeet.

When I came back, I went to the same school. I felt sad. Lots of people stayed back. There were lots of killings. People died and they were floating around in the water. It was a good thing that I didn't see anyone dead. I have seen a person die, but it was out on the street and the man just had a heart attack and fell over.

I used to be really bad. Curse. I was mean to my sister. But I learned some stuff in the facility. I took it home with me. I figured if I changed, things would be better. I definitely will not go back to my ways. I was brought through hell.

I didn't go on the last field trip to the Maya Angelou Museum with YEP. But I think I'll go on the next trip. I like the YEP girls' group after school. We talk about girl problems: how to change, who to talk to, dating. You know, girl talk.

At my next court date, the judge may take me off probation. Even off probation, I'll probably stay with the program here. They want to take care of you.

8 Outsider Insights

Michelle

During daytime hours, Rachael's Women's Center in Washington, D.C., is home to countless homeless and formerly homeless women. Rachael's offers women shelter, food, showers and a place to do laundry, as well as case management and programs that give them the tools to take control of their own lives.

Rachael's began in 1979 when Washingtonian Kathleen Guinan and volunteers rehabilitated a run-down house in the northwestern part of the city, transforming it into what they called a "place of hospitality and hope."

Today, thirty-two years later, women are filing into Rachael's to join others who are sitting in the living room socializing. It is getting close to lunchtime and the aroma of the chicken pasta dish wafts into the spacious home's living room. A woman who has been doing housecleaning chores says that, even though yesterday's rain is gone and it is bright outside, she hopes it gets warmer. It has been a long harsh winter in Washington, and an unseasonably cold spring. Even the famous cherry blossoms were nipped.

A tree is painted on one dining room wall, its branches extending to the adjacent wall. Words decorate the tree: peace, friends, laughter, strength, nurture, support, joy, faith, compassion, tolerance, love.

The sign on Program Director Michelle Durham's door two flights up says, "Life isn't about waiting for the storm to pass. It's about learning to dance in the rain."

There is such a wide, diverse population of women who come to the house, from those who need daily support to those who need occasional clothing or a meal. There is an outreach program on Mondays and Thursdays when staff and volunteers go out to talk with women who are still out on the streets, to give them water and clothing and encourage them to come to the center. They also talk to men about the services available to them.

Some are struggling with mental problems. Others have housing problems, problems with their shelters. The city is quite diligent in its persecution of the homeless.

The wide benches around the government buildings have been replaced with skinny metal ones. It's to discourage people from sleeping on them. Homeless people carry lots of bags. If they are visibly homeless and are sitting in one place too long, the police say, "Move along."

There is a huge national trend toward the criminalization of the homeless. There are complaints from business owners. It has to do with small crimes. Often the police target is someone being vagrant, maybe drinking, and if they say something inappropriate, someone will call the police. The women here don't go downtown at all now. They avoid the downtown area. It's unfortunate. People should feel free to go where they want.

Sometimes women have carts with their belongings. They try to sleep. The police will tell them that they can't be in the park or other area, that it is a secure area. Some of these women have trauma issues, and they are confronted by big men shining flashlights in their eyes.

Another day center is three blocks away, but Rachael's is the only place just women can come to. Other day centers made the choice to be co-ed. There is an area across the courtyard in the back of Rachael's where men spend daytimes. But the men are not allowed inside Rachael's. In the courtyard, there is an unwritten agreement: the men are on one side, and the women are on the other.

I've been with the center since 2002. I started as a case manager and became program director in 2006. It's been a learning experience for me.

I always knew counseling would be my work. I went to Marymount University in Arlington, Virginia, for a master's in counseling psychology. I began my career in the locked wards of a hospital working as an administrator dealing with insurance companies. I had an opportunity to work for a community program for women with disabilities. I saw I could be of service in a hospital setting, but more so in a community program.

For most of our women, the majority of the money they have goes toward housing. They are paying for everything. It costs $1.70 to ride the bus one way. Imagine: you go to the doctor, then to another, then to a lab. I don't know how the women do so much with so little. Every day they surprise me, and themselves.

There are so many life challenges—substance abuse, trauma, even addiction, mental health problems. Before I came here, I had a picture of folks experiencing homelessness, but I had to change my mental language. It is more than being without a home. It's what they are emotionally and physically experiencing. A lot of women consider Rachael's as home. It's where they come when they are hurt or angry or upset. The door is always open.

We have women we don't see for two to three years. Then someone from 2006 will come and say, "This is my car. This is the key to my house where I live now." Sometimes they e-mail and say, "My children are living with me again," or "My mother is back again." Some want to know if they can still come to visit Rachael's if they have a job and a home. And they can.

Most people do not think about what it is to be needy until they are themselves down. One day in the life of a homeless person: what do you eat, how you travel, where is there a safe space for you? A woman may not want to go to a shelter because she was attacked last time.

Rachael's House has a low-barrier program. You have to be appropriate, not violent, no physical touching. You must do chores if you are going to have lunch. Women sit at tables to eat as a family. We want them to come and have a sense of ownership. We want them to experience a sense of peace.

A meal coordinator prepares a hot breakfast and lunch every day, Monday through Friday. Saturday breakfast is continental. The D.C. Central Kitchen Program brings four to six pans of food Tuesdays and Fridays. The cook freezes what we're not using and serves those leftovers for Saturday lunch. On Sundays, the women rely on other food, available mainly through churches.

The women love the meal coordinator's cooking. They love the way she makes spaghetti. She cooks veggies just right. We are Capital Area Food Bank members. They buy a lot of food, and we buy food at Costco. As far as fresh food, some is donated by Whole Foods. Sometimes they have a 5 percent-for-the-day program and we get the money. We pick up breakfast sandwiches and such that Starbucks donates. At Panera's we pick up bread and bagels. Overall, there is a variety of food, even for people who don't eat meat.

For breakfast there are twenty to thirty women, at lunch twenty to twenty-five. We serve more breakfasts because some women work. They come to lunch Saturdays, too. At the beginning of the month, there are fewer people because they get their government assistance checks. On Sundays, Bethany's around the corner is open. The churches in the area offer a meal.

AA meetings are Monday through Saturday at ten. We strongly encourage people to go to this. There are women who come every day. We can refer them to substance abuse treatment, for substance abuse recovery housing. It is easier to go through detox there.

We rely so much on volunteers. We get quite a bit of community support, although sometimes it can be touch and go.

Our staff and volunteers give workshops in-house on how to land jobs and they work with the women to develop resumes. We have a daily house meeting to tell people about opportunities. We post jobs on the bulletin board. The quicker they find out about them the better. We check the e-mail all day. There are a lot of referrals for programs, community training programs with a small stipend, or that pay the participant's way to and from the training.

Most often the jobs are in fields of office assistance, maintenance and the medical field. We help people get their GEDs and are constantly making referrals. Some have a work history in jobs they liked, like with hotels or hospitals, and who cut the staff. They may have had jobs they have done consistently well but have no computer skills, so we teach them those. The Jesuit Volunteer Corps comes every week to help us with training.

There is a great need for clean clothing. In the basement we have a clothing room with shoes, underthings and winter coats. We also provide them with essentials like feminine hygiene products, soap, and toothpaste. Many women come here with just the clothes on their back. Flip-flops in the winter. When you are fleeing, you can't take anything.

Large women like me have a hard time finding clothing. I've donated when I find things in my size, as have my friends and family. I am always hearing "They don't have anything for me" or "They never have my size." There's one place that has larger sizes, that's about all.

People drop clothing by. Churches do clothing drives. Downtown offices do clothing drives. One time a law firm called and said they were donating coats. We expected maybe ten coats. They brought two carloads of coats, boots and hats.

At Christmas, Gifts for the Homeless, which was organized by lawyers and law firms in Washington, shops every year for sweats and winter things. They bring ten to thirteen boxes—sometimes in the spring, too. Sometimes we get really low on clothes. We send out e-mails or our church friends bring things by. That's the struggle of nonprofits. You have to keep homelessness in front of people: constantly remind them that there are men, women and children who are sleeping outdoors tonight.

Karen

Karen sits in the living room of Rachael's Women's Center, the house that's open daytimes to homeless women in Washington, D.C. She spends many of her daylight hours there six days a week. She is a native Washingtonian.

I'm forty-one. I had been working since I was fourteen. I was working a job on Amtrak, mostly on the Eastern Coast. From here, no further than Boston.

I lost my mother. I just took a bad spill from there. I got into a depression. When she got sick and before she passed away, I had to relinquish my job. The insurance wouldn't pay a lot and I got in debt because of my mom. I lost the house. I couldn't pay the taxes. There was limited family help. I have one brother. My relatives, they all have families of their own.

I've been homeless for a year. I'm trying to re-establish my life. It's a shame there aren't more facilities like this. I don't know why there are no programs for people in need. It's a shame. There are lots of programs for drug addicts or families with children. But there are no programs for people who have just fallen. If they did, that ways more people could get help. They could be retrained. When you get in this situation, society looks at you in a different way. It puts you in a certain mental state. You feel like you're not even from here. Your own homegrown base looks at you like trash.

I live in a shelter twelve blocks away. I come here to Rachael's every day except Sunday, no matter what the weather. It is more of a bother in the rain and snow. Sundays I go to a church program at First Jericho (*City of Praise Baptist Church*).

I try to keep the faith. People need to know the numbers of homeless people. They need to hand-pick certain people to talk on their behalf. It's terrible to feel like nobody cares.

I've tried for a job. I'm staying at a shelter now with a curfew. That makes it hard to get a job where I might not get off until after curfew. The people hiring say, "That's not our problem." Everyone wants to work prime hours. Sometimes you get an answer from employers. More often they say, "If you don't hear from us in two months, you don't have the job."

You won't get interviews if you are stigmatized. Women don't want to give the shelter phone number for employers to call. You don't want them to know you are homeless or they won't hire you. And most employers call during the daytime when the shelter isn't open. We can use Rachael's number as our contact. Anyone who answers the phone just says hello and does not identify the place. That person then takes a message and gets a phone number to call back.

I go to the computer lab at the library every day. They allow you forty-five minutes online. There are a lot of people down there. They used to be open much longer. It used to be open nine to nine. The hours have changed dramatically. Everybody has got budget cuts and restraints. It's really a challenge. But do people really want to see people out on the streets?

I looked into getting a job again with the railroad. It's been five years. I worked for them for ten years. Sometimes I get online and try to see how to get an interview. Jobs are only open someplace else. They look at the reasons why you leave.

I've tried for jobs with restaurants and hotels in this area. Safeway. I have to think about transportation. I can't have a job too far away from the shelter. There are no bus transfers. Tokens are sold only to programs. To go to a doctor's appointment, you have to show proof. It's hard to even get around for a job search. You have to have the right clothes and shoes. I can't walk everywhere. I have tendinitis in my feet.

It hasn't been easy, but I don't blame anyone. It's a long, long struggle. I see places advertising for workers and get an application. Then I see there are more people working there and I haven't heard anything. Mostly they want you to apply online.

If you are carrying a bag, you can't use a bathroom. We need places with showering facilities. There are so many social services, but who do they actually help, you wonder? There needs to be a restructure. Congress fights over amounts of money we will never see in our lifetime, but no one has money for the homeless.

It used to be better when Mitch Snyder was alive. Once he passed away, we don't have an advocate to educate the people. There is nobody here to represent us, the people who want to be part of the system—the system they already have been a part of. If you texted to Americans about the situation, how many responses would you get? It would be 55,000 in one second for a pop star.

D.C. is such a small city. I see all the developments of businesses. The building I am in right now is downtown. I worry for us all the time. The shelter ladies wait outside, waiting for beds. Look at the *Washington Post* today. It talks about homeless people in tourist centers right downtown. The businesses say homeless people are an eyesore.

There are areas where you are not allowed to walk. It's always a challenge. People look at you and don't realize how much you have tried.

At the shelter, if a client commits an offense, even something minor, the police may come and arrest them. Or they put them out. They have to just walk around.

I think there is enough for everybody. People should invest in companies that provide simple shelter for everyone. I lived a life where I had a car and had much more, but now I just want a place to come home where I can eat and sleep. Most people want so much. It's the American Dream.

Being homeless has changed my views. Homeless people don't want more than a place to call their own. Stick a key in the door and call it theirs.

There are a lot of different issues for why people are homeless. Arrests, drugs. But most people can do menial jobs. Look at the people who come to this place.

I'd like to start a dialogue for understanding of people dislocated from families or jobs. For people to see how we are all connected.

Being homeless takes a toll on your psyche. You've heard the expression that God puts no more on you than you can bear? Sometimes I wonder. Don't we all?

Eric Price

Eric Price is sitting on one of many benches in Sacramento's Loaves and Fishes Friendship Park. The park is a safe area for homeless people in Sacramento. Services grouped around the park range from meals to a library and showers to pet kennels. Eric is surrounded by at least 200 other homeless people who are waiting for a loud speaker to announce the beginning lineup for lunch in a nearby dining room.

I just got here a couple of days ago. I'm homeless from San Francisco. I kinda walked here from San Francisco. I don't know why, exactly. The Lord made me come here, maybe.

I just got into the shelter across the park. I was staying in one down the street. You can stay seven nights and after that you have to stay out three nights until you can come back, depending on bed availability. It means you might be on the streets at night.

The one I am in now you can stay as long as you abide by the rules. They are strict that you have to be in at a certain time. If you are able to be employed, you should be looking for a job. They have counselors and programs to help you. If you are not getting anywhere with one program, they will send you to another one.

I was living in Antioch for a while and commuting about fifty miles every day to San Francisco. I was going to the California Culinary Academy in San Francisco to be a chef. In fact, my daughter is bringing my knives to me this weekend. When I was commuting, I also had a job working after school. I had to be at work at two and then I got off at eleven. I did that for a whole year.

I have a sixteen-year-old daughter. My daughter and her mom became homeless. She had remarried and her husband kicked her out along with my daughter. Her mom lives off the system. So my daughter and her mom had no place to go. I had a one-bedroom apartment in San Francisco at that time. I gave them my place. I knew I could survive in the streets.

I have had a good relationship with my wife and daughter. I have been close to my daughter since day one. I have kept in touch. They are still in my place. I knew I could survive out here. I wouldn't go back to the city though. I was robbed a couple of times in San Francisco when I was out on the streets. I had a job, but I couldn't take it in the city any more. I would sleep at the Safeway at 24th and Mission. I would put my shoes next to me. One day I wake up and see homeless people running off with my shoes.

I had a membership to a 24-hour fitness center, where I could take showers. Food-wise I was doing OK. I just was not making enough to get another place. The cost of living in San Francisco is too high. Between the weather and the people, I was ready to leave. When you are living on the streets out there, the people are so rude. I kinda needed a change.

I was living out of a backpack that was stolen. I fell asleep on BART. I wake up and, boom, my backpack is gone. That was the last straw. I talked to the Lord. I said, "I need to reset what I am doing."

I am from the Concord-Walnut creek area. I thought about going to Hayward. Someone said I should come to Sacramento. Maybe the Lord. Are you a Christian? I'm a Christian. One side of my family was raised in the ghetto, in Palo Alto. They turned out different. The other side was from the suburbs, where I grew up. People tell me I sound educated, but I have seen both sides.

So people in the city stole my ID when they stole my backpack. I took BART out of the city to the railroad station. You had to show an ID to get on a bus or the trains. I looked down at the railroad tracks and said, "I guess I'm walking now."

It took me three days, forty-five hours, to get here. I slept under bushes and trees near a brand new housing complex. I slept on the side of a fence and at a picnic area. But mostly I just kept walking. It was about 90 to 95 degrees—pretty warm. I didn't know anything about it here.

I thought I was going to die. I was parched. Dehydrated. I had to walk through pastures. There were wild animals. Coyotes. I found some out-houses they had out there with a sink. Really. It had a pump and a little faucet. I didn't know if it was drinkable. It was for the workers, so I assumed it was clean. I saw fruits and vegetables growing along the way. I picked some apples for the moisture but they were not ripe. I thought their juice would do until I could get to water. At a house, I sneaked water from a garden hose. I got water from a gas station. One night, I ran into a bar that was about to close. They had coolers and I got two bottles of water.

I got to Brentwood, Oakley. I followed close to Highway 4 all the way to I-5. In Stockton, I saw a bus map. I knew I couldn't walk on the freeway. I followed the train tracks to Franklin Road. I walked through Elk Grove and followed the train tracks to Sacramento. I saw a Goodwill and bought a couple of shirts and pants.

I was in a Sacramento ghetto. I mean, it was really run down. A bad area. I wanted to go where the homeless were. Somebody said there was a shelter. I took the light rail to Eighth Street. I asked: "Is there a shelter around?"

People said, "You want to go to Mission Gospel."

The homeless people guided me.

Once I was here, I found there was a lot of help. I am seeing this as an avenue to get myself together. They stole everything I had in San Francisco, so I have to get a social security card, a California ID, bank cards. I'm waiting for IDs to come so I can start looking for a job.

When I came here, I got infected with TB. The shelter downtown where I was, they let you stay while you are getting a TB card. To go to other shelters, you must have a TB card and a shot. I found out when they sent me to a clinic to clear me that I had contracted TB.

I was homeless in San Francisco but not around this type of population. I was a loner. When you take a shower at the Mission, you are taking it together. You are in one room with sixty guys sleeping. The mattresses are plastic. They just put clean sheets over the mattresses.

To get into the shelters, you have to go on a waiting list. The Salvation Army, Volunteers of America, they are all around here. You call in every day. There is a signup sheet for all of them. Every day you come in and are checked in. Some of the shelters have waitlists that are three to six months out. But, because I kept on top of it, I found one within a week. They saw that I was trying to get stuff done.

Where I am staying, Volunteers of America, is like the Hilton of shelters. You can take showers all day and they offer three meals a day. They are there to get you out of here so someone else can have your bed. There are housing programs. Counselors ask you: "What are you doing this week to get a job?" I'm probably one of the few who is trying to do that. See that guy over there? He is kind of in the same situation and we hang around together. We say that whoever gets a place first, you can come stay with me.

The shelter has a pay phone. Once I got here, I found that employers won't answer to a pay phone and that I should get a cell phone. There are lots of restaurants here, though. My best bet is to get a post office box. I also applied for food stamps and General Assistance. Then, if I get GA, I can use it to buy a cell phone. Now it's just a waiting game. GA gives you money on a card and a voucher to get an ID card. It's normally $23 to get a California ID. You can get it for $7 through here.

A lot of people here are living on the streets. Loaves and Fishes feeds 700 to 900 people a day. A lot leave and go out on the streets.

In this complex around us they have lawyers, clinics, showers. They give out clothes, blankets. Free food. You would never starve out here. It looks like a flea market sometimes with people bringing food and clothes. There are so many people working here. There are kids working out of high school. Eight hours a day. Loaves and Fishes has regular employees with volunteer cooks. There are people who are working off tickets or fines or whatever. The court sends them to work with the homeless.

There is a local phone here. It extends from Auburn to Elk Grove for free. And 800 numbers. People call anyone from a doctor to a probation officer.

There is a lottery system for washing clothes. Once a week you can win the lottery and when they call your name, you have twenty minutes to get your dirty clothes together and they'll do it. I keep my own clothes. A lot of people here circulate clothes. The shelter I'm in has eighty beds. I'm number seventy. They do laundry there every week in twenty-bed increments. For example, Monday is one through twenty.

I come from a clean background. At my shelter, you have to take a shower before bed. You're kicked out if you don't. Everyone has PJs.

There is a free clinic here. Anybody can go there. There is a doctor on duty from eight thirty to two thirty.

It's crazy down here. There are a lot of felons. I met a lot of different people. Fortunately, I don't have a record, but from Loaves and Fishes, you can go right across the street for legal help if you need it. They'll help you set up court dates. There are free computers and a library. They do jail visitations. They help with warrants. This is a whole center set up to survive. At St. Francis, you can get free bus passes for a month. There is a shuttle through Wheels to Work. Three times a day they come here. They will take you to the unemployment office, the DMV, a clinic.

It's like a whole other city out here. You can eat donated pastries. They have a store where you can buy noodles. It's a trip.

A lot of people around here are on something. I'm not on drugs. I never messed with drugs.

They are here for whatever situation—their family got tired of them strung out on drugs. But they like having no bills, no car payments. You get involved in drugs and it takes over.

There is fighting, too. In some ways, it's like being in jail.

In the shelters, they lose five to ten guys a day who go back out on the streets. They have been on the streets so long they can't cope. They don't like curfews, bed checks. They don't like being told what to do. They feel like they are being treated like kids.

Some people are comfortable with the homeless lifestyle. A lot of them don't want to bathe. They have no urge to brush their teeth. There are a lot of mental issues. The longer you spend here, the more you see it.

I'm so against people getting something for free. People bring things here like pet food for the homeless people who have dogs, hot food for them. They get no type of thank you. I talked to workers who have been here since the place started. They tell me how to beat the system but I tell them, "No, I don't want that."

Nobody judges anybody here. From what do you do and what did you do to get here, nobody asks. I talked to some older guys around here. They say to me: "Where are you going today? Man, you are really lucky. You've got everything to look forward to. I messed up. I went to prison." Then they get out and they are around people all day who don't care about helping themselves. After a while, their self-esteem is gone.

I can't do this. It's crazy out here. I don't want to be homeless again.

This weekend my daughter is going to bring my last two checks from my work in San Francisco. I have the best kid you could ever have. She's loveable. Very sensitive. I didn't call her for a week while I was getting here and getting settled. She went through the city looking for me. When I called her, she said, "Don't ever do that again."

She told everybody then: "My dad's OK." She let everybody know.

I only have eight hours of restaurant work for school and then I'll be done with school. I'll graduate next January. I have already updated my resume. I took Wheels to Work. They train you on interviews. They have a program that puts your resume in the right form. My resumes go out this weekend. But if the place where you are applying heard that you were using a pay phone from a shelter, that's it. They won't hire you. That's why I'm getting a cell phone with my next money.

I landed here, and I'm starting all over again. Nobody is slamming doors, from medical help to housing. There is not a way you couldn't get out of here if you wanted to. Even felons. There are services that find employers who are willing to give them a chance. Volunteers of America have their own housing complexes. I'm going to get a two-bedroom for two years in a complex for $300 a month. Two bedrooms so my daughter can come to visit.

They told me, "Save your money. Once you get a job, we'll get you in this complex. There are people who want your bed at the shelter."

They give you every opportunity to get out of here.

Donna

A woman's voice carries a Beatles tune out into Friendship Park, where Sacramento-based homeless people, mostly men, are milling around.

> *And then while I'm away*
> *I'll write home every day*
> *And I'll send all my loving to you.*

Horseshoes clank in a far corner of the park. People are getting into lockers where they've stored their possessions. Some are sitting at tables and chatting under the latticed gazebos. Others are sleeping on benches. One group is smoking under the trees that offer some comfort this warm summer's day, while a few are eating snacks at the picnic tables on the grass. Donna pauses from her repertoire of sheet music to talk about her past. She is less open to talking about her present.

My grandparents liked music and owned instruments. I had a grandma who played the guitar.

I'm what's called a displaced caregiver. I trained up to be a medical assistant at one of these trade schools on Jackson Road. I learned how to give shots. Actually, I was a straight A student. I found out at the end of the course what I was taught was reserved for RNs to do.

I learned fifty shots. When my diabetic father lost his feet, I took his blood sugar. My mother had MS. They were in the house I grew up in, in the living room in hospital beds.

They got to watch their favorite shows like the *Dukes of Hazzard* and James Garner. They were big 49ers fans.

The house I grew up in is out in the country with an elementary school across the street. They bought the house and 1.9 acres in 1951 for $500. It had been a vineyard. It was full of grape stakes.

There was a dairy on both sides where I grew up. My grandparents were in a trailer on the north side of where my family lived. We had two cows, Pepper and Bossy. My father would milk them after work. He was a butcher. At the end of his life he was a union rep for the Amalgamated Meat Cutters working in a shop on T Street. We used to tease him because 4th and T was where there were the ladies of the evening.

All of us girls were supposed to be boys. My older sister was supposed to be a boy. I was supposed to be a boy. My little brother was born on Father's Day, June 16, 1947. My little sister was supposed to be a boy so my brother would have a boy to play with.

My grandparents had green thumbs. My parents didn't charge them rent. They had a little cocker spaniel and so many flowers, you couldn't believe it. Zinnias, dahlias, foxgloves, gloxinias, gladiolas, all types of ferns, tulips and grape hyacinths, morning glories. It was fun. My granddaddy used to take big glass medicine bottles and put food coloring in them and set them next to the flowers to catch the light.

I would look out to see what he was doing every morning. He was out in the fog in a sleeveless t-shirt. There would be little baby toads en masse all over the property, about a half-inch long. Thousands of them. It happened two or three times in my life. We had polyhemous moths that were huge. It was fun out there.

We vacationed in Yosemite in the summer. Dad had two pictures of everything he wanted to take. The same. If it was the falls, there were two of them. My mother complained, "Couldn't you put the kids in that one?" There were little bears that came up to Curry Village, up on their hind legs. Our parents told us not to feed the bears, that people who feed the bears were stupid.

I had an aunt in Oregon. She came with a group from the Midwest in the Depression in the Dust Bowl. She owned property in Oregon. She gave it to her oldest daughter. It was in view of Mt. Hood. Everything was tidy and nice. She raised corn. There was mint in the air. It was so pungent. Overpowering, really. She had an outhouse. That was another overpowering smell.

My uncle worked at a sawmill. Toward his retirement, he fell down in front of a saw and cut his hands off. But he was that type of person: he yelled to get ice. They put his hands on ice. The surgeon did something experimental. He sewed his hands into his stomach. Then he put them back on his arms. He had some use of his hands.

I had an uncle in Shingletown, California. He made a way-tall totem pole. He sold bricks for people to have commemorative things under the totem pole. Fifty dollars a brick or something. He ended up marrying his financier. Anyway, so, he's a bit of an accomplished artist. He built his own home and another totem pole that snow gets on. He has a view of Mt. Shasta. He felled timber so he could see Mt. Shasta.

We have a relative in Oregon who is also a seasoned artist. She paints seascapes. She also paints saws. I have one cousin who was the only one to become a millionaire. If you turn on the show *Deadliest Catch*. He has ships. One named *Time Bandit* and a huge one named *Grisly*. They actually canned crab on the surface of one of his ships.

Unfortunately, I lost both my sisters. My older one, when she was about four, she got cancer. She had what you call horseshoe kidneys, just one kidney in the shape of a horseshoe. It doesn't function as healthy as two. My mother said only two out of twelve survive. They gave her a heavy dose of radiation. It scarred her stomach. When my parents didn't know if she was going to survive, they ended up buying her a pregnant horse. She had always wanted a horse. She was a black horse. She had a white-looking baby that was half workhorse and we named him Golden Boy.

My sister survived until 1990. Prior to losing my big sister, my little sister had acquired an Arabian. It was dappled grey with pink skin underneath. She rode along a row of low telephone poles and was killed. They found part of her eyeglasses embedded in one of the poles. She was twenty-five.

That's partly why I decided to care for the folks full time. They had lost both their daughters. I wanted them to stay in the house with their memories of their daughters.

The last time Mom was home, in 2006, I brought her home from a convalescent home. My son and daughter were there. It was for Thanksgiving and we had everything, except whipped cream on the pumpkin pie I made. She also came home on her birthday.

It's been an interesting go. I ended up caring for both parents. Mom could use her Amigo mobility scooter inside the house. She had complications from MS but not like Annette Funicello, who couldn't see. Mom could see but she couldn't walk.

After my parents passed, I made an agreement with a man from the AM-PM convenience and gas store at Watt and Fruitridge to work there. It was about a minute's drive from my house. I got Kaiser coverage. I got an ingrown toenail taken care of. I ended up being head cashier there on the swing shift.

That's all I have to say about it. I'm currently unemployed.

Things change on me. I'll show you this Indian shawl I have in my suitcase, blue and green. See the little pieces of metal decorating it? When I first got it, it didn't have this one, or this one. It's called the princess effect, when things change around you. I have seen changes in murals, a picture in a frame at my daughter's, this swimsuit that has more color than when I got it. I don't usually talk about it. Here is a copy of *Little Women* I got from the library. It now has more illustrations.

I don't have a home. The kids have done well. My son is in the Air Force.

My daughter is currently living in a house that has no room for Mummy and that's all fine. I incurred debts my kids don't have to take responsibility for. I have to take responsibility. I don't want it to fall into their laps.

You don't have to spend a lot to get a Bible. This is from the Dollar Store. I lost some things in my room. There was some calamity. I cherished that Bible. But this one is no less valuable. May I read to you from the King James Bible? It starts at 1 Corinthians 13:3:

> 3 And though I bestow all my good to feed the poor, and though I give my body to be burned, and have not charity, it profiteth me nothing.
>
> 4 Charity suffereth long, and is kind; charity envieth not; charity vaunteth not itself, is not puffed up,
>
> 5 Doth not behave itself unseemly, seeketh not her own, is not easily provoked, thinketh no evil;
>
> 6 Rejoiceth not in iniquity, but rejoiceth in the truth;
>
> 7 Beareth all things, believeth all things, hopeth all things, endureth all things.

8 Charity never faileth: but whether there be prophecies, they shall fail; whether there be tongues, they shall cease; whether there be knowledge, it shall vanish away.

9 For we know in part, and we prophesy in part.

10 But when that which is perfect is come, then that which is part shall be done away.

11 When I was a child, I spake as a child, I understood as a child, I thought as a child: but when I became a man, I put away childish things.

12 For now we see through a glass, darkly, but then face to face: now I know in part; but then shall I know even as also I am known.

13 And now abideth faith, hope, charity, these three; but the greatest of these is charity.

This place helps a lot of people. There would be a lot more people in trouble in California if they didn't exist. Somewhere for us to go to live for a bit where there is a toilet, things of interest, water, out of the weather.

I will be sixty. Sometimes I think:,"If I can just get below 200 pounds." I would like to be a member of a 24-hour fitness center. I was paying $22 a month and not using it. That's not a lot of money. I could use it some day and maybe it would keep me out of the hospital. I'd love to go swimming.

I could do that and maybe be in a safe place when it gets dark. I don't know what the solution is for the rest of it. I could sleep in the park in the day in the summer and swim and be in the fitness center at night.

Clint

The head of the Rocky Mountain Youth Corps is delivering a gift to Taos Men's Shelter director Clint Murphy in May 2010. It is a sign that middle school and high school students in Taos, New Mexico, made and painted. The students persuaded the two hardware stores in town to donate materials and have come every Thursday morning to paint, do plumbing, build shelves and make curtains in the dormitory for the new shelter.

The activities are part of a transitional learning program for kids who have been kicked out of school and are referred through the juvenile probation courts.

The men's shelter, newly reopened the month before, is looking homey with couches and chairs pushed near the television, dining tables, a big refrigerator and microwaves to warm up the food the volunteer cooks bring every night.

We have twenty beds here in the dormitory off this room: ten bunk beds. There is a one-person bath. Down the road we hope to extend that. In November of 2007, the men's shelter initially opened on some property owned by the county. We knew it was temporary because the judicial system was going to do an expansion of their buildings. In July of 2009 we had to shut the doors. There was no place to put the shelter building.

We tried to get various lots, like one over on Salazar Road that would have been good. But there was a lot of opposition. Heated town meetings. It was fear. They didn't want that perceived element, even though it was zoned a mixed residential area. They objected to one registered offender when they already had six offenders living in the area. They were afraid men would be drinking on their lawns or approaching schoolkids as they waited for the bus. People have a subconscious fear of becoming homeless. It's primal. If people see it exists, there is a real shut-off there.

The plan was to move the shelter to private property. Tom Blankenship, the program director, secured the place and entered into an agreement. But then in August of 2009, someone torched the old building. It was not a random act. It was deliberate, an easy target.

So then we had a place to put the shelter, but no building. We started shopping for a new building. The school district gave us this one for free. But seventy-five grand needed to be put into the site and for infrastructure. Fifty thousand for the building and twenty-five thousand for the infrastructure. It was a mobile classroom. You can see where we retained the chalkboards. We got a break from Phoenix Mechanical, which did the plumbing and heating work.

We had closed the old shelter in July. The old building burned in August. We moved the new building onto this site on the first of December, using donations to finance the move. But it was not ready for occupancy until April 21 of this year. We gave hotel vouchers to as many men as we could over the winter. Some had to sleep outside. Slim lost his toes to frostbite. People were forced out of the area. Santa Fe had a full house because of the overflow.

Now we have an average of twelve to fourteen, consistently at least. They are not necessarily the same people. We've had thirty new clients since we opened. Fifteen previous clients.

When they leave the shelter, the men go in all directions—to Santa Fe, Albuquerque and Denver. A lot were born here, though, and don't want to leave. A lot of people travel through Taos. They stay in a vacant lot or in the forest. A lot of people want to come to Taos, but I'm not sure the climate factors in for the hardcore homeless. Many have got a circuit. They go to Tucson or Phoenix for the winter. They are here a day or two on their way through.

We get local people who are marginally housed. They use our services for a night. We have let in people who have been drinking. We had a .08 limit, but we haven't enforced that rule. But we establish firm boundaries if we let them in: "You can go directly to bed if you are drunk." In the morning we tell them, "If you show up like that again, you won't be able to stay here." We have more leeway than, say, St. Elizabeth's in Santa Fe. They have a .000 breathalyzer at the door.

The homeless population is just as varied as other people. The root causes of homelessness? There is a lot of mental illness and substance abuse. A lot of shelters work to cover that fact up because it doesn't sell.

We give case management referrals. If they are competent to work and are having trouble finding work, we try to match their skill sets with employment and put together resumes. Some men are on benefits and are not working. Tri-County Community Services works with us to get them jobs and housing. If there are substance abuse issues, we refer them to detox.

Hitching, walking, some have cars. There is no problem. They get here, even if we are a little off the beaten path. They wind up at the door at all hours of the night.

Women sometimes come to eat dinner. It's random. They show up with the guys or they have heard about us. We also refer them to resources. We even let them take showers.

Some people come for social interaction. They all crave human interaction. There is a hierarchy among the residents, but generally it's good and I see dynamic interactions.

It's harder to find people who might be able to take advantage of the shelter here because people live in campers, cars. Marginal living, like out on the mesa without water, et cetera. I think there is a Western attitude here: "I can pull myself up by my bootstraps." We try to foster independence. We have a lot of projects around here. They do a garden, build fences, feel useful. Homelessness is a huge destroyer of confidence.

I worked for the Forest Service as a structural and wildland firefighter. I had my winters free. I had been homeless myself, and I saw an opportunity to volunteer and then they talked about an opening here. I had been trying to get out of firefighting, which I had done for ten years. It was hard to maintain a family life.

They asked if I would like the job. I told them I didn't have a degree in social work, but they said they needed someone who could handle emergencies. I work here just about all the time now. There are fourteen men under case management and I am the sole case manager. I am here fourteen hours a night and then there is all the stuff to do during the days. Twenty hours a day is typical. When we closed the old place, I was fried.

Besides me, there is the relief manager, the executive director, a bookkeeper and the board of directors of the nonprofit. I'm glad we have that status. We are able to operate more freely than a government agency.

Most people exist about one paycheck away from being homeless. The difference is that most of us have family support. It's hard here in Taos because the Hispanic community finds it hard to understand homelessness. They take in family members who have no place to go. If people are homeless they think they must have really screwed up. There are a lot of Anglos from other places, so the people here think they must have done something really bad. We try to dispel this image and make people aware of who the men are.

There is a range of people, people who want to work, or not. They can stay for seven days, then they come under case management and have to conform to that. Right now we are being funded as an emergency shelter. Residents can stay ninety days. We have four beds designated as transitional.

The Mortgage Finance Authority under the Department of Housing and Urban Development, the Daniels Fund, and private donors fund the shelter. The shelter's budget is $100,000 a year. Churches, organizations and individuals donate all food. A local gallery, Nightingale-Wilder, hosts a December fundraising called Hearts and Stars. We have letter-writing campaigns, car washes and bake sales. Just about anything to raise money.

A local nonprofit, Viva Bicycles, is partnering with the shelter to provide bicycles for the men who want them. Cid's grocery store has a program where, if you bring your own bag, you can drop a chip for the charity of your choice in a can. We have a can there. (*The shelter phone rings and Clint answers it.*) What's your situation? (*Inaudible conversation.*)

Santa Fe has another one for us. We are not overtaxed with a lot of clients, but the person who wants to come is constantly inebriated. He has to go to detox. My fear would be that he would be back out on the street immediately. He's in the position where he wants off the streets but he is not ready.

I was a drug addict and an alcoholic. It was a lifestyle choice and why I was homeless. I traveled a lot from the time I was seventeen till I was twenty, mostly from Seattle to San Francisco and back. I am from Oregon. My family was really supportive. That's how I got clean.

I generally stayed outside. I was really isolated, but by my own choice. I was not in a mental state to interact. I didn't eat much. When I did, it was usually out of garbage cans and off outdoor restaurant patios.

There is a lot of excess in this country. There is always food in the garbage. Even here, in a dumpster in Arroyo Hondo, I found a good working bicycle. Here, in one of the poorest of the poor states in the country. Finding a bicycle in the trash in a Third World country would make somebody's year.

John

It's a spring evening and the door is open to the newly reopened men's shelter in Taos, New Mexico. In the common room of the converted school modular unit, nine men are finishing their evening meal. John has just polished off a pork-and-bean dish.

It's good to have a meal. I came to the shelter to sleep for a couple of months in December and January, but I try to keep my own counsel and not depend on them. I have my own dysfunctional truck. It's a pretty good bedroom in winter.

I pretty much stay in Taos. I have commitments here, and friends. I have had a number of apartments. I have a number of commitments with different people. That makes me want to stay here. I like it here. Culturally, it's the most diverse place in North America.

I create little jobs for myself. Recently I have been reading the I Ching for people in town. I ask for a spiritual service donation. You can't put a price on spiritual service. I'm a poet. Entertaining and fun. Everybody knows it. I'm stuck in a role. I really think I can pull on this Dylan Thomas thing forever.

I'm originally from Detroit, but I have been all over the underground forever. I moved back to Detroit and was there for twenty years, from when I was sixteen to thirty-six and on. Married for eleven years off and on. My kid's twenty-five. My ex-wife is crazy. We lived together in Detroit. After we divorced, I saw my kid in the summers.

She's my baby. She lives in Athens, Georgia, and is studying to be a paralegal and ultimately will get a law degree. She first went to a junior college and had a bookkeeping job. She figured out she didn't like it and that there was not money in handling other people's money, but in being a lawyer. I ask her about having kids and she says, "Forget it, Dad. Maybe when I'm thirty-five, if then."

I'm fifty-six now, soon fifty-seven. I was born in a good year in Detroit because Ford, Chevy and Chrysler all came out with automobile models with unique styling features. I was born to a loving pair of stable Catholics. I delivered papers. I shoveled snow. I was an altar boy.

Mom and Dad were dancers after World War II. They were the white couple who went into all the black joints on the west side of Detroit and danced to Dizzy Gillespie and John Coltrane.

I was number three of eight children. I stay in touch with all my brothers and sisters. I'm the risk-taker. Mike is smart. Annie is cute. I'm wild. Tom is conservative. Cathy's a bitch. Joe's confused. Mary Ellen is Mom. Tim is going to rule the world. He is a consultant to Arnold Schwarzenegger on alternative energy. Tim is going to be the energy king.

I don't know about a permanent place. I'm looking for a spot to land. I'd like to start riding a bicycle. I can't see paying any more money into the oil game. I'm an adventurous kind of guy. I'm stark raving sane. But if you don't live life you're dying. I've been up on top and down on the bottom.

Jobs? One time I wrote a list of them. It was six pages at fifty lines a page.

I was working in the French Market in New Orleans selling Guatemalan hats. A spunky old lady with a nice aura came in. I told her, "I'm a palmist," and she held out her hand. It was a quickie exchange. She said, "That's the best quickie I've had in ninety-eight years."

I'm real garrulous. I speak English better than everybody else around here. In poetry, I try to take very individual experiences and find the universal in them. I want universality. That way I can relate to people and they can relate to my poetry. (*He reads a couple of his poems. One is called "Milt and Roe," about his parents' flirtatious natures. The other, "Stark Raving Sane," is partly about the experience of being out on the streets.*)

I have been involved in the theater. I was a facilities manager and an MC and other roles where I was paid to be erudite and entertaining. I have a friend who is a producer. He wrote *The Texas Chainsaw Massacre*. He paid me to write a play about a night in a men's homeless shelter. He is getting a grant so we can produce the play and raise money for homeless shelters. It has four people in it with multiple roles. The working title of the play is *Symphony of Snores*. We are working on copyrighting it.

I am nowhere near normal, even for hippies. You've got to let it all out or you are denying reality. Be honest and straightforward.

Client C

A man, who wants to be identified only as Client C, is spending nights at the Taos men's shelter.

Just call me His Cosmic Eminence on his mission to save this planet.

How did I get to Taos? In 1994 I got out of the military. I'd rather not say which branch. I was discharged because I was an alcoholic. My mother was in Memphis, but I didn't get along with her. I met a friend from New Orleans who was living with his lover. They were both dying of AIDS.

They wanted to go to the Rainbow Gathering in Wyoming. We went to pick up people in Hurricane, Utah, and go up to the gathering. We walked in a quarter of a mile at night. People came along carrying apples and bananas—Little Foot and Lover Frog. They were from Taos.

My friend's lover, Will, died, and Greg and I decided we would go to a Rainbow Gathering outside Taos in the Carson National Forest. After the Rainbow Gathering we stopped by Little Foot and Lover Frog's house way out on the mesa to take showers. We said, "Oh my God, this is Taos? This is gorgeous."

Little Foot needed a person to take care of his music business. I came to Taos to do that and he started an intentional community. He was looking for a tax shelter. I looked at land for him, something that would have access, privacy and water. I got room and board for doing it, but for money I knew I would have to do something else.

I went to work for one of their friends, Owl, at the Pottery Garden. That's how I got into clay. I made porcelain wind chimes at 5 cents apiece. (*He laughs loudly.*)

I know that's not very much per wind chime, but I can do them really fast.

I went down to Raymond, New Mexico, at the foot of the Zuni Mountains. It's an hour south of Grants. There wasn't anything out there except a bunch of dirty, hungry fairies. I lived at a mountain sanctuary, a rural permaculture community, for three years. Then that Y2K crap started up. I started feeling guilty about my mother in case everything fell apart, which it didn't.

I went back to New Orleans to work in a French restaurant in the French Quarter, where I had been. I loved the New Orleans winters and the sanctuary in the summers. Until 2005, when Katrina hit and I lost everything. All I had was the clothes on my back and my backpack. I lived in Albuquerque for a year. Some guys let me stay with them. I couldn't get stabilized.

But I love Taos. The shelter opened and I came here. I'm not sure what's going on in my life right now. I possibly will work as the relief manager for the shelter. The ashram needs a caretaker. Or I am considering going to UNM (*the University of New Mexico–Taos*) to get a nursing degree.

That might be it. Or is this just a rehearsal? (*He laughs.*)

I came here with my nose in the air and my tail between my legs.

I went to the sanctuary in 2009 and then to the Rainbow Gathering in Cuba, New Mexico. There was too much alcohol. I've stopped drinking, and it didn't click. It was too dark. I called it the Drainbow Gathering.

I stayed down in the sanctuary until Thanksgiving, then came up to

Taos. Now it seems like what I was called for is to be a healer. I was a surgical technician in the military. I would really like to teach healing arts—herbs, energy work, an eclectic blend of work. I'm more interested in teaching.

I'm amazed at how diet is not stressed. Preventative, that's where it's at. You don't have to heal from stuff you never get sick from.

I just finished house-sitting for a month for a woman who owns a million-dollar house near Ranchos de Taos. I was so nervous. "Don't break anything," I kept thinking. I told her, "You don't even know me." But she said she read my energy. She liked me.

I'm living here now. My little agenda scheme is to take out a student loan, only to go in the fall. There is a man here who is considering leaving, so the board of directors said maybe I could work here a couple nights a week.

I put down the bottle about nineteen years ago. (*He pulls a clear flat box from his pocket. Inside sits a round piece of metal that says, "To thine own self be true. Recovery."*) I asked my sponsor why I got this chip for nineteen years. Why not twenty? He said I've been sober for as long as I was drinking. I started drinking when I was fourteen. I quit at thirty-three. Nineteen years now.

There are new AA meetings that have started up in town at Wired Cafe. It's for atheists and agnostics. I call it the satanic meeting. They hate that. I ask them, "Hey, how are those satanic meetings going?" and they get mad.

(*He laughs loudly again.*) That's my Shamanic power tool: humor. There was a time when the laughter stopped. I had an abusive childhood. No wonder I fucking drank. I suffered every level of abuse. At sixteen, I persuaded my mother that it would be in her best interest to throw me out. I pumped gas in high school. I went to school when I was in the military. I joined when I was twenty-five—delayed enlistment. I started as a busboy in the New Orleans French Quarter. I faked a French accent. They ate that shit up. You put something pretty on the plate and hope they leave you a dollar. After a time I could do every job in the place. I made my way up to maitre d'. I could do it all.

"The right of everyone to adequate standard of living ... the right to adequate food, clothing, housing and the continuous improvement of living conditions ... the right to live somewhere in security, peace and dignity ... adequate privacy, adequate space, adequate security, adequate lighting and ventilation, adequate basic infrastructure and adequate location with regard to work and basic facilities ... all at a reasonable cost."

Article 11, Universal Declaration of Human Rights
Adopted by the UN General Assembly, 1966

Paul Boden

Paul Boden is executive director of the Western Regional Advocacy Project in the San Francisco Bay Area. WRAP "is grounded in the experiences of those who live with and work on homeless and poverty issues every day." The organization's mission is to "expose and eliminate root causes of civil and human rights abuses of people experiencing poverty and homelessness in our communities."

HUD *(the U.S. Department of Housing and Urban Development)* recently issued a memorandum defining who is homeless. People who are living in single-room occupancy hotels *(SROs)*, people living with friends or family because they have lost their homes due to foreclosure, and people in various other living situations now no longer qualify as homeless. We don't have fewer homeless people. The government has just changed the definition.

The federal government conducts point-in-time headcounts. Local volunteers are asked to go out and count the people they find sleeping outside. So they pick a day and do homeless counts in places like Montana and Minnesota. What day did they pick? January 25. Would you go out in Montana on a winter day and do a headcount of homeless people? Instead of as many as 3.5 million homeless, they came up with around 760,000 from their headcount.

Then HUD and the Inter-Agency Council on Homelessness massage the data to determine whatever outcome they want. The Department of

Education said there were over 1 million kids in the United States going to school who don't have somewhere to sleep at night. HUD is saying that the total number of homeless in this country is 760,000. You figure that out.

Homeless people are outside. Always outside. No privacy. Danger. Boredom. Extreme weather. The worst: no sleep. The shelters kick you out at 6 a.m. and let you back at 5 p.m., maybe. The police prod you awake or arrest you if you lie down for any length of time.

So, sleep in the shelter? Too much noise from people coming and going—to the bathroom, from the outside. Too many people having bad dreams and screaming out. Too much snoring or coughing from diseases homeless people pick up.

I have experienced homelessness. I spent years out there. I'm a native of Long Island. My mother died when I was sixteen and I found myself on the streets. Eventually, I came to San Francisco and started volunteering at the drop-in shelter I was staying in. In September of 1983, I was hired as a case manager because I could help people navigate the welfare system.

I was the first director of the Coalition for the Homeless in San Francisco. I saw that local battles are important but at some point you need to start hitting up the feds. We have a government that has cut housing budgets for the poor for decades. Fewer homes. More homeless.

The Reagan administration did away with affordable housing funding in the 1980s. He slashed federal funding for social programs for poor people and funding for affordable housing production. This is the main cause of mass homelessness today.

Reagan-era neoliberalism policies supported the idea of privitization of state-owned enterprises and deregulation. Corporate America was designated as the protectorate of the people. The government began to take a corporations-first approach. The idea was that if corporate America did well, wealth would trickle down. The trickle-down effect doesn't work except when they are peeing on us.

HUD's budget shrank from $83 billion in the late 1970s to a little more than $18 billion in 1983. We began opening shelters. Homelessness has been a part of the fabric of our society since then. They claim they are trying to address and end homelessness at the same time they are cutting funding.

From 1995 to 2011, we lost 290,588 existing units of public housing and 360,000 Section 8 units, with another 7,107 scheduled to be demolished since March 2011. At the same time, thousands of jail and prison cells have been created. Since 1996, HUD funding for new public housing units, the safety net for the poorest, has been nonexistent.

In 2008, homeowner tax breaks cost the U.S. Treasury about $144 billion. Seventy-five percent of these expenditures benefited people with incomes of more than $100,000 a year. Total federal funding for low-income housing was $46 billion. Rents that are charged for low-income housing are too much for homeless people. They can't afford it.

Now in 2012, HUD's budget is $37.4 billion. That's a $3.7 billion cut from last year's budget. Public housing funds were budgeted at $3.96 billion, a decrease of $760 million in the last three years. Capital for maintenance of public housing for 2012 is $1.8 billion. That's a decrease of $625 million in the last three years. Maintenance for HUD public housing costs between $20 and $30 billion a year.

Congress did not address this. They created the Rental Assistance Demonstration. It is supposed to convert 60,000 public housing units to private or nonprofit-owned housing, but the bill didn't provide any new funding. HUD is supposed to use existing resources and cut other public housing operating and capital funds to fund the new program.

Then there is all the interagency effort that is supposed to be coordinating to confront homeless issues. It is just a front—agencies issuing PR and talking about plans. There's Bush's homeless plan, now it's Obama's homeless plan, San Francisco's mayor has his campaign. They love to do studies. They love to have conferences. They love to have webinars. That's the latest. You could spend half your time on webinars about homelessness.

We should stop talking about ten-year plans. Of course, you don't hear anything about the latest ten-year plan because it is eight years old now.

During this period of foreclosures, the press was saying we were seeing a new homeless population. It's not new. The new are the old in a few months.

Housing is a PR tagline: "Our program works because we put people in housing." But who? Overwhelmingly they are talking about single adults. But what about families? An SRO unit for an adult is ten times cheaper than one for a family. Then they just appear on the media and show how much they care. They don't say they are dismantling programs. But we are seeing better PR to claim they are addressing the problems. They never address the fact that homelessness means *without housing.*

Some $3 million was allocated for the Interagency Council of the Homeless. They put out PR to announce everything they were doing. They issue reports, have quarterly meetings with advocates. It's $3 million for propaganda. They are not actually doing anything. The Coalition for the Homeless is a powerless little dweeb. You Google "national homelessness" and fourteen national coalitions for the homeless will come up. One for vets, one for families, et cetera. You can see how off-focus we are: fourteen separate groups instead of one.

Families with children account for the largest increase in the homeless population. Under President George W. Bush, homeless assistance increased, with the idea of targeting what they called the chronically homeless, mostly single adults. But the chronic-homeless initiative took attention away from families and children and focused on policies that mayors wanted that would get unruly people out of their downtowns. Meanwhile, homelessness among children, youth and families increased and continues to increase.

Local ordinances have been created by people in power who wanted to get rid of homeless people. The federal government lets cities enact these ordinances because they call it a local issue. They can't arrest people for sleeping in public places because it is against the Geneva Convention. "Camping" they call it now. It's so ironic. Like you're going on a nice trip. So people have begun to think in terms of homeless encampments. You can't make it illegal to do something you are absolutely required to do, like sleeping, so they renamed it camping and have defined where people can do it and made the places where they do it illegal.

The application of these laws is very racist. Take it from a white boy who used to be homeless. It would have been different for me. I would have gone to jail for some of the things I did but I was not big, black and mentally ill.

It's the same thing. It's fear. Fear of the poor and homeless. People are scared shitless. Where do homeless people go when they take them away? People are just happy they are gone.

Business districts are increasingly taking control of more and more public space. San Francisco has six bids that would take a whole section around the Union Square Business District. The major thrust for the business districts is safety. Management corporations hire security companies to do studies and show so-called successes after they make the area what they call secure. This is so the security companies can say, "Look how good we are. Look, this guy is gone. Our ambassadors have removed him."

Oakland has hired Block by Block now. Businesses use these security companies to control what happens within their area. Block by Block is hired to protect their interests. When you cut through it all, you can see how businesses are running these business districts just like shopping malls. It was the same mentality. Make sure there is a safe shopping area so you white people can spend all your money.

The problem is that homeless people are arrested, told that they are breaking the law for minor infractions. They can't sit, sleep or stand or they are dinged. When you hear people talking about how it's necessary to take a stance against aggressive panhandling, et cetera, these are the business districts that are becoming more prevalent. But what most people are being charged with are not violent crimes. They are charged for sitting, standing. What can you do? You can't sleep. You can't sit. You can walk. Keep on walking.

We did outreach and put out a fact sheet. Over 700 homeless people were documented with respect to the increase in business district policy with street people and the police. The uniformity of the response was

From the Website for Block by Block,
an SMS Holding Company, Oakland, California

Security Ambassadors are under the direction of a single Operations Manager and management structure. Security Ambassadors are responsible for patrolling on foot and bike to serve as additional "eyes and ears" of the Oakland Police Department, while serving as a visible deterrent. Ambassadors will report all activity that is deemed to be out of the ordinary and engage low level quality of life crimes in order to seek compliance through verbal request. All Ambassadors will provide a high level of engagement with workers, residents and visitors to improve perceptions of safety…

amazing. The disproportionate impact on the mentally ill really stands out. About 78 percent had been arrested or harassed for loitering, sitting on the sidewalk, sleeping.

Our April 1 "No Fooling, National Day of Action for the Right to Exist" focused on fourteen cities in the U.S. and Canada simultaneously protesting the ongoing criminalization of poor and homeless people in our communities. We are launching a nationwide organizing campaign focused on human rights and issues interconnected with them.

The new privatized jail cells aren't making a profit if they are sitting empty. Customers mean money. You'd better fill them up.

Now there is a court system set up just for the homeless. Talk about the road to hell being paved with good intentions. Just stop arresting them in the first place. Yes, in the criminal justice system now there are separate courts for the mentally ill, addicted, homeless. So they have set up a whole industry of separate systems. You can imagine the division between black and white. If you are poor, you get no lawyer. If you are rich, you get a lawyer.

In San Francisco, if you are homeless and plead guilty, you get services they dangle in front of you, like a shelter bed or a case manager. When the City of San Francisco first started the system, they were giving out hotel rooms. As soon as the TV cameras went away, so did the referrals to hotels.

And they didn't add any shelter beds to the system. The court-referred homeless people were just taking up beds. It just meant that people not going to court had few options because the city was not adding to the number of beds available.

People need to get education about these issues. You don't get it from United Way commercials. "We don't know who you are, but we love you"? The bottom line is that people need to start thinking about poverty and justice. We have the largest prison system in the world and the prisons are all filled with poor people.

We criminalize our way out of social issues by demonizing poverty. Really, lock up all the poor people. Then this commodity in the prisons becomes the enemy. How sick is that?

Our latest Western Regional Advocacy Project report is called "Without Housing: Decades of Federal Housing Cutbacks, Massive Homelessness and Policy Failures." In it we urge people to educate themselves about the connection between mass homelessness and the unavailability of affordable housing and to examine the criminalization of poverty in light of human rights.

We have to get past the mindset of charity versus responsible justice. We have to get to the place where we say, "This is how a community of people is treated." Is it really OK to say to a homeless group of people that they can't sit, stand or sleep? Housing, health care and education—they all intersect with the issue of homelessness. If we worked out these issues, we would work out the issue of homelessness.

9 Homemade Green

Bob Dixson

In 2007, a tornado with 205-mile-per-hour winds leveled 95 percent of Greensburg, Kansas. Bob Dixson was elected mayor the next year. Before the storm, Bob and his wife, Ann, lived in an old Victorian-style house. He was also Greensburg's postmaster.

I had been out working in the yard, May 4, getting it mowed, kind of picking up. The weekend following that, my son was going to have his college graduation party here in our yard. So I was starting in preparation a week in advance when I saw the clouds coming in.

My wife and I came in the house, had a nice supper, and were just sitting in the chairs visiting and went on about our evening. We were watching a movie so we didn't have the TV news on. After the movie was over we switched over to the networks and they had across the bottom of the screen "Storm Warning." So I got on the Internet and looked at the city service radar and watched that for a while. Then, when the sirens went off about 9:15 or so, I knew it was time to go to the basement.

I'm usually the one who likes to go out in severe weather and stand in the alley and see what's going on. This time I knew. I just knew. It really surprised Ann that I had the gut feeling to get to the basement.

On the ledge in the family room on the built-in china hutch, I had a little container and I always put my billfold there and my medicine and several things. And I had one of those plastic Dillon sacks and I raked all that in there, and she grabbed her purse and we went to the basement.

I was told to do it. The Lord told me to do it. The Lord told us to do it.

So we went down to the basement, and sirens were going off. The lights went off. I said, "Oops, must have closed the highway just south of town because it took out the power lines."

And I said, "Shoot, I forgot. I forgot the flashlight. I'll go up and get it."

She said, "No, I know right where it's at. I'll go get it." So she ran up and came right back down—and then it hit. Oh my gosh.

We remember debris hitting the house and windows popping and our ears popping, and there was a tremendous amount of noise. And then there was a lull. The National Weather Service says as much as three minutes. And then the backside hit us. We were right in the core of the tornado. Right in this block here, it tore up everything so bad.

There was a couple over here I just heard about the other day that it hit and instead of bowling their whole house down, it scooted it. And then there was that lull and they thought it was over, and so they ran across the street to the people they knew who had a basement, and barely got in and the backside hit 'em.

So we were huddled down in there. My daughter, our oldest daughter, had, when she was back visiting us one time, bought some of those area rugs, and we were storing them. We pulled them up over our heads. I said, "We'd better get these up over our heads in case there's some debris flying. We don't want to get hit."

So we didn't have no debris hit us, no bruises, nothing. The noise had died down. It was raining. I could feel the wet down below us. I said, "Ann, we ain't got no roof left." And, of course, we hadn't looked out 'cause there was some hail in the air. Not enough to hurt us.

It took away the floor, everything. The only thing left when it got done was this concrete step here you see in the photo. This was all stacked right over there. Three stories of it. Debris that had been the house.

The actual basement was only about five and a half feet from the ground. The house was built in 1912. I stood up and Ann stood up and we looked out of the basement to mass destruction and devastation. There were no streetlights left, but we could see with the lightning. Just like in a horror film.

We had lived in the house about ten or eleven years. It was our second home we lived in. Our other house that we lived in was east of the Bridge School and it got totally destroyed. We moved to Greensburg in '85. I moved here to be postmaster. U.S. Postal Service.

I stood up in the basement and looked out and just went, "Holy cow!"

Well, I don't think those were my exact words, but I mean, you couldn't even get up and down the streets for all the trees and the debris and everything in them. Just a few minutes later, the neighbor from over—two neighbors over—just on the other side of the block, came over hollering, "Can anybody help?"

They did need help. We was just getting ready to get out of the basement when we had … there was a water line that was just about so tall. And it was sticking through the concrete. It had ripped everything else out. So I stood on it. I threw those rugs on it so I stood on it and we got out and we pulled up and went immediately across the street to our elderly neighbors to see if they were OK and found they were all right. But the real eerie part that I found out afterwards was all the horns and emergency flashers and things like that on vehicles had shorted out.

Right at first there I thought, "Wow, emergency services sure got here quick!"

But it wasn't that. Phone lights were on, you could hear a few horns around, but the dome lights were on because it had shorted 'em out. Oh my gosh, but the vehicles were there. Or had they been strewn around? The cars were there. My pickup was parked right here and this tree was right through the middle of it. Oooh.

Her car was left in the garages and it sucked the garage off and it left the car. My pickup had some limbs in it. I couldn't even sell it, you know, on carquest.com or whatever that is. You know, they say, "Slight wind damage." That's a joke.

We just started around the block. Our neighbor back here, he was trying to find us, and he headed out around to the south, so we weren't around and he didn't see us. Didn't know where we were at. There was mass confusion because people are really big neighbors and they were out looking for people. If they didn't see you, they didn't know what to think.

We started right down here where you turned the corner. There was a gas station across the street here and Dodge City came in from the side here and Bradley in from the east side. They needed to start accounting for everybody. All the emergency services came in from Dodge City. Everybody. Their chapter of the Red Cross, the fire department, everybody from the west side started this way, the communities that started to respond.

And everybody from the east was working out of the parking lot over on the east side. Mullinville and Haviland opened up their high school gymnasiums. They sent school buses over and started bussing people to those gymnasiums, and anybody that needed medical attention, depending on what side of town they were on, they went there.

It ended up we lost about ten people, or was it eleven? It was initially nine and it went up. We had a gentleman that passed away a couple months afterwards. He really suffered, too.

It's hard to say why people died. We had a gentleman that lived just half a block down here, an older man, a sweet guy. We had a little house just across the street here that had a cellar outside and Claude said, "Are you locking that?"

I said, "No, not if you need it."

Then I said, "Claude, come over to our house, you know?"

They found him out in the yard under some debris. Maybe he was just trying to make it. Or he got sucked out of his house. Nobody will ever know. We'll know someday when we all get to see the big picture replayed to us.

Then there was a gentleman across the alley right over here that didn't have a cellar or storm shelter. No, I take that back: they think he was on his way to the storm shelter and didn't get there fast enough.

So we had two die just in this block here.

We had about twenty, twenty-five minutes' warning. I can really sing the praises of the storm spotters throughout central Kansas and the Dodge City National Weather Service and their staying on top of it and issuing warnings and tracking it as well as they did.

Twenty minutes' warning was nice. If it had been two hours later—we're an older community—and people had been in bed, they may or may not have heard it. This was before the ten o'clock news, so everyone was pretty much aware. The TV stations out of Wichita and all the local stations were covering it mid-afternoon on. The conditions were deteriorating.

It was probably on the ground for twenty to twenty-five miles before it got to us. It came from the southwest. And then it broke. This one almost looked like it was going to miss us. Then it turned northwest and came straight at us. Then about five miles northeast, it started again. Another cell. It took off through the little town of Trousdale. A lot of farmers lost a lot of stuff. National Weather Service out of Dodge City says there were actually four cells that came through.

This particular one was EF5, the biggest that was ever recorded under the new system. They know by the damage it did to old structures, like a school that was built like a fortress.

I'd say about 1,000 people went to the gymnasiums afterwards. We had about 1,400 or 1,500 people. Some people could have been out of town.

There were a lot of us like my wife and myself that had friends out here west of us on the farm and they told us to come stay with them.

There were farmers who didn't lose their farmsteads and several down here just south of town that lost just as much as we did, if not more in equipment. Everything. Beautiful farmsteads with windbreaks and everything that now look like the top of this table.

Everyone just poured their hearts out. That's what we do. We human beings take care of each other. That was very evident by all the communities and assistance that came from all over the state of Kansas in some form or fashion. That's what we in Kansas and Midwest America do to help each other. Somebody is in trouble, you help them. It's no different than when I was a kid and if a farmer had health problems and it was harvest time, everybody went over and cut his wheat. You just took a day and there might be twenty combines over there, but that's what we do in rural America.

I was just speaking with my cousin last night and we were talking about that spirit. That she felt in rural farm towns, you know, particularly in the Midwest.

It did put it all in perspective about what's really important. You know, stuff is just stuff. Some of it probably needed to go to the dump. Some of it needed cleaned out anyway. Ann doesn't like it when I say that, but when you lose all the pictures, and you lose family heirlooms, you know, some furniture and some plates and things like that. Just gone. But in the midst of everything it shows you what's really important for us all.

We lost everything. It was just easier to 'doze our lot off and start from scratch. We were all in the same boat. It didn't matter what your social or economic status was in the community. It was gone. We got back to our roots. We got back to where we started. We were naked to the world. We were all just people.

We had the clothes we had on and there was more hugging and compassion than you've ever seen. It was fantastic. You had to see it. It's really been a blessing to this community. There was a reason for it but the Lord had shown his strength through the midst of this.

Now this house that we've built is not a beautiful home. It's not quite … it's a beautiful house, but we're still in the process of making it a home. We've started planting some plants. We've got to plant some grass and get it to where it starts looking like a home.

I think it was really harder on my children, who, well, none of them lived here. They lost everything. They lost the school they went to, the houses they grew up in. They lost the church they went to. They lost the theater. They lost the drugstore with the soda fountain. Everything that was stable in their life memory-wise, they lost. It was gone.

They were all here by six o'clock in the morning or earlier, from Lawrence and Manhattan, and my other daughter and her husband were about forty-five miles away. They kept us all out of town for two days. We snuck back in the morning afterwards just to assess things. We salvaged a couple of photo albums that weren't too bad. We got them spread out at the farm. The deep freeze, it was bent like this, but the top layer was still solid. We threw some away but saved a bunch of meat. Beef and pork out of that, and we found a few mementos. Then they came by and said, "We're evacuating the town."

They had to account for everybody. They had the cadaver dogs in. And as soon as those dogs would smell something, new scents, they would have to go back and research the scent. But when we were in our house, they were smelling us because we were messing around so we had to get out. And we weren't the only ones. It irritated a lot of people. They thought they could save more. Because it was raining. You know, three or four days afterwards. It was just like today, overcast, misting, and a lot of people thought they could have saved some stuff if they had let us stay in town. But they did what was right for the best interest of everybody.

And sometimes that ain't popular. I had no problem with it because I didn't have anything much I could save anyway.

When they let us back in and all the kids, sons-in-law and daughter-in-law, were all here. The kids started through this whole rubble. It was in layers a little bit. They would lift a wall up a little bit and start throwing stuff away and they found a bunch of Ann's jewelry. We found some things. After about a day and a half, I was tired. I was ready to just push it to the street and haul it off. What do you save and what don't you save?

After four days, the kids finally gave up. I realized at that time it was like a grieving process for them to go through this. It was like a funeral.

I realized they needed that time. Now we've got tubs of stuff in the Quonset out at our friend's farm. When we need to go through it we could, and I bet two-thirds of it we're going to throw away because it's that damaged. But the kids want to save it. The rock from the old fireplace, they saved that rock and put it on this fireplace. They wanted that.

That green platter that's up on the mantel? My oldest daughter's a ceramics artist, and in the hallway you went in our front door and there was oak columns and then up the stairway this plate was hanging up on the wall. Decorative. After the tornado hit, there was an area about as big as a table and it had no debris on it. Perfectly clear on the concrete driveway. That plate was sitting in the middle of that. There ain't a chip out of it. There isn't a crack in it. There ain't nothing. Now how did that happen when ten feet away we have a pile of rubble that's this deep?

And everybody in town has a story like that to tell. Everybody has a story about how things came to be.

Some people knew right away they were going to rebuild. Some people have been talking and, especially our older friends and neighbors, as they were getting older, they had mentioned for a couple of years before that they were going to move closer to their kids. Or other family. Those kinds of things. Or they might move to Pratt. It's got a little more medical and shopping, and it's got a big civic center.

That just made the decision for those few people. We've got a few young couples that have made decisions now and are in the process of building houses. They have kids in school so they have a different perspective. They live over in trailers out in FEMA-town.

FEMA came in and put up trailers on the south end of town, but that took a while. I don't know where everybody was staying but they were staying, and soon as they got a FEMA trailer they moved in. There was 250 trailers to start out with, something like that. When people move into their new homes, they haul them away. There's a hundred and something out there right now.

Ann is a magistrate judge. Kiowa County magistrate judge. She has eight more years before she retires. She has to live in the county. I'm retired from the Postal Service. The first thing we asked ourselves was what are we going to do when we retire. Where do we want to be? Well, this is home. Neither of us was raised in Greensburg, but our kids went to school here and grew up here. The decision was made. We're going to stay in Kiowa County after we retire.

We could go to another place across town and then we said, "We own the lot right here. Why would we do anything different? This is our home. This is our piece of property."

That Sunday before the storm had hit we had been looking at a little piece of property out the edge of town. You know, just everybody longs to get back to a simpler way of life and part of that is being in the country.

Two days after the tornado, we got on the Internet and requested a catalogue from a home manufacturing plant up at Clay Center.

People's rebuilding depended on what kind of insurance policy you had. The insurance companies were all here immediately and ours was an easy settlement because there wasn't anything left. We had our insurance money within weeks. We were covered well, but none of us had any idea that construction costs were so high.

Even if you have replacement cost, a lot of the insurance companies, well, it's not stick for stick to build back. In a lot of cases it's what your appraised value was. What could you buy a house for—the same square footage in the same community you're in?

Did you know I was mayor? April 1. I take office May 5. If you found out from Stacy at city hall, she's my oldest daughter. On Labor Day they moved back. Her and her husband both got jobs here and they want to be part of the rebuilding process. They wanted to be part of something new. I never thought they would want to come back and be a part of Greensburg. There are some younger people moving back. People who have gone off and found jobs, good-paying jobs, and found out that they're not rewarding to them and that money isn't everything. And there's a spirit here and we've been very blessed. People have been drawn to Greensburg because of our heart and soul and heritage.

And because it's exciting. Discovery Channel came to us. We talked with them from square one. We were still in the cleanup stage from the destruction. They were staying over in Dodge City. They said, "We look forward to coming over here every day."

Ann said, "Why?"

The gal said, "It's just exciting. There's just something always going on here."

Ann just told her this is the Holy Spirit and people are being drawn here because the Lord's leading them here. And the lady from Discovery said, "We come from vastly different religious backgrounds, but each of us knows there's something special going on."

Those were her exact words. And to me, that's what's drawing young kids. It's not about the storm now. It was old news months and months ago. It's about the rebuilding. It's about being part of getting back to roots.

It's about new growth, our green initiative. It's about being a new pioneer. It's about challenges and getting out of your comfort zone. It's about being rewarded for risk taking. It's not about, "Oh, it's a secure job and I don't really know but, you know, it's secure."

And that has been part of the downfall and part of the fabric of our country. The pioneer spirit has been lost. As a general thing. There's pockets of it.

My goal as mayor is we need new jobs and new businesses. Whatever they might be. People want to come to town, we're going to have a brand-new school. Brand-new downtown area. I just see a place where your children can ride their bikes and walk to school safely. A spot where you can make a reasonable living and have a gardening spot in the back yard if you want. A spot where grandparents want to move to be a part of their grandkids' lives. And I don't feel that's a pie-in-the-sky dream. I just think people are being drawn here for those specific reasons. I'm excited about the opportunities.

That's the reason we decided on day two after the tornado to stay here. The Spirit was here the night of the tornado. You could tell by the way that people treated each other. The hand of God was right over us, protecting us.

There were nine churches. On the highway over there, Faith Tabernacle. Then there was Bible Baptist ... anyway, all gone. Wasn't a one of them salvaged. We had community church services under a big service tent. We had community meetings just to pass information along. That was really the hub, the big tent, all summer long.

You could go to a dedicated AM radio station and they had running announcements on it, where to get assistance, where to do this, where to do that. The Salvation Army had their vehicles up and down the street passing out snacks and water. County health nurses from all over the state came and were pushing grocery carts down the street and giving tetanus shots. It's those little things you don't think about.

Once in a while, because it's been a trauma and everything, somebody just breaks down and gets mad and says or does something that they really didn't mean. We're all cognizant of that because we have had the same thing happen. And so, we just got to love each other and when we do snap at each other, it's not because we're irritated at each other, it's because something has surfaced. The trauma has surfaced.

I was raised in a household where you did community work. You did volunteer work and civics was taught. You have to be involved and engaged in what's going on. And if we're not, we're just sponges. We just absorb. We don't put anything back. I think we're all called to leave this place better than we found it.

We have to decide what legacy we're going to leave. That's part of our green initiative, or whatever term you want to put on it. We just have to make less of a footprint on our environment than we've been making.

We have to be good stewards. This is biblical and this is the original green. Be a good steward of what the Lord has given us and entrusted us with. And that's the bottom line.

That's going green; that's what green is. Are you good stewards of what you've been given?

Jenny Kivett

Less than a year after Greensburg's devastating tornado, students from a program called Studio 804 on the University of Kansas campus took on a project to build a sustainable building prototype for the town. It was to be completed on site by the anniversary of the tornado and was the kickoff to Greensburg's plan to become America's first green city. In April 2008, the students from KU's School of Architecture and Urban Planning were building the town's new arts center to Leadership in Energy and Design (LEED) Platinum standards, the highest designation of green building. It was the first of many LEED Platinum buildings to follow in the town, and the first one in the state of Kansas. Jenny Kivett was student project manager.

Some of the students who are here building the arts center are going for their graduate degree and some are in the undergraduate program. It's about half and half. I'm twenty-two and a graduate student.

We started about a month ago, March 17. It hasn't rained until this week. It has been really windy. Uncomfortable. It's gone back and forth, cold and hot. Normally we build a house for our project rather than a community building. Studio 804 has done a design and building project for twelve years. The first seven were built on-site in Lawrence through the Tenants to Homeowners program. It's a program for someone who needs a house.

We build for handicapped access, ADA regulations always, a sustainable design. Building in place is a big step for us. The last four projects were modular buildings. We build it whole, then break it into pieces. Some we had to build in Kansas City because there was not enough space in our building in Lawrence.

We put the homes in old neighborhoods, a jewel to revitalize the area. But we lost our building site this year. We were disappointed. But then students drove down here to Greensburg, and we went to city meetings to propose what we would like to do for the town. We were told at Greensburg city meetings that they would be unable to fund it, that we would have to find support for financing. Previously we had been financed by entities like El Centro in Kansas City, an organization that boosts economic opportunities for Hispanic families, or through a Kansas City community development corporation interested in renewing the downtown.

I'm so glad we didn't stop because Greensburg couldn't fund it. We were planning and simultaneously looking for a donor. We stayed and eventually they started a not-for-profit. They decided it would be interesting to work with us.

We originally thought we'd build a house, the way the city was starting to rebuild. We could do a house as an example. It could be a residence with a sustainable bath, kitchen and living room. Then we thought it could be a community center or an office building. It was decided it would be an arts center.

LEED Platinum is the highest level of certification. It costs more money up front, but it eventually reduces costs and is better for the environment. We wanted to do LEED Platinum certification. Not necessarily something that could most easily be done, but something that will benefit the community.

This building is 1,660 square feet. It is the biggest we have done since they started Studio 804, the most ambitious. It also is different than anything we've done in the past. There is a lot of paperwork. We never considered LEED Platinum in other projects. This was four sites instead of one—four sites on this block. The houses were here before the tornado. It was kind of sad digging. We found toys, shoes. We are now digging a trench for the trench wall. We have a wind turbine and photovoltaic panels. There is a geothermal heat pump, which we never would have considered before because of the cost.

The agreement is that they get the building we produce. Our group and the city are both working to find donations. Wherever we don't have it covered, they will. Building materials are donated through private donors. We do a lot of cold-calling. We are chipping away at it. We are getting $5,000 to $10,000 a day.

Our labor is all volunteer. There is no cost for professional fees. It dramatically reduces the cost—about $200,000 to $250,000.

We did research on water reclamation for the water system and the gutters. I enjoyed the concrete work. The people you see here all worked on research. The design was done as a collective, even though we researched each part that we were in charge of.

We are all responsible for different parts of the building. Simon is in charge of the concrete, Zach the geothermal pump and HVAC systems. Lindsey is in charge of roofing. She is doing it in gypsum. Justin is in charge of fundraising efforts. Katie will be doing furniture and cabinetry. Corey is doing doors and windows.

There are passive systems too. The walls are 3½ feet thick. The sun comes in and warms up the concrete. There will be a green roof with sedums that will help insulate and reduce the heat island effect. That effect happens when buildings and roads are constructed and there is less open land, so it creates temperatures that are at least 10 percent hotter than in rural areas. There will be cross-ventilation in the building as well.

We got wood for the building from the Sunflower Ammunition Plant Redevelopment. It's an Army ammo depot west of Kansas City left over from World War II and the Korean War. They had buildings they used to store the ammo in. We planned to take some of them down and use the reclaimed lumber. The legalities were complicated because chemical remediation had to be done on the salvaged wood to make sure there was no explosive residue. The lawyers decided on its viability. It was finally OK'd in the final months of last semester. We got it and have big plans to use it on future projects as well.

Now it will be the exterior here. There is glass around the wood so it is set off a few inches because it is sixty years old. The glass provides UV protection. The other wood we have used is certified by the Federal Stewardship Council, which decides when wood is acceptable for use in sustainable building. Six mills in the country provide what you need for LEED Platinum credit.

I want to be a professor of architecture. That's why I am getting a master's degree. I'll get my license and work for a while. But after doing this process, I'd maybe like to be part of a small firm instead of a big company.

We are staying at Pratt Community College, thirty miles away. We're tired, but personally I am enjoying it. I don't want it to end. I'd love to do it as a career. We leave Pratt at 6 every morning. At 6:30 we meet in Greensburg. We work until 8 p.m., then go back and shower. We still do work on computers when we get back to Pratt. We stay up to 12 or 1, seven days a week. There is so much work to do every day.

It was fun to be here when the water tower went up. It was like a parade. We were having lunch in the Boy Scout shed and could see them putting it up. It was an event. People were crawling all over our building waiting for it to happen.

There will be a city walk-through and appreciation night for the opening of our building after everything is in place. Townspeople come every day and make us feel very welcome. They bring cookies and drinks. The Red Cross comes two times a day. Everyone says how much they appreciate our work. We had not realized it would affect the people so much.

I'm from a small town of 1,100 people, so I understand. You don't have to help, but why wouldn't you help?

Missy Cannon and family

After the tornado in Greensburg demolished their house, Missy Cannon, her husband, Shawn, and their two children Maddie (nine) and Josh (eight) lived in Kinsley, Kansas, for the summer, then returned to live in a FEMA trailer on the edge of Greensburg.

For nearly ten years my family and I lived at 320 W. Illinois in a two-story Victorian home on the north side of town. Our daughter was one and our son was about to be born when we moved there.

I'm originally from Jefferson City, Missouri, and moved to Kansas in 1984. My husband is from Wyandotte County near Kansas City. We met at K-State and got married in September of 1994. I work at the elementary school. My husband is a graphic designer and works in Dodge City as media manager for the Dodge City *Daily Globe*.

When the tornado warnings started, my son, husband and I were at the house. Our daughter was across the street at a sleepover.

Shawn and I had been planning to clean the garage. Spring cleaning. One of my husband's co-workers was a storm chaser and told him before he left that it was supposed to be bad weather.

That day was so gorgeous before the dark clouds rolled in. We saw lightning, but Maddie had asked if she could spend the night across the street. We said sure. Shawn was taking pictures of the storm clouds for the paper. The sirens went off. He came to the living room, then told us to go downstairs.

Josh was playing video games downstairs.

Josh: The day of the tornado turned into one of the worst days of my life.

Missy: The guys were out on the porches looking at the weather. Someone from Coldwater called and said, "There's a bad storm coming your way." In about two or three minutes, the lights went out. Shawn came running down and I asked him if we need to take cover. He said yes.

There was wind, cracking windows. We covered ourselves, quick. It was a cellar-type basement. Nothing huge came down on top of us. In the northwest corner windows blew out and the second level came down.

Josh: I have a little tornado scar from my sister's tea set, where a metal pan hit my head when a shelf came down.

Maddie: I was at a sleepover at Tatum's. We were playing Barbie dolls and they called us to eat. Their mom was watching the Weather Channel and it said a big tornado was going to go through Greensburg. Then we heard sirens. We all got in a circle. Their dad put blankets over all of us. First the windows crashed and we all screamed. We were hanging on to their mom's leg. We heard it stop and we ran to the bathroom across the hall. Tatum and I were both crying. We didn't know if everybody was OK. Then I heard my dad and I saw my mom.

Missy: All I could see was from the lightning and I kept thinking that the house was not over there. I don't remember climbing over trees to get to the neighbor's. "Oh my gosh, it looks like a bomb went off," I said. But our family was not harmed.

Neighbors gathered in the streets to make sure every family was accounted for. Emergency Management made us move toward the highway because we could smell gas. We were taken to the KDOT building until we could be bused to surrounding shelters. There was no way to let our families out of town know that we were all right.

We stayed in the town of Haviland, where they set up a shelter in the high school gym with my stepdad and mom and uncle. At the shelter, they had cots, pillows, blankets. They had wrestling mats for beds. Everybody was talking. You'd see friends and say, "Good—they're OK." One of the teachers who was on the recovery team told me all the kids and teachers were fine.

We thought the tornado had just hit our side of town. We thought everybody else on the other side was probably OK, that ours was in the eye. When we found out the whole town had been hit, we thought how fortunate we were to have so few lives lost. It still amazes me.

The National Guard guys were among the first to be called in. When the sun came up, they had a feeling they would be pulling body after body out. House by house. But the number was so low. We lost eleven people out of more than 1,500.

Maddie: This is my baby who made it, Sarah. And Josh has Buddy, the dog. It was hard to get through to get them. Mom and Dad got back into town on Monday, and I said, "Go get Sarah."

Missy: Debris hit the cars and destroyed them. I had been cleaning that day before the tornado and set my rings on a hutch. My father, uncle, husband and a firefighter friend went in and found my wedding ring, my anniversary ring and then my engagement ring in the hutch drawer. It had opened just enough, then shifted when it fell on the ground.

We went to Pratt. My stepdad's friend offered us a house to stay in. My mom, uncle, Shawn, me, Maddie and Josh. Then all the relatives started to come, and friends. Eight to ten guys worked on the house to flip the walls. Plus Mom's and my uncle's houses and our family's restaurant and gift shop on Main Street. That week was a blur.

By Friday we had found as much as we could. Then we bulldozed. We tried to sort things out. The house we lived in after the tornado was in Kinsley, an A-frame on a lake where they were drilling for sand. After one week, Shawn's work donated food, toys and clothes. We lived there for the summer. It had a wonderful view. The kids and dogs went swimming.

We traveled a lot that summer after the tornado and visited many relatives. We went to Hawaii and joked that we might stay there and not come back. The last week of July we got this FEMA trailer and on August 15 school started. There was a moratorium on building where our lot was because they were building a road there. "So what do we do?" we asked.

We thought about moving closer to our relatives and had many states to choose from, but the more we thought about it, the more we said, "This is home." We had that connection. We thought we'd give it a try and see what we thought. By October, we had started plans for a house on a corner lot. We are in the process of building on a new lot at 320 Bay Street.

A lot of people shuffled lots. We built on the south side of the highway. "So-and-so used to live there," we say as we drive around. It's part of rebuilding Greensburg. Some are not coming back. Some people have two lots now. We bought ours from people who chose to build out in the country. We knew it was going to be a struggle, but we wanted to be a part of it. One big issue was: Is there going to be a school? To get the school up and running. The superintendent, principals and the board understood. If they hadn't understood the need to rebuild the school, we wouldn't have had kids. People would not be starting over and bringing them back.

Some people are surprised we're not building a two-story house. Well, that idea is kind of gone. The old one was nearly a hundred years old.

Because we are all in the same boat, we're all excited about so-and-so's house going up. Others asked us, "How do you do it day after day?" But as soon as I get out of school, I look around. "Look, a new house has come in there." Who is not going to want to come to a state-of-the-art brand-new town?

There were tornados in Texas in February. The school counselor had the kids write cards to the students: "We know what you're going through." They raised $4,000 to send them.

So many gave to us. We're at the point where we can give back a little.

On our side of the block, there was one house standing. The rest were flattened. I still come into town and want to turn onto our old block. It was just a year ago that we were there. Sometimes it seems like a bad dream. Maybe I'll wake up and be there.

I've learned lots of patience.

Josh: Patience is not my thing. I hate patience but everybody needs it sometimes.

Missy: The kids at school cut out two hundred stars of bright colors—purple, yellow and so on. They put "love," "peace" and "hope" on them and they decorated them. There is one on each corner of each block. It's encouraging. When you feel blue, it brightens you up.

Missy Cannon is back at home after work at the new Greensburg school. Her son Josh, now twelve, is on the couch watching TV. Ironically, while Missy is reviewing the aftermath of the Greensburg tornado, Josh is listening to an announcer talk about a wide funnel heading for Tuscaloosa, Alabama. The next day that tornado was deemed "catastrophic." It claimed sixty-four lives in Tuscaloosa and Birmingham.

Missy: It gets to you when news about another tornado comes on. It does. The TV takes us back to what ours was like.

And when we were in the FEMA trailer, we heard thunderstorms and hail. "Are we going to have a tornado again?"

The year after the tornado, south of town, there was another one just as big. It got to right outside Greensburg and then lifted.

The kids in town are still leery, but they don't panic. Volunteers would come the first year we were in the trailers, and sit to calm kids when a storm was coming. They felt safer. We practice for a tornado. There is security in knowing they have a place to go. We talked to the kids about it. How did they feel when they went to the shelter? They thought another tornado might take everything away again. They would envision that everything was going to be gone again.

We could have lost a lot of kids had they been at the school when the tornado hit. I can't think how many we would have lost.

Even though my husband and I still really miss our old house, we are fortunate we could build again the way we wanted.

The green aspects of our house are the spray-in insulation, the windows that are energy efficient and the energy-efficient appliances. We have a water system, tankless water heater and dual flush toilets. We have a safe room directly under the porch out front. Six inches of concrete and six inches of sand, then four more inches of concrete and the steel door opens inward. It was definitely a priority. The safe room was built first, and a couple of times when we were still in the trailer, we came over here when storms were predicted.

There are people who didn't come back, even though they survived the tornado. But also, if they had a house that was worth $50,000 to $60,000, it now costs $120,000 to $190,000 to rebuild new.

After the tornado, my uncle went to Hutchinson. My mom and stepdad went to Pratt. It was too hard for them to move back. The devastation. They didn't want to build new homes. My mom and stepdad's house was on an area they took to build the highway.

I'm glad we stayed. It's the only place the kids know and have grown up. Several of our friends moved back. Had our kids not felt comfortable in the trailers, or going to school, or felt safe, we might have moved. It was a big issue. But we didn't want to uproot them even if we would have been closer to family.

We work the same places. My husband works for the *Globe* still doing the web and ads. I work at the school, K–5, which is phenomenal. It's not so hard to get up and go because we can be inside a new green building. After the tornado, it was a campus of twenty-two trailers. Now it's brand-new just this year. The kids moved in the fall of 2010.

Every day there is another FEMA trailer pulled out. You've got to stay positive. There are lots of new faces. There are close to three hundred students, pre-kindergarten through twelfth grade. New young families are coming to town.

It's amazing to see how many volunteers are still coming out to help with lots. Whatever needs to be done. Our town wouldn't look near as well without them.

I guess everything happens for a reason. Sometimes we don't know why or how, but I'm a big believer in that now.

Catherine Hart

In 2011, Catherine Hart was cofounder and program director of Greensburg GreenTown, a community-based nonprofit that showcases the town's green initiative in rebuilding. In 2012, Catherine moved to Joplin, Missouri, another tornado-torn town, to become general manager of Joplin GreenTown—an affiliate of Greensburg GreenTown that is helping incorporate sustainable principles into the rebuilding effort.

My husband and I live north of Greensburg in Stafford County. We have been working here since a week after the tornado, when the city of Greensburg announced that they were going to build sustainably after a tornado destroyed over 90 percent of the town.

We came up with a concept paper we had independently developed and shared it with community leaders at the first post-tornado meeting, just a week after the storm. After hearing then-mayor Lonnie McCollum announce the green vision for the recovery, we were excited about the possibilities and started working with the city and county officials, business owners, and local residents to incorporate sustainable principles into their rebuilding process.

First we needed to help residents understand what it means to come back as a green community, to depoliticize what it means. Many people in this conservative community were afraid to be branded as "tree huggers."

As is the case with people anywhere, they didn't want to make changes they were not comfortable with. Some people thought that "green" would mean that building would cost more, and we worked to help dispel myths about that and offer people options for making their new homes more energy efficient. There was not so much resistance to green as there has been the need to educate on what sustainability means. How will it affect people's daily lives? There were tons of community meetings with outside experts, architects and other consultants.

For the people here, the idea of taking care of resources and the land was a no-brainer. And people like the idea that things can be built with reclaimed and repurposed products.

The organization we established and manage, Greensburg GreenTown, is a grass-roots nonprofit that is supported through sponsors and partners and memberships. We're striving for Greensburg to be a model green town for the future.

Our first demonstration building project was the Silo Eco-Home. A Florida-based contractor, Dave Moffett, came to town shortly after the tornado and offered to build a model concrete house that he had devised to withstand 200-mile-an-hour hurricane-force winds. He wanted to share that technology with our town, and he made it happen. We named it "Silo" after the town's grain elevator, which was still standing when all else was lying in rubble.

The six-inch-thick concrete walls enable it to withstand high winds, and there are lots of green features inside that show people who visit what sustainable living technologies are all about.

When people from all over the country—and all over the world—hear about Greensburg's efforts and want to come see green building, we have a place for them to come and tour and spend the night. After the storm, when the city announced that Greensburg was building back sustainably, visitors would come to town wanting to see all these new green houses. Obviously, you can't ask residents to open their homes for tours over and over again. So Daniel *(GreenTown's founder and executive director)* came up with the Chain of Eco-Homes concept. The Silo Home is the first in the chain to be completed. The home offers a bed-and-breakfast where you can rent a guest suite, and it houses GreenTown's administrative office and the town's Green Visitors Center.

After that, we cosponsored an international competition with FreeGreen.com. We solicited designs from architects, students, and other designers for the next link in our chain of eco-homes.

We challenged competitors to come up with innovative wall systems, building techniques, and technologies to demonstrate sustainability to the thousands of visitors who are now coming to Greensburg annually.

We got 150 entries from thirty-eight states and thirteen countries. The winner was from New York, a design from Michael Stevens of Steven Learner Studio. His design uses German technology for the wall system in what he named Meadowlark House—after Kansas's state bird. The house will feature a superinsulated shell that's airtight and can withstand 180-mile-an-hour winds and an 8.0 earthquake.

Meadowlark House is also being built to passive specifications, which are a relatively new idea in the United States. European passive designs were first developed in 1990, and there are over 25,000 such homes there. There are fewer than two dozen in the U.S. This type of home is designed to use 90 percent less heat in the winter, and there is no need for air conditioning.

Dieter Junker, the man who developed the HIB *(Highly Insulated Building)* system, came from his home in Germany to help assemble the blocks that provide such excellent insulation and protection from our winds. The blocks are 100 percent biodegradable and toxin free. They assemble easily, sort of like Legos. We are the first project in the United States to use this system. He brought his German partner with him to assemble the blocks and help build the home with a local contractor and crew. It only took two and a half weeks to raise the home's walls.

GreenTown is representing Greensburg outside the community to people who are interested in the Green Initiative. We offer information, resources and support to people throughout the U.S. to make it easier for homeowners, builders, building supply companies and local businesses to do their business as green as possible.

When people come to visit, we share our community-wide tour book and green tour map, featuring all major green projects in town. The tour book is also available for download online. We maintain a library about green building and living. We have offered classes online and through workshops both in Greensburg and around the area. Staff travel throughout the country giving presentations about the Green Initiative, and people find the story very inspiring.

There has been an amazing amount of press on Greensburg's efforts to rebuild, from three seasons on Planet Green, which is a part of the Discovery Network, to recent appearances in *Reader's Digest* and *Dwell* magazine.

The Greensburg story really resonates with people—they are amazed at what this small farm town has been able to do.

10 Finders/Seekers

Wayne

From the balcony of his Colorado Springs apartment, Wayne Keller views the dramatic sandstone rock formations in Garden of the Gods National Park. Pikes Peak, white-capped much of the year, crowns the vista. While Wayne, sixty-two, appreciates the view, he does not feel at home there.

I've never felt at home anywhere. My mother was a schizophrenic but not diagnosed until she was in her eighties and I was in my fifties. She saw the doctor in 2004, just months before her death. She took her own life. You couldn't stop a freight train. She was going to write her own exit.

It was not an easy childhood. I'm the middle of three sons. One brother was three years older. He was an example of what I didn't want to be like, in any way. My other brother was seven years younger, a loner, and one never depended on him for anything.

My father was German, from Stuttgart. My mother was Scotch/Irish and constantly fought with him and pulled us aside to tell us how much she hated him. She was not terribly loving, but she was extremely controlling. She tried to divide us from our father. There was a lot of screaming and yelling. She told us later, "I stayed in the marriage for you three boys." Sure, I thought, and screwed up three boys in the process. I never had a childhood really.

I grew up in my own world. I was the only reader in the family and was reading books far above my age level. I would go through those summer reading lists like Grant hung around Richmond.

My grandmother was and is my guardian angel. She was the ultimate definition of unconditional love. Grammy showed me how to sew. She explained how if you were born with a talent, you must use it. She took apart shirts of mine for the patterns. For my thirteenth birthday I wanted a buttonholer. My father said no. My grandmother got me two.

I am an extremely fortunate and most grateful person to have been given the sound encouragement, love and understanding at a very young age from an unbelievably loving grandmother. She made my life's path very clear to me.

Our family was like gypsies. We moved thirteen times while I was growing up. Here in Colorado Springs. I can remember the names of the streets where we lived: Corona, Roswell. I was born on Las Animas. Mohawk Drive, Weber, El Paso, Royer, Madison (a house by Bonny Park), and "The Green Acres Estate" in Black Forest. In hindsight, I see my parents as miserable people. If there was love left over from the house they just bought, they thought it would serve them as well.

One time I said to my mother, "Why do we take these things out of the boxes? They're all labeled for next time."

We never had a mortgage. We always had cars, houses and dogs. My father bred Alsatians. He was not fun, dour, but he had a good work ethic. He was cold, not a hugger. My mother wasn't either. Hugging was an acquired skill for me. I remember a little girl once trying to hug me behind a building at school. She finally said, "You don't really like this, do you?"

My parents divorced when my little brother was fifteen. My mother never remarried. My father died eight years before she did.

I moved out of the house at sixteen. I had my own apartment on Nevada Avenue, where I pressed my own graduation robe. Sometimes I would get lonely, but then I would think of things about living with my family and I would snap out of it.

When I was just a skinny eleven-year-old kid, I announced to the entire family and relatives while watching *Gunsmoke*, "I'm going to work in the studios, motion pictures and television." My father laughed the loudest. Years later when I walked down the set of the main street in Dodge—it was a dirt road with building fronts and nothing behind them—I thought about his laughter and I said, "Well, I made it to Dodge."

My first year of college was at the Pasadena Playhouse in California, where I was in technical theater, designing costumes. For one year I went to Los Angeles City College, because they had an excellent theater arts department. At Pasadena Playhouse a fellow student kept following me around. I found out what he wanted and decided it was what I wanted too. We became lovers, but after a time I got into a pattern of leaving and coming home and starting a feud. He would ask, "Is this necessary?" I realized for the first time this was all I knew. I didn't know you could live without strife. I was accustomed to my ever-changing mother. As a child I would think, "I wonder who she is today. Dark, light or medium?" I had had no capacity as a child to figure that out. To this day I still have to remind myself I'm OK.

Coming out of the closet? My time spent in any closet has been looking for clothes to wear, not who I am.

Why do some gay men make themselves so odd? Why the need to discuss yourself all the time? Acceptance of the fact would save everyone's time and be much more enjoyable for all. I'm not on a mission. I've never been in a gay parade. I'm not out to change people's lives. My name is Wayne Keller. I happen to be gay. But that's not the main event.

It's no one's business anyway. Who cares? Some people run around looking for approval. How terribly limiting and exhausting.

I worked at the Pasadena Playhouse for a year. At nineteen, I was at poverty level. I still knew I wanted to work in the entertainment industry. One day I got out the phone book and called NBC. I asked for the wardrobe department. I got a Mrs. Jo Jones—head of the whole wardrobe department. I said, "Mrs. Jones, I would like an interview with you." I knew nothing about how things worked there at all, from job positions to pay, openings, nothing.

She said, "Yes, Mr. Keller. I'll tell the gate to issue you a pass to get into the lot." It was like I was in a movie. When I got to the wardrobe department, it felt like home, as if I definitely belonged there. I love clothes. There were racks of them.

I showed her a few things I had done, from high school and the two colleges. We didn't talk about my past jobs. Afterward, I gave my name to Molly at the reception desk and asked if I could have a look around. I went to the cutting room, special effects department, and the photo gallery. The place is like a big hangar—with a huge ceiling because they have to transport sets. You never know what weather changes might be happening outside or when your day might finish. It's another world.

I went back to the loft where I was living. I didn't have a phone. Later that afternoon my landlady came running down the hall telling me I had a call from NBC.

NBC is a class act. Rhett Turner (*production manager*) was on the phone and said he understood I had an interview with Jo Jones that afternoon.

Then he said, "Would you like to come to work tomorrow morning?"

Mrs. Jones liked me, I thought. She must have seen I had some ability. I had told her I had been sewing since I was six years old.

I didn't know what I would be doing. I was sent to a setup room. Each stage has one where you pull clothes for the dressing rooms. I went into Jimmy Durante's the first day. He was a rough little fellow. I couldn't understand what I was supposed to do. There were all different tags for such and such a scene. I said to Jody Evans (*now a film producer*): "I need help here. I don't know when to get people ready to go."

"Oh my God!" she said. "You need a run-down schedule." Otherwise I wouldn't know what clothes to put on him. Or when.

I was a dresser first. They changed the name of the job to handler, but it entailed the same skills. Eventually I became a shop steward and head of the wardrobe department. I loved it. I was home. I could deal with people. You are halfway home if you can please people. You have direct interaction with actors and actresses when you are designing and putting their clothes on them. There were prima donnas, of course. There was an actress who one day didn't want to put on the dress for her scene. She told me, "I don't wear that color."

I told her, "Your character doesn't shop at Neiman-Marcus. You are playing the part of a Kansas farmwoman who wears housedresses from J.C. Penney and the Sears catalogue. You are playing someone else. Can you act or can't you act?"

There is rivalry in show business between the East and West Coasts. Bernadette Peters, who had starred in a number of musicals on Broadway, moved to Los Angeles in the seventies to concentrate on television and film work. When she appeared on the NBC set, everyone thought she was a lightweight, with that cute little mouth and the way she talks. She was adorable, but she was like Goldie Hawn, both smart cookies.

I worked on so many television programs: *The Golddiggers, The Andy Williams Show, Rowan & Martin's Laugh-In, Sanford and Son, The Helen Reddy Show, The Tennessee Ernie Ford Special, NBC Follies, All in the Family, Hallmark Hall of Fame* and *Cameo Theatre*. As head of the workroom at NBC, the sketches came to me, and I put the machine ladies to work making costumes.

I ventured out and did film toward the end of my thirty-year career. I worked on *American Pop*. It was an animated history of music from pre-jazz to the eighties. Ralph Bakshi directed it. It's little known that animators like Disney would first look at the movement of real humans in real costumes. They study the movements for the repetition of frames, then do the animation. The last show I worked on was at ABC, *The Barney Miller Show*. I liked Ron Glass and Ron Carey—he's dead now—but I didn't like Hal Linden. He was quite a challenge.

I admire Sally Struthers. I went to school with her. I think Norman Lear is a genius. I don't care much for Billy Crystal—so sort of full of self. Maureen O'Hara was the most beautiful woman I ever came across— Irish, red-headed. There were some bitches along the way. Marlo Thomas was one you don't forget.

When I first started working, I found little spoons in the pocket of Redd Foxx's clothes and I thought they were gourmet spoons. They were gold, so I put them in the safe. I was green as grass.

I remember Cyd Charisse had huge black glasses. Gorgeous legs. She spent hours and days in makeup. Lily Tomlin was no beauty. She had high gums and little sparkly eyes. She wrote all her own work, like for Edith Ann and Ernestine. She said, "I want to do male impersonations." I told her, "You do it." She was brilliant.

I've known some great ones—Gene Kelly. Jimmy Stewart. I worked on a Dean Martin roast with him. Jimmy Stewart was lovely—six foot four and really thin. George Burns was adorable. I worked with him on a Ronald Reagan roast when Reagan was governor. He was in one of the trailers outside of the stage. He had these darling little glasses. I had to say, "Mr. Burns, it's time to go to makeup," and I'd lead him there. He lived to be a hundred and two, you know.

He gave me a tip about cigars: buy the cheapest. You don't have to keep puffing.

You get surprises. Some actors are wonderful workhorses. It's in their blood. More are called because they want the fame and glory rather than the craft, which is a shame. I also got a taste of the stage when I worked briefly in a theater. It's like a whole family. When the show is over, it's a death. Home is the show. You bond and then you break up. In television, they use the same people and it's ongoing.

I quit in 1990. The quality of TV was going down. Now TV is trash. Reality TV is the worst.

I enjoyed many years doing exactly what I loved doing—basically chopping up fabric, stitching it together and making people feel good in front of a camera.

I had a relationship with an English man and lived in England for a few years. I developed a cottage industry doing slipcovers and drapes. I was into the horsey set. I showed, did jumping. It got old. I once spent a whole day boxing a horse (*trying to get the horse into a trailer*).

An aunt called me when I was in England and told me my house in Malibu had burned down. It was set by firemen—one who had wanted extra time firefighting, the other to be a hero. There was nothing left. I lost all my sketches, all my photos of the stars, books signed by Dior. It was so final. Just ashes. Like a body. But nobody lost their life.

I came back to Colorado Springs in 1995 and had a major heart attack. Angioplasty didn't work, so then I had a triple bypass. I was forty-seven years old. It was a long recovery. Now there is life after the bypass. I joined a rehabilitation group. I'm not alone out there. I thought this just happened to old people.

I started traveling to the places I wanted to see—Italy, back to England, a long relationship in Argentina.

But meanwhile my mother was on a downward slalom. She couldn't adequately take care of herself, although she still lived in her own house. I was asked to have durable power of attorney and be executor of her will because, she said, "He's the smartest one I've got."

I was at a seminar in Denver when I got the word that she had killed herself. I hurried back to Colorado Springs and came in by the back door of my mother's house. She was out in the garage, lying near the exhaust. She had started the morning with a full tank of gas. She wanted to get the job done. My older brother was at the dining room table, heaving, overly dramatic. I comforted him and patted him. I always try to make peace with a situation. I have been known to be the strong one.

I made good money at the studio, but I also inherited money from my mother. Life is stranger than fiction. Her death has made my life comfortable. Who knew she had money? I bought a Mercedes. I never got to thank her. Do you know that feeling? Never got to tell her of my gratitude.

Personal relationships haven't been what has carried me through the ups and downs of my life so much as my professional relationships and my work. It has been wonderful. Today, I have no regrets. There are some things I would approach differently.

I never socialized with people in the wardrobe department at NBC, though. My father said, "Never put your pickle where you get your nickel."

I'm puzzled by people who don't know what they want to do. When I was young, I couldn't understand why we were cutting up frogs that had been in formaldehyde. How would that contribute to the direction I wanted my life to go? On the other hand, when I feel something I want to do and it doesn't hurt anyone else, no one can talk me out of it.

In the Bible it talks about how so much is given, God-given talents. It is terrible when people don't develop them or just piss them away. I think hard times create the greatest opportunities for learning, the greatest outcomes. Entitlement gripes me. There are gurus who tell you that everything you want is in the air, for free. People who tell you there are secret formulas. I'm sorry, but you have to work for it. You don't just deserve it.

I'm a sucker for giving money out to people who are less fortunate. In the blink of an eyelid any of us could be there. We are all out there scraping. You cast a seed and you never should be concerned about it coming back. You couldn't write the script about how it will come back to you. A gift.

We only truly receive after we give—when you see a need or it is asked of you. The ones who receive are ourselves.

The closest I got to feeling at home was with a man I was with while in Richmond, Virginia. I found togetherness. I found a person who needed me. But then after a while, I found him to be too needy, a wounded soul.

I know what I want in a relationship now. And what I don't want. It will not be a person with indirection. Why would I get in a car with you if you don't know where you are going?

Right now I am more or less enjoying being alone. I'm much more relaxed. I don't have to answer to anybody. I can have whatever I want to buy, do what I want. Get into my jammies. Say no to going out for the evening. I am ready to leave Colorado Springs. I'm looking for a lighthouse keeper's house on the East Coast to buy. That's where I think I'd like to write a book and spend the rest of my life. But there are complications in dealing with the government to buy a lighthouse and tender's cottage. But I'm definitely optimistic.

For me, home involves another human being. A good, healthy, loving, sharing relationship with another person is what makes a home for me. When people go home they should feel they are in an environment where they are supported and listened to. Two people make something between them. A union doesn't work alone.

If you have a life's work that involves pleasing people, you are halfway home.

Truong

*"that he will build a house without doors that those who enter will lose
their way that in the finding they will call home"*

Truong Tran

the lost book, from *four letter words*

*Truong Tran's artwork varies from playful to intensely thought-provoking. He
used both extremes in his last exhibit, a two-man show titled "At War," in which
war scenes and war's accoutrements mingled with images that normally evoke
pleasurable sensations in a viewer.*

*Behind plexiglas in "Four Seasons, Four Processes," pictures of nature alternate
with flickering peeks at war. In "How a Baby Grows Up," Truong creates contrast
with a photo of a naked baby lying on his stomach facing us, reaching for a ring
on the floor in front of him, and a companion photo of a soldier in camouflage in
the same pose. While the warrior lies in a grassy field surrounded by pine trees,
the barrel of his gun points directly at the observer.*

Most of my artwork derives from found images, reclaimed images dis-
carded by society. In the past, I've incorporated vintage print porno and
nature photos, put together like a quilt. Natural man woven into nature.

I have published five books of poetry, but the world of poetry drove me
into the world of art.

In one book, *four letter words*, a vellum sheet obscures a poem. It is a
symbol of my life in exile. I'm in exile from my place of birth, Vietnam,
but I have had more experiences here that make me feel in exile. Leaving
Vietnam was not that traumatic for me. I was going on six in 1975 when
my parents, brothers, sister and I left. My memory is that I was very en-
chanted with the United States. The first movie I ever saw here was *Star
Wars*.

To escape Vietnam, we went to a port where Korea was evacuating its
citizens on a tanker. My mother's sister's husband was an assistant to the
ambassador in Korea. She had a photo of him and pulled it out and said
she was his sister. When they found out she was lying, they were about

to drop our family off on an island off the coast of Vietnam. We staged a protest and they let us go on to Korea.

Korea was never a permanent resettlement area for Vietnamese refugees. They wanted Vietnamese refugees to leave. Eventually we ended up coming to the U.S. through the sponsorship of two Bay Area families.

I grew up in San Jose. San Jose was practically rural at that time. The community we lived in was predominantly Vietnamese. My high school French teacher was Vietnamese. I didn't learn a lick of French, but I spoke a lot of Vietnamese with my teacher.

My parents were driven people. They went right to work starting a new life. My father had been a military officer. Here he drove a van for National Semiconductor and then became a computer operator. My mother was a seamstress and got clients through her church, Holy Family Catholic Church. She eventually had her own business and had enough money to buy a house. My mother had an uncanny ability to go into a high-end department store and study the couture, then reproduce things based on memory.

I helped her with the business by translating for her because I spoke English. The first time I thought I was gay was when a slew of young men were being measured for disco suits. This contributed to my recognition that I was gay.

My family couldn't figure me out. My brother was the representation of the gay son. I was someone that they were in a quandary about. They couldn't really figure out how I fell into that spectrum. So for the longest time they insisted that somehow my identity was tied to my intellectual pursuits.

When I was ten, my mother started working for the phone company, Nortel, as an assembler. She was able to buy a house. She's retired now because her eyes are bad. She doesn't really understand my art, but she tries. In fact, she collaborated with me on a piece. It's a combination of knitting she did and wooden balls I added.

She thinks I am odd and quirky, but she indulges me. She has done a lot of translating into Vietnamese for me. The language in poetry needed accent marks and I always get them out of context.

When I was a teenager, I thought of myself as creative, but not a poet. More like a fiction writer. In high school, I was a horrible student with a horrible GPA, just regurgitating class requirements. I hardly passed.

I was even put into a remedial English as a Second Language program when my family moved my freshman year. I spent three years yawning through ESL. I was trained to fear poetry. We had to recite it from memory in front of the class.

My father would have been pleased with whoever I chose to be, but there was a side of him that was practical. He suggested I go to trade school. Probably his thinking was that I would have something to fall back on. This was in comparison to my brother, who was starting med school. But when my father came to the conclusion that I was going to pursue writing poetry with some sort of abandonment, he was all in.

With $50 from my own bank account, I enrolled in junior college to take a creative writing class. I felt really connected to writing. After that I transferred to the University of California at Santa Cruz. My father was happy and proud. At Santa Cruz, I knew I was a writer and I started writing poetry.

After that I went to San Francisco State for my MFA. This from a person who had had no plans for college at all. The very fact that I am now teaching at two universities is crazy. At San Francisco State, I was still a good, but not the best, student. I figured out how to excel. I had no interest at that time in teaching. I ran away from the academic environment like a bat out of hell.

I spent 1995–96 doing social work with Refugee Transition, a nonprofit to help refugees become self-sufficient. The next year, I moved to another nonprofit under a literary organization, Poets and Writers. Then a dot-com company contacted me and asked me to work for them doing international greeting cards.

I took the job of writing greeting card punch lines. It was a fledgling business, but about 80 percent of the cards were my text for the next five years.

I was asked to be an editing director doing paper greetings with a Cleveland company called Egreetings. I said no, and instead lived off my savings. I survived.

I didn't work at a job for the next two years, and then started teaching writing through the Kearny Street Workshop. It's the oldest Asian arts organization in the Bay Area. One of my poetry students was Itzolin Garcia, a young Latino-Jewish poet who found a connection with the Asian community. He wanted to pursue art but felt pressured to pursue a doctorate at Stanford University. It probably would have led to his teaching poetry.

I remember our conversations about his inner conflict with this life decision. He wanted to be a poet. He found it highly romantic. I was already a poet by then. I thought being a poet was boring and hard work. I still feel that way. He wanted to find a way to be in that world himself. He could have done that.

Unfortunately, he took his own life. His mother asked me to preside over the funeral.

When I started writing poetry, I found that I was expected to address the notion of identity and to deliver what I had to say in an immigrant's voice. I tell my students they don't have to do that, that it can be limiting.

At the same time, that obligation is something that you have to write through rather than bypass. I had to write according to the person I felt I was. I have gotten to the place in my own written text and visual work where I resist the expectation of others.

Immigrants often are caught up in a limbo existence—the place of belonging to no place. I have several nieces and nephews who have never even been to Vietnam, but they will always be recognized as "other," both there and here.

I now teach at two universities. I thought that academia was my milieu, but I had disillusionment at one school that made me feel shut out of that community. The conflict was around the issue of diversity. That they play at diversity in academia is not acknowledged. It is probably one of the most racist atmospheres in our society. Words like *diversity* invoked by those in power? They pit people of color against one another and invoke diversity.

I worked on a book about it. I sat on my experience, wrote it, rewrote it. I wanted to extract anger. It took two years to process. I wrote the book in an effort to take the literal into a metaphor.

When I felt I had no way to voice what I was feeling—no way to articulate it, and that I was angry—I started to create art.

The metaphor for me was this idea of exile—from country, exile from place, and now, exile from the word. I think art is a self-imposed exile from the word for me. I am choosing not to write. I'm doing a project of erasures. I'm taking my first book, the book that I wrote in academia for an MFA program, and I'm erasing everything.

That's my only way of writing now: to erase the language that came before. It stems from the fact that I do not trust language in this latest phase of my life. It's really interesting. It's caught on that this is my project and everybody is really interested in it. I'm getting all of these different literary magazines and universities asking me to write essays about it. But I'm erasing myself. I'm erasing my language because I don't trust it—and you're asking me to articulate it. It becomes a challenge. That's the struggle that I have, because ultimately we return to language.

So I think it's an individual art practice. I'm working with that in my first book, *Placing the Accents*, which I wrote as a grad student. It was a book very much rooted to this idea of identity poetics. It's a book I'm proud of, but at the same time, twenty years later, I'm reflecting on that book and questioning how much of it was me writing and how much was written because of a voice in the world that said, "This is who you are. This is who you're supposed to be. And this is what you should be writing." And I wrote exactly that. But now I'm reading it and I'm not entirely trusting.

I'm using a Sharpie and creating black lines. I'm not giving myself the luxury of adding or rearranging words. I am merely erasing, in the hopes that what is left feels real to me.

What you'll see in the final version will be black lines. I come back to the idea that this is more a visual project than a written project. I want to implement a book to be published as a French fold. French books were bound in the olden days so that you'd have to cut open the bottom of the pages to get to the book. I'll publish a book so that when you open it up, all you will see are black lines. Whatever words are left won't sit on these pages but will sit inside so that, in order for the parts of the poem that are left to be revealed, you must cut open each page. Whatever is left becomes different poems, but they're minimal—minimalist poems. I'm more interested here in what's remaining. First, what happens when we encounter a book of these black lines? Then, what happens in the violent act of cutting open something to get at something else?

I like to teach. I like my students. I have a connection with them. I want to convey to my students that they are in this time writing. You write out of necessity in some ways. I don't think you write just for the sake of writing. Writing and art are just ways of thinking, and you write so that you can think. You make art so that you can think. It gives you a different way to enter into a subject. It gives you a different way to inquire about the world that you exist in.

I worry sometimes about my students when they're young. They're so invested in the product, with the poem—this shiny object, in a sense. Sometimes the thinking is not really embedded in the work. That's the same reason I had to extract anger from my book. Because the anger is not the product of the book. If we are to really think about that work, then I have to question my own anger. I have to question the venom inside the book as well. It isn't just a one-directional trajectory.

I've always wanted to create art that speaks for itself and struggles not on behalf of anyone. Wherever I've gone, I've been part of the struggle, part of expectations. But what I create stems from my own desire to represent.

I did a show about war. One thing I concluded was that I didn't have the perspective of the soldier in there. It's easy for me to be critical of war, but I thought it was important for me to have the other side.

I met a soldier at a poetry reading. Alex asked me why I chose to make art. I said because it was in me. I had to get it out.

He agreed to let me photograph him. In return, I wanted his commitment that he would write his story, and I would facilitate the writing of that story. This was the one time I wanted to step back as much as possible as the writer. I wanted to be, in a sense, a reporter, and give Alex the opportunity to have his voice.

I felt he was giving of himself in such a vulnerable way. When I photographed Alex, we took photos of him clothed and unclothed, and ultimately I left it up to him what he wanted to do and he said, "Let's use the nude images. I'm in civilian clothes right now, but it's just another uniform." He wanted to remove the uniforms, the various uniforms.

I am always trying to redefine the notion of identity. I went back to Vietnam. It took a day or two to understand that I am exiled from that life. But I am comfortable with that.

I am criticized all the time that my work does not speak to my Vietnamese identity or my gay identity. How can I not have a gay identity? I live with that 24/7.

We are all so caught up in identity and the container of identity. We have all exiled ourselves. I stopped considering the notion of looking for a home in academia. When you get close, look across the threshold and see the reality of that world. It is devastating.

Writing has a public persona for me, maybe because I have been so much a part of that world. I think art is my world, although not as a public persona. It completes me internally. I get to choose with whom and when to share it.

■ ■ ■

Resources

Antelope Trails Vendors Organization: Since 1995, this organization has helped provide small business for the Bodaway/Gap Chapter area arts and crafts artists on the Navajo Nation. Vendors rent table space from ATVO on heavily traveled tourist roads to sell their jewelry and other handmade items. Profits from the table rent are used for scholarships to send local students to college, universities and trade schools, and for monetary assistance for funerals and school trips.

Asian American Institute: A Chicago-based organization designed to empower the Asian American community through advocacy, research, education and coalition building. The group was established by activists, academicians and business leaders in response to the growing need to create pan-Asian policies among Chicago's diverse Asian American communities.

Battered Women's Justice Project: The organization "promotes systemic change within community organizations and governmental agencies engaged in the civil and criminal justice response to domestic violence in order to hold these institutions accountable for the goals and safety and security of battered women and their children." The Battered Women's Justice Project Criminal and Civil Justice Office seeks to coordinate agencies and their policy development so they can engage in effective intervention.

Citizens Against Violence: A Taos (New Mexico) County nonprofit program addressing the needs of victims of domestic and sexual violence by providing a 24-hour crisis hotline, an emergency and transitional shelter, and advocacy. The organization provides child and adult counseling and support groups, helps with criminal cases, assists with health care needs and performs outreach through prevention and educational programs.

The Crawford House: The only private, nonprofit residential treatment facility specifically for veterans in Colorado. It provides emergency housing for veterans who are homeless and receiving mental health care and a temporary living environment for veterans in VA-provided substance abuse rehabilitation. It also provides low-cost transitional boarding houses for homeless veterans and case managers who do followup and ensure that vets leaving the program are employed or have applied for disability and have long-term health care in place.

Crossroads Hospice: A hospice and palliative care program active in seven states that focuses on a person's quality of life at the end of life. It surrounds the patient and family with a team of professionals and a volunteer who deal not only with physical distress, but with emotional and spiritual issues as well. With the motto of "Expect more of us. We do," the hospice organization has unique services that include a care system with lower-than-average patient-to-staff ratios ensuring daily visits, a watch system to monitor patients' developments, a grief recovery and bereavement program, a veterans recognition program, and an "ultimate gifts" program that provides "a perfect day" according to the hospice patient's wishes.

Emergency Department Case Management Program: This program at San Francisco General Hospital targets frequent users of medical and emergency department services at the facility and provides professional services, support and care to a diverse, vulnerable and socially disadvantaged patient population. It addresses medical, substance abuse and psychological problems. Most of the clients are homeless. Case managers assist with housing, financial entitlements, primary medical care, mental health and substance abuse referrals, and other social services. The program has seen a substantial reduction in emergency room visits, a reduction in clients' psychosocial problems and an improvement in clients' self-determination.

Emory-Tibet Partnership: Motto: "Bridging two worlds for one common humanity." Founded in 1998, the partnership between Emory University in Atlanta and the Tibetan Government in Exile has been "committed to bringing together the best of Western and Tibetan intellectual traditions for mutual enrichment and the discovery of new knowledge for the benefit of humanity." The Emory Tibet Science Initiative, started in 2006, is a comprehensive science program for Tibetan Buddhist monks and nuns to nurture "a dialogue and cross fertilization between science and spirituality, as both are essential for enriching human life and alleviating suffering on both individual and global levels."

Forgotten People: A nonprofit organization dedicated to the well-being of Arizona Navajo people living on 2 million acres in the western part of the Navajo Nation. Its mission is to ensure that these people have access to safe drinking water, sanitation, low-cost housing and solar electrification, and that they can maintain sustainable agriculture practices. Most of the population speak only Diné, practice their traditional religion, and survive by sheepherding and weaving. Forgotten People's aim is "to teach people how to change from reactive to be proactive to take control of their destiny."

Fostering Opportunities Dollars for Scholars: San Diego County–based nonprofit, tax-exempt scholarship foundation established to expand post secondary educational opportunities specifically for former foster youth in San Diego County. The foundation is all volunteer and, with support from the community, awarded 305 scholarships to 211 students from 2002 to 2012. With 1,000 volunteer-drive chapters nationally, Dollars for Scholars works to help local students achieve postsecondary success. Dollars for Scholars is part of Scholarship America, a national organization that has helped 1.7 million students go to college since 1961.

Hope Center Community Development Agency: The not-for-profit Hope Center works in concert with the community, faith-based and civic organizations, government officials and private entities to coordinate redevelopment plans for East Biloxi, Mississippi. Founded by William Stallworth, Biloxi councilman for Ward 2, two days after Hurricane Katrina destroyed the area (and now called the East Biloxi Coordination, Relief and Redevelopment Agency), the center first obtained funding for immediate needs for food, shelter and basic medical care for thousands of suddenly homeless families. It has evolved into a center where residents can get technical and logistical support in rebuilding their homes as well as share their hopes and concerns for their community during the rebuilding efforts.

Hospice Volunteer Association: Ever since the hospice and palliative care movement began, volunteers have provided a compassionate connection with dying people. According to the association, their presence "often becomes an important element in that person's final journey—a crucial existential, spiritual and developmental time to bear witness to the ending of a life." The association was formed to ensure that the spirit of hospice volunteerism be preserved and not dissolved by ever-increasing financial pressures on hospice organizations.

International Tibet Network: A global coalition of Tibet-related nongovernmental organizations to maximize the effectiveness of the worldwide Tibet movement. Network members are committed to nonviolence and regard Tibet as an occupied country and the Tibetan Government in Exile as the sole legitimate government of the Tibetan people.

Loaves & Fishes: Loaves & Fishes–Sacramento feeds the hungry and shelters the homeless. It provides safe and clean areas for men, women and children seeking survival services. Loaves & Fishes relies solely on private donations. Based north of downtown Sacramento, the organization provides a park called Friendship Park with services for homeless people surrounding the area, including a dining area, an urgent care clinic run by the Sisters of Mercy, a legal clinic, a lawyer to assist with Social Security disability issues, a women's empowerment program and a pet clinic. Sacramento Homeless Organizing Committee's office is located on the edge of the park. The group advocates for homeless equal rights and the safety and well-being of homeless people, and puts out a bimonthly newsletter.

The Lower Ninth Ward Neighborhood Empowerment Network Association (NENA): Originally a New Orleans relief organization after Hurricane Katrina, NENA now helps with individuals' rebuilding efforts, supports local small and entrepreneurial business developers and contractors and subcontractors doing business in the Lower Ninth Ward and other parts of Greater New Orleans. As part of its program, NENA provides pro bono on-site architectural construction administration and assistance with permits to residents as they rebuild their homes.

Muslim Women's Resource Center: A Chicago-based organization whose goal is to facilitate the needs and expectations of immigrant and refugee women and the resources available to them by governmental and non-governmental foundations. The center has expanded from helping Muslim women to serving all immigrants and refugees. The center provides, among other things, citizenship education, employment counseling, English as a Second Language courses, youth care and empowerment services, and care for the elderly.

National Association for the Education of Homeless Children and Youth: A grassroots association of educators, parents, advocates, researchers and service providers who work to ensure enrollment, attendance and overall success for children and young people whose lives have been disrupted by the lack of a safe, permanent, adequate place to live. The association says that every year, about 1.5 million children and young people experience homelessness in U.S. towns, cities and counties.

Rachael's Women's Center: The philosophy of Rachael's House is to offer a homelike environment during the day that is a place of "hospitality and hope." The house, in Washington, D.C., provides safety, shelter, meals and laundry for homeless and formerly homeless women and offers services that give them the opportunity to "bring forth their forgotten or lost potential." Rachael's also reaches out to individuals living on the streets to help them gain access to services and benefits available to them.

Sisters of the Road: The group's mission is to help build relationships among poor and homeless women and "alleviate the hunger of isolation in an atmosphere of nonviolence and gentle personalism that nurtures the whole individual, while seeking systematic solutions that reach the roots of homelessness and poverty to end them forever." Along with its philosophy of nonviolence, Sisters rejects any form of humiliation. It incorporates a "dine with dignity" program that provides a safe place to eat and enjoy a meal of healthful food.

Taos (New Mexico) Men's Shelter: Provides "safe haven for men who have nowhere else to go and whose circumstances bring them to the door." Community members provide a full evening meal. The shelter offers overnight sleeping accommodations, shower facilities, laundry services and support service guidance. "Our shelter is a humane and effective solution. It saves public funding by avoiding the expense of incarceration or emergency room care."

Twenty-First Century Foundation powered by Tides (Network): Leading U.S. foundation rooted in philanthropy that impacts minority communities, institutions and families. It brings together investors, donors, and doers committed to addressing the challenges facing Black and "new majority" communities domestically and internationally. Its three key issues are "the empowerment of Afro-Black-Latin Americans and immigrants of Afro-Latino descent; corporate social impact fueled by employee-led philanthropy; prevention of emotional, physical, economic and sexual abuse of Black, Latina, Asian, Muslim/Middle Eastern and Native American girls; efforts that dismantle the on-ramps that lead to human trafficking."

Veterans Remember: A Colorado Springs–based network of active duty soldiers, veterans, families and supporters of soldiers and veterans, and the community at large, who come together periodically to tell their experiences in war and their experiences back from war. "We talk and we listen. Both are equal in value. All experiences are honored, no matter what they may have been in the military." The group welcomes participation of spouses and families of soldiers and veterans, "and all those who wish to understand the effects of war on soldiers and their families in these healing dialogues."

Western Regional Advocacy Project: WRAP was created to "expose and eliminate the root causes of civil and human rights abuses of people experiencing poverty and homelessness" in San Francisco Bay Area communities. Its mission is to unite local social justice organizations to work together in a cohesive and effective manner, to influence the federal government to restore affordable housing funding and to develop solutions to end homelessness. Campaigns include programs to promote civil rights and housing rights.

Wounded Warrior Project: Helps injured vets with their rehabilitative and transitional processes. Its mission is to provide unique, direct, "ever-evolving" programs and services to meet the needs of injured service members, including outdoor rehabilitative retreats, peer support, combat stress recovery programs and family support.

Youth Empowerment Project: A New Orleans–based nonprofit started in 2004 as the only program in the state focusing on providing re-entry services to young people returning home to the region from juvenile facilities. The Juvenile Justice Project recognized the urgency to help formerly incarcerated children and address the high recidivism and early death rates of this population. YEP helps these young people obtain their GEDs, develop job skills and find jobs, and mentors them and does intensive case management. Many staff members come from the same neighborhoods where YEP youth now reside. YEP has grown from helping its initial 25 clients in 2004 to 1,200 in 2012, and developed more centers for aftercare and educational programs around the city.

Acknowledgments

Thank you to writer and friend Blair Hyde for her patient critiques of past writing—who let me show all vulnerabilities, listened with care, nurtured my ideas, and helped me grow.

Thank you to:

Kansas City writers Juliet Kincaid, Gail Fortin, Julia Lednicky, Crystal Bevell, Dana Pflumm, Dave Bondank, and Liberty Speidel who said, "That book idea sounds good—and timely."

Thank you to fellow New Mexico writers Heidi Smith, Jean Admire, Bill Stone and Chris Robert for listening so carefully, understanding where I wanted to go even when I didn't, and for giving invaluable feedback.

To Rev. Hollis Walker for the task of being my editor again and re-upping our friendship.

To friend Jan Winbigler, who organized me, reassured me when I doubted myself, and mirrored my vision back to me—only better.

To almost-sister Tracy Thomas for goading, guidance, and love.

Abundant gratitude to my editor Steve Hiatt, who heard what I wanted and redirected the book to get there. Thank you for the persistence and ideas to take this book from a journalist's venture to the realm of intimate, personal accounts.

Thank you to:

+ Bianca Neumann, who took the weight of website design and other technical concerns off my shoulders. Also to David Lim.
+ John Gibson, Jurgen Reinzuch, Laura Shubert, and Hannah Tyson for your comments and, more important, the questions that made me rethink the book's presentation.

+ Kathy O'Brien, who provided inspiration in her work with the San Francisco General Emergency Department Case Management Program, helping homeless people in San Francisco in an innovative way.

+ Scott Montgomery and Marc Rand for providing your incredible space for me to bounce my thoughts around in.

Thank you to my life coach, Deb Holt. Your wise words kept ringing in my ears. You were right: a book is not something that you impose your will upon. It is something that comes through you.

Thanks to my friends: Anne Blackman, Cathy Clark, Susan Gibson, Lynn Hager, Kande Korth, Sig Lindel, Edeen Martin, Suzanne Stassevitch, Sue Strebe, and Karrie Williams, who supported me in so many ways and who understood that I was driven to do this.

And to recent pals: Judy Mangina, Bonnie McManus, Linda Meier, and Sandra Williams.

Great love to Sister Annie Loendorff for providing a home for so many through House of Menuha and for further offering a place of great understanding in her heart.

Thank you to my partner, Keith Palmer, for believing in me and seeing me through harder times than writing any book could ever be. Wherever I am with you, that is my home.

CPSIA information can be obtained at www.ICGtesting.com
Printed in the USA
LVOW13s1149060414

380488LV00002B/86/P